To Marre

with my best wishes
for big life and true
my happiness,

Benh G. Goldstein

For Decades I Was Silent

JUDAIC STUDIES SERIES

Leon J. Weinberger
General Editor

For Decades I Was Silent

A Holocaust Survivor's Journey Back to Faith

Baruch G. Goldstein

THE UNIVERSITY OF ALABAMA PRESS
Tuscaloosa

Copyright © 2008
The University of Alabama Press
Tuscaloosa, Alabama 35487-0380
All rights reserved
Manufactured in the United States of America

Typeface: Caslon

∞

The paper on which this book is printed meets the minimum requirements of American National Standard for Information Sciences-Permanence of Paper for Printed Library Materials, ANSI Z39.48-1984.

Library of Congress Cataloging-in-Publication Data

Goldstein, Baruch G., 1923–
    For decades I was silent : a Holocaust survivor's journey back to faith / Baruch G. Goldstein.
        p.   cm. — (Judaic Studies Series)
    Includes bibliographical references and index.
    ISBN 978-0-8173-1619-8 (cloth : alk. paper) 1. Goldstein, Baruch G., 1923– 2. Jews—Poland—Mlawa—Biography. 3. Holocaust, Jewish (1939–1945)—Poland—Mlawa—Biography. 4. Holocaust survivors—United States—Biography. 5. Mlawa (Poland)—Biography. I. Title.
    DS134.72.G65A3 2008
    940.53´18092—dc22
    [B]

                                                                        2008003091

In memory of my beloved parents, Israel Meyer and Tirtza Beilah Goldstein, and my sister, Rachel, and brother, Shmuel Alter, who perished in the Shoah, November 1942 / Kislev 5703

O Man, you have been told what is good and what it is that the Lord requires of you—only to do justice, to love kindness and to walk humbly with your God.

—Micah 6:8

Contents

Preface

For decades I was silent. I had lived under the Nazi regime for five and a half years. I experienced and witnessed horrors beyond imagining and suffered the consequences of that period for many years thereafter. Yet I could not speak about what Nazi Germany had done to my family and to my people. Perhaps I was focused on creating a new life for myself in America and attempting to put the painful memories of the past behind me. But I do remember also wondering how a survivor might truly be able to translate into words his or her incredible experiences. How could I possibly describe the pain of the losses of my dearest family, the psychological impact of the brutality I had witnessed, the evil of the perpetrators, and the suffering of the victims before they were murdered? How could I describe the sorrow of having seen cities once vibrant with Jewish life being made *Judenrein*, free of Jews?

My thinking changed about thirty years ago after the Jewish Community Center in Worcester, Massachusetts, invited me to give a six-session course on the Holocaust, a program in which I would also describe my personal experiences during the war. I accepted the invitation reluctantly, but to my surprise the course was well received. The participants showed great interest in the subject, and each session elicited meaningful discussions about the history of that period and how it had been possible for so many Jewish communities to be completely wiped out. Above all, the participants wanted to know the details of my suffering, my losses, and my survival. After teaching this course, I concluded that even if I failed to convey the full extent of the horror, I was still going to tell my story. The time had come to break my silence.

Since that first class I conducted, I have had the opportunity of speaking about the Holocaust and my personal experiences to thousands of people in Massachusetts, Connecticut, New Hampshire, Rhode Island, California, and Oregon. I have made myself available to universities, elementary schools, high schools, and many organizations and congregations—Jewish and Christian—that expressed interest. As a survivor, I have felt duty bound to testify and to give a voice and to honor those who were silenced and denied a chance to cry out and express their pain. In my talks I claim no heroism, no special wisdom, no unusual physical strength. A great many victims were wiser, stronger, and more heroic than I, yet did not survive. To this day, I cannot explain why I survived while so many others did not.

I have lived my life with an acute awareness of my experiences under Nazi terror and the consequences of that period. Rarely does a week or month pass by without my making some kind of reference to the Holocaust, whether I verbalize these feelings to others or keep them to myself. I value, weigh, and scrutinize all the experiences of my life—the successes, failures, celebrations, and misfortunes—with memories of the Holocaust as the backdrop. Of course, I am also conscious and grateful for the blessings of life and for resilience, which most survivors have demonstrated in creating meaningful lives for our families and ourselves. And so I have made it my practice to speak not only of the horrors and suffering but also of our responsibility to learn from our past for the sake of our future. For more than three decades now, I not only have tried to teach the history of the Holocaust but also have urged my audiences to focus their energies toward creating a more tolerant and kinder society.

For some years now, I have been encouraged by my family and friends to write my personal account of the Holocaust. As I now prepare to share my story, I wish to express my deepest gratitude to them for having been an integral part of my life. I am grateful for the happiness they have brought to me by their love and friendship, even at times when my heart was filled with sorrow. It is my hope that they and all who find this book of interest will share my story with their children and grandchildren and with generations thereafter.

I am merely one voice, but I wish for it to be heard so that I may contribute, even in a small measure, to *tikun olam,* the mending of the world. This is my dream, and I continue to hope for the coming of the Messiah, when the words of the Hebrew prophet Isaiah will be realized: "In the days to come, the mount of the Lord's house shall stand firm above the mountains and tower above the hills, and all the nations shall gaze at it with joy. . . . And they shall beat their swords into plowshares and their spears into pruning hooks. Nations shall not take up swords against nation; they shall never again know war" (Isaiah 2:2, 4).

And while we are waiting for that time to come, may we, every one of us, contribute to this messianic age by eradicating racism, hate, prejudice, and bigotry. Let us all try harder to spread goodness, kindness, acceptance, tolerance, and love. Let us all accept the fact that we all belong to one race, the human race and that all of us are the children of the same God, who created us all.

Acknowledgments

In May–June 1995 I celebrated the fiftieth anniversary of my liberation from the Nazi Germany concentration camps by writing a short article to mark the significance of that jubilee occasion for me. It was not intended for publication but to share with family and friends my thoughts and memories on that occasion. At that time I started thinking seriously about writing my memoirs were I to be blessed with years of life and the strength needed for that task. I have felt an obligation to tell my story and share a much-needed message for our times, a vital lesson we all must learn from the Nazi reign of terror in the years of 1933–1945. I began to collect my memories, some of which I had lived with for half a century and others that I had shelved in the innermost chambers of my heart and mind. I had to search hard for them and write about those emotional memories with pain and tears.

Most of the book is about my own personal experiences and of my own firsthand knowledge of the facts as they were. Also in this book are many accounts of a historical nature that are usually dealt with by professional history scholars. Nevertheless, I found it impossible to write my story without touching on historical facts that are of significance to my personal story and, I think, of value to the reader. For those facts I relied on the writings of well-recognized historians. I do not claim to be a historian.

Now, some thirteen years later, after many lengthy interruptions beyond my control and after many revisions, I am pleased to have reached the moment of acknowledging my gratitude to the many who have extended so graciously their assistance to me in bringing this project to a reality.

I am most grateful to Chava Boland of Jerusalem for editing the first draft of my manuscript and for her support and encouragement. Special thanks to her for introducing a number of excellent ideas, which helped me to restructure the manuscript to my satisfaction. I am grateful to Rabbi Miriam Berkowitz of Boca Raton, Florida, for her support and editorial suggestions. And I am very grateful to Heath Lynn Silberfeld of Gainesville, Florida, for editing and preparing the manuscript for publication.

My special thanks go to Rabbi Leon J. Weinberger, PhD, professor emeritus in the Religious Studies Department at The University of Alabama, for introducing me to The University of Alabama Press. To Dr. Weinberger I express my gratitude for reading my manuscript and for recommending it to be published by the press. The support, kindness, and courteous communication the staff gave me are of special value to me.

I wish to express my thanks and appreciation to my children, Meyer and Sue-Rita; to my grandchildren, Jonah, Liza, Sarah, and Daniel, for their support and encouragement; and to my cousin, Dr. Herbert Kleibard, for his guidance and practical suggestions.

I am grateful to all my friends who read the manuscript and offered suggestions, support, and encouragement. Each one of their comments inspired me and strengthened my resolve to have my story published. They all are entitled to share in the joy and satisfaction of seeing this book in printed form. Of course, the responsibility for errors and shortcomings of this book is entirely mine.

Extended Family Members Who Perished in the Holocaust, 1939–1945

Grandmothers

Toba Devorah Goldstein   Malka Kleinbard

Uncles and Aunts

Shimon Noson and Miriam Goldstein   Moshe and Berakhah Berko

Moshe Yoel and Sarah Goldberg   Tzerko Sokolover

Aaron and Bailche Goldstein   Yehuda Leib and Sarah Kramer

Moshe and Tzvikah Eichler   Yitche (Yitzhak) and Rose

Hersh and Rose Kleinbard   Kleinbard

Cousins

Hava Gisha and Jacob Markewitz   Shmuel Noson Goldstein

Rivka Goldberg   Zisel Goldstein

Israel (Yisrolek) Goldberg   Rachel Eichler

Malka Goldberg   Yermo Berko

Hayah Goldberg   Shifra Berko

Shmuel Alter Goldberg   Hayim Sokolover

Sheindel Goldberg   Simha Sokolover

Devorah Goldstein   Rachel Kleinbard

Sheindel Goldstein   Hayim Kramer

Sheindel Goldstein   Braina Kleinbard

Cousin Jacob Goldberg—survived the Holocaust,
died on April 13, 1980–27 Nissan 5740
A victim of the Holocaust

Grandfathers

Shmuel Alter Goldstein   Hayim Kleinbard
Died before the Holocaust
In Loving Memory

For Decades I Was Silent

Introduction

The letter began *"Taierer Fraind"* ("Dear Friend"), and as a man who had lost all his friends and loved ones, this was a phrase I had never expected to hear or read again. The year was 1947, two and a half years after my liberation from the Nazi concentration camps, and I, a twenty-four-year-old survivor, found myself still in transit, longing to immigrate to Palestine. I had just arrived in Rome, where I knew almost no one, to continue waiting for the opportunity.

The writer, a Miss Rivka Golinkin, introduced herself as a friend of my aunt Sonia Ulick, whom she had befriended on her vacation trip to Los Angeles. My aunt had shown Rivka some of my letters, and Rivka was moved to help bring me to America, she wrote, if that was what I wanted. I was living then in a fog of despondence. Although the war had ended more than two years earlier, I was still very much a refugee. After the liberation, I had traveled from Czechoslovakia to Hungary, then to Austria, and finally to Italy, where I had spent two and a half years in displaced persons camps, with no real home, no family, no sense of stability, without plans for a normal life in the future. My life was permeated with frustration and loneliness, and the expression of friendship from a stranger touched me very deeply.

My intentions after the war had been to immigrate to Palestine as soon as possible, but after spending years of waiting for the opportunity to reach Palestine, I did not know what I wanted. I responded to Rivka's note and expressed gratitude for her kindness and caring. Maybe I would consider going to America, I wrote back. And from there began our correspondence.

Rivka's letter had arrived after a long and dark period in my life. That letter became the beginning of a healing process that ultimately helped me to live a full life again. Please allow me to share my story with you.

I

Origins

The city of Mlawa is located in the northern part of Poland, between Warsaw and Danzig, in the district of Mazowsze. Both my parents, Israel Meyer Goldstein and Tirtza Beilah Goldstein, were born there, and on April 23, 1923, I became one of the first of the next generation of Goldsteins to be born in the city. I was named Baruch Gershon after my mother's uncle, who had been known as Boruch Gershon *der Sofer* ("the scribe"), and they nicknamed me "Butche." A year and a half later, my sister, Rachel (Rachela, in Polish) was born. We called her "Ruchcza." And then, about a year and a half after that came my brother, Shmuel Alter, whom we called "Shmulik." I do not know when, from where, or who of my ancestors came first to Mlawa.

No one knows exactly when and from where the first Jews arrived in Mlawa, either. According to an article by Yehuda Rosenthal, who has done extensive research on the history of Mlawa, Jews lived in Mlawa for at least four hundred years. The earliest available information dates back to 1515 and refers to a Dr. Brasius, a Christian who was accused of preaching Judaism to Christians. A claim was made that the doctor observed Jewish holidays and customs and had leanings toward Judaism. We can assume that he was under the influence of Jews who lived there at that time.[1]

A more specific document, dated 1543, was found in the archives of the city of Plock, then the capital city of the Mazowsze region. It mentions the names of Berachja or Baruch (Polish: Bugoslaw), the Parnes (the chief or leader of the Jewish community) of the Jewish community in Mlawa, along with Dr. Lewek, the Parnes of the Jewish community in Plock, as having reported a decree of the Polish king Zigmunt August the First, on August 1, 1541, which made ritual accusations against Jews. This proves that there were Jews in Mlawa in 1541 and that they had a Parnes who took care of the Jewish affairs in the community in connection with a case of blood libel.[2]

By 1569 twenty-three Jewish families were living in Mlawa, and by 1578 there were thirty-four families. Their main sources of livelihood were the livestock trade and various crafts. The fires that devastated Mlawa in 1659 and in 1692 and the accusations of disloyalty in 1670 caused the number of Jews in Mlawa to decrease. Growth in the region's economic activity during the last third of the eighteenth century brought more Jews to the area. The 1765 census showed seventy Jewish families and 487 Jewish poll-tax payers (head tax paid by Jews) in Mlawa and the neighboring villages. Jews owned fifteen houses in the town itself. The 1781 census showed a Jewish population of 718 individuals.[3]

After the Prussian conquest in 1793, the city of Mlawa was granted a *privilegia de non-tolerandis Judaeis* status, which forbade Jews from living in the city. The Jews then moved to Zabrody, an area just outside Mlawa. In fact, there were 3,164 Jews living in the surrounding towns and villages. They made up 10 percent of the total population.[4]

Stories used to circulate in Mlawa that the renowned Rabbi Levi Yitzchak, the *tzaddik* of Berdichev, Ukraine, had once spent a few days in the city when the Jews lived in Zabrody. This could have been between the years 1772 and 1785. From that we may assume that Hasidim (pious Jews) were already in Mlawa. A century and a half later, that visit was still a source of pride to the Jews of Mlawa. Jews would walk to the synagogue in Zabrody on the high holidays to pray where the *tzaddik* of Berdichev had prayed. The Zabrody synagogue existed until World War I.[5]

With the establishment of the Grand Duchy of Warsaw in 1806, Jews were allowed to return to Mlawa. By 1808, records show, 137 Jews living in Mlawa, constituting 15 percent of the total population, but they were not completely welcome in the city. About twenty years later, restrictions were again placed on Jewish settlement, and in 1824 a special Jewish quarter was established. With some rare exceptions, Jews were permitted to live only in the Jewish quarter. Yet, in 1827, 792 Jews made up 36 percent of the total population of Mlawa. The restrictions on residence and land ownership by Jews remained in place for almost forty years; they were abolished in 1862.

The Jewish population increased considerably once the railway from Mlawa to Warsaw and Gdansk was opened toward the end of the nineteenth century. Many Jews earned their livelihood then from the trade in grain, livestock, wood, and army supplies. Between 1857 and 1897, the Jewish population of Mlawa grew from 1,650 to 4,845, representing 41 percent of the total population.[6]

The influence of Hasidism manifested itself among the Jews of Mlawa from the beginning of the nineteenth century. Toward the end of the nineteenth century, the influence of the Mitnagdim, opponents of Hasidism, gained strength. (Although both groups are considered Orthodox in comparison to other branches of Judaism, they differ in some respects. The Hasidim emphasize meticulous observance of God's commandments but worship with ecstasy and joy; the Mitnagdim use a more scholarly approach to religious behavior and attitudes.) By then the Jewish population had grown to more than five thousand people. Rabbi Wolf Lipszic became rabbi of Mlawa in 1870. The last rabbi of Mlawa, Rabbi Yechiel Moshe Segalowitz, a Mitnaged, was appointed in 1901.[7]

By that time Mlawa had become home to a large and active community of Jewish intelligentsia. In the late 1890s a Zionist group called Hovevei Zion—Lovers of Zion—was organized there. During the same period, while pogroms were rampant in Russia, the Bund (Jewish Socialist Party) and the Po'alei Tzion (a Zionist workers' organization) wielded considerable influence among Jewish workers, youth, and intelligentsia. The renowned author Joseph Opatoshu (his brother, Feivel Opatowsky, was my Yiddish teacher), the Yiddish and Hebrew writer Yakir Warshawsky, the publicist and influential leader of the Bund, Victor Alter, and the accomplished engineer-mathematician Moshe Merker were born and began their careers in Mlawa.[8]

While I was growing up in Mlawa, about six thousand Jews resided in the city out of a total population of approximately twenty thousand. Although it was not a particularly large city, it had a very active cultural life and was one of the more progressive cities of Poland at the turn of the twentieth century. Religious Jews made up a significant portion of the city's Jewish population in the early part of the twentieth century.

Among the religious Jews were different groups of Hasidim in Mlawa, each with its own specific religious philosophy of serving God. Each group of Hasidim had its own rebbe or *tzaddik* and considered him to be the greatest spiritual leader. The Hasidim would follow his leadership with great devotion and would seek his advice on all important matters of life. Each Hasidic group had its own place of worship, known as *shtibl*, usually consisting of not more than one or two rooms. Thus Mlawa had many different Hasidic groups along with the Mitnagdim, who remained philosophically opposed to the Hasidic movement altogether. Despite their disagreements, however, these groups shared common basic beliefs and a strong commitment to religious observance.

The number of Zionists of all convictions continued to grow in the twentieth century. Among the groups were the General Zionist Party, the socialist Zionists, and the right wing and left wing of the socialist Po'alei Tzion movement. There were also the religious Mizrahi Zionists, and when Ze'ev Jabotinsky separated from the general Zionist movement and founded the Revisionist Zionist movement, there were Revisionists in Mlawa, too.[9] All these organizations actively supported the idea of the Jewish people returning to

Palestine, the Land of Israel, to rebuild the land, which had been neglected for thousands of years, to build new settlements and farms, and to reestablish there an independent Jewish state. The persecution of Jews and the spread of nationalism in the nineteenth century contributed greatly to the creation and growth of the political movement of Zionism.

Anti-Zionists made their voices heard in Mlawa as well. The religious organization Agudath Israel held onto the traditional idea that Jews should wait for the coming of the Messiah to take them back to the Land of Israel en masse. The Bund in Mlawa also opposed the Zionist movement. This secular group believed it best for the Jewish people to remain in the countries of their birth and work for social justice and equal rights for all citizens. They believed that Jews should maintain their love and commitment to Jewish culture, the Yiddish language, and Yiddish literature instead of attempting to renew the ancient Hebrew language.

Thus, virtually every Jewish religious and political movement was represented in Mlawa. Moreover, each movement had its own youth organization. For example, there were the Hashomer Hatza'ir (socialist Zionists), Hashomer Hadati (religious Zionists), Hashomer Haleumi (national-general Zionists), and Betar (revisionist Zionists). Many of Mlawa's youth joined the Hakhshara ("preparation"), a movement of young people who learned agricultural and industrial skills to prepare to immigrate to Palestine and assist in the rebuilding of the Jewish homeland there. A sizable number of people from Mlawa succeeded in their efforts to immigrate to Palestine before the beginning of World War II, despite the hardships they then had to endure there from the hot climate, the lack of water, and the malaria epidemics.

Non-Zionist youth groups were also active, such as Tze'irei Agudath Israel (Young Adults of Agudath Israel) and Pirchei Agudath Israel (religious non-Zionist youth). My parents were not politically involved, but I guess they leaned toward Agudath Israel. I used to attend Pirchei Agudath Israel meetings, even though I personally had more Zionist leanings and would attend the occasional meeting of the Betar club of the Revisionist youth. Some young Mlawa Jews even held membership in the underground Communist Party, which completely rejected Jewish tradition and Zionism. I knew young Jewish Communists who served jail sentences for their political activities because the Communist Party was illegal in Poland.

Many social service organizations functioned successfully in the city, too. Managed and staffed by volunteers, these groups assisted families in need. Among them were the Beis Lechem (food for the poor), Bikur Cholim (help for the needy sick), Hakhnosas Orchim (food and shelter for strangers),

Hakhnosas Kallah (help for poor brides), Gemilus Chesed Kasse (interest-free loans for the needy), and Hevra Kadisha (the burial society).

The Jewish community was well organized, with officials elected to the Jewish *gemainde* (council), which represented all organizations—religious and secular, Zionist and non-Zionist. Preelection months were a particularly lively and busy time, when all the organizations attempted to win as many seats as possible to serve on the *gemainde*. Printed materials included the *Jewish Weekly*, printed in Yiddish in Mlawa, and *Dos Mlawer Lebn (Jewish Life in Mlawa)*. When I was growing up in Mlawa in the 1920s and 1930s, all of the above became a part of my awareness and my fond memories.

The center of the city was the market square, with the city hall in the middle. In that building were nine stores rented by Jewish merchants. My father's store was one of those nine. Next to the city hall was the Catholic Church. From the four corners of the square began four major streets that branched out in different directions. A little street close to the city center was an important center for all Jews in the city, and it is also ingrained in my memory with fondness. It was Shul Gass (Synagogue Street), where three synagogues stood. We frequented this street more than any other, as these three synagogues constituted the spiritual center of the community. In each of those sanctuaries, Jews gathered for prayer, meditation, and study. Those structures, each with a distinctive character, each different from the surrounding homes, spoke to the hearts of every Jew in the city; they were bridges connecting Jewish hearts with their God and with each other.

In the center of the street was the shul (synagogue). At its left was *alter bet midrash*, the "*old* house of study," and to its right was *naier bet midrash*, the "*new* house of study." With its high ceiling and impressive Aron Hakodesh (holy ark) on the eastern wall, the shul was the largest of the three buildings. Two sets of stairs, one on each side of the sanctuary, led to the holy ark. The shul's architecture and internal decor were artistically designed, expressing dignity and awe. This was the official and formal community synagogue. It was open for worship only on Sabbaths and holidays. This was where the rabbi and the elite of the community prayed. The official hazan (cantor) led the services on the Sabbaths, and a choir accompanied him on holidays and special occasions. I was a member of the choir on numerous occasions. The Jewish community paid a salary to the cantor, who was also a *shohet*, one who slaughters chicken and cattle ritually to provide the community with kosher meat.

One of the special occasions on which the Jewish community gathered at this shul was for Polish Independence Day, celebrated every May 3. We would also gather for other Polish national occasions and Jewish community celebrations. The rabbi would deliver a lecture on the significance of the day, and the hazan and choir would sing the Polish national anthem. A representative of the local government would always honor us with his presence on Polish Independence Day.

The *alter bet midrash* was a place of continuous daily prayer and Torah study. There one would always find individuals and groups sitting around long tables with open volumes of the Talmud, deeply engaged in study from early morning to late at night. Minyanim (groups of at least ten men to constitute a quorum) met for morning services beginning at dawn and would continue one after the other until the late hours of the morning. Before one minyan would conclude, another would be ready to start. The same was repeated in the evenings for *minhah* and *ma'ariv* services (the afternoon and evening prayers). At times, a traveling *magid* (preacher) would deliver his fiery *drosho* (religious discourse) there. People would come to listen to the *magid's* philosophical and inspirational interpretations of Jewish classical texts, exhorting the people to follow God's way and not to digress from his teachings. Other times, a traveling hazan would draw large crowds to listen to him sing his cantorial creations of the liturgy. Here one would always find individuals and groups praying, studying, reciting psalms, or discussing local events and world politics. The *alter bet midrash* was always open and welcoming, and when people were there they felt like they were in their own homes and in the presence of God.

The *naier bet midrash* drew a different crowd, mainly those from the various Zionist movements, the *maskilim* (enlightened individuals), and the more modern and younger crowd. Here, too, one could find individuals and groups involved in the study of Torah between *minhah* and *ma'ariv* every day of the week. It was open daily, but for morning and evening services only. It was a newly built structure, beautifully painted, with pews, and it was well kept. The worshippers were more modern, too, in dress and lifestyle. At two long tables, groups would study religious texts for a short period between *minhah* and *ma'ariv*. Two beautiful murals were painted on the northern and southern walls with scenes from the Land of Israel, reflecting the Zionist commitment of the worshippers. On one mural was the statement *"Tziyon b'mishpat Tipade Vshave'ha bitzdakah"* (Zion will be redeemed with justice and those who return with righteousness—Isaiah 1:27). On the opposite wall the statement said, *"Hazorim b'dima b'rina yiktz'oru"* (Those who sow in tears shall reap in joyous song—Psalms 127:5).

Several other places of worship, Hasidic *shtiblach,* existed in Mlawa, all of them close to Shul Gass. They typically were small synagogues, consisting of a room or two where Hasidim prayed. Some were open for prayer and study on Shabbat and holidays only; others were open every day. In those, too, you would find Hasidim praying or sitting in groups around long tables studying. My father prayed in the Radziminer *shtibl* on Sabbaths, and on weekdays he prayed in the *alter bet midrash*, for there was no minyan at the *shtibl* for daily services.

I had a large extended family in Mlawa, including my two grandmothers, Toba Goldstein and Malka Kleinbard, and many uncles, aunts, and cousins. I never knew my grandfathers, though. My mother's father, Hayim Kleinbard, died before I was born, and my father's father, Shmuel Alter Goldstein, died not long after I was born.

My parents owned a small textile business in the center of the city, which provided adequately for our family. We were lower-middle class, and I sometimes sensed that we were better off than some of the other families I knew. I also knew of occasions when we faced serious financial hardships. Anti-Semitism was very prevalent in Poland in those years, and it was no different in Mlawa. Various anti-Semitic movements called for Poles to boycott Jewish-owned stores. I remember the posters carried by the Jew-haters, such as "Do Not Buy from Jews!" or "Each to His Own!" encouraging the Polish people to support the boycott of Jewish merchants. I also saw posters saying, "Jews, Go to Palestine!"

I recall one morning in 1937 or 1938, when I was a student in Warsaw walking to the yeshiva. I stopped at a newspaper kiosk and saw the headlines of one of the newspapers, *Dos Yiddishe Express*, announcing in big letters, "POGROM IN MLAWA." The article described how a group of hooligans had attacked the Jewish merchants the day before. It must have been on a Tuesday, one of the two market days when Jewish merchants were displaying their wares for sale. The police dispersed the attackers after some loss of property and some fistfights. No one was arrested, but I was concerned about the welfare of my family. Soon thereafter, family friends who traveled frequently to Warsaw informed me that my family was safe but that some Jews did suffer minor injuries. The fear of acts of anti-Semites became more real to me than ever before.

Of course, Jews were affected economically throughout the country by the boycott. It was deeply felt by the Jews in Mlawa, including my family, because much of our business and employment depended on trade with the Polish population, especially with the nearby villages on market days. On those days, the boycott activities increased against Jewish businesses. Yet we never felt poor. There was always enough to provide for our basic needs. We maintained a positive and hopeful outlook, and life continued normally in our home under all circumstances. My siblings and I grew up happy and secure with unquestionable love from our father and mother. Our frequent get-togethers with cousins were especially enjoyable, and we looked forward to those gathering with joyous anticipation

Both my parents were kind, gentle, and soft-spoken people. My mother often helped my father with his business affairs, and my father helped around the house and assisted my mother in raising us, three energetic children. I recall with fondness my father polishing our shoes on Thursday nights when we were sleeping so that they would be nice and shiny for the Sabbath. This meant we could not enjoy stepping in the mud or splashing in the pools of water in the streets on Fridays. I recall as a child being sick once with a high fever. I kept waking up during the night, and I found my father sitting near my bed reciting Tehilim (Psalms) with pious devotion, praying for my recovery. I also recall with fondness how my mother used to take us to the milk farm to drink the freshly milked liquid. My mother often invited friends and their children to come with us, and we all had fun.

When growing up we also felt hated by the Polish kids, who would call us "Christ killers." For a long time I truly did not understand what that meant. We were also occasionally attacked physically on the way to or from school. My father or mother would report such incidents to the police, who filed reports, but I do not recall any action ever taken by the police.

My father belonged to the Radziminer Hasidim, followers of the rebbe (Hasidic rabbi) of Radzimin, Rabbi Aaron Mendel Gutterman. The Radziminer rebbe was descended from the Modzitzer rebbe's family, who were descendants of Rabbi Yechezkel of Kuzmir, a disciple of the Ba'al Shem Tov ("The Master of the Good Name"), the founder of the Hasidic movement. I remember my father taking me to the train station once when I was just a child to welcome the Radziminer rebbe to our town. A huge crowd of Hasidim had gathered to greet him. When the rebbe disembarked from the train, my father placed me on his shoulders and asked me to yell out, "*Shalom aleichem moreinu v'rabbeinu!*" (Welcome, our teacher and rabbi!). My father took me to visit the rebbe while he was visiting in the city, and the rebbe put his hands on my head and blessed me. I cherished that moment for a long time. This rebbe died just a few years later, when I was still a young child, and it saddened me.

Our home was a truly religious place where the spirit of hopefulness and kindness was an integral part of daily existence. My parents maintained an unwavering belief in God and a strong commitment to the observance of *mitzvoth* (religious commandments). My father attended prayer services three times daily, and my mother attended services in the shul on Sabbaths and festivals only. My parents taught my siblings and me to observe our religious traditions without question and to maintain our belief in God and his Torah. "God is near us," they would say, "and he will never forsake us." We were taught to believe that God, the creator of the universe, had chosen our destiny as a people and that we were to believe in the coming of the Messiah, who was to bring a time of peace and true happiness for the Jews and all humankind. On the Messiah's coming, the Jewish people would finally return to the Land of Israel, their homeland, and hate would cease to exist in the world. All of Jewish history was leading toward that time. Meanwhile, we were to learn to accept what happened to us individually and as a people, for everything happened by the will of God.

These ideas were reinforced in the schools we attended. My brother and I attended the Talmud Torah for our elementary education. The curriculum in that school included general studies, the Polish language, history, math, and geography, as well as religious studies, the Bible, prayer, and Shulchan Arukh (Jewish religious laws). The school days were long, six days a week, and kept us occupied year round, with the exception of the Sabbaths and holidays. During the school years we became fascinated by and imbued with a deep love for the biblical narratives and the values of our tradition. We were trained to believe that God chose us not to be treated better but to hold us to a higher standard than other nations, and therefore we must try our best to be as close to perfect as possible. God's world is imperfect, we were taught, and it was our task to help him perfect it by observing *mitzvoth*, performing good deeds as written in the Torah and expanded on by our sages. Because God expected more of us, we learned, he permitted the other nations to oppress us with expulsions and persecutions. My sister attended public school and received her religious education in the Beis Yaacov School for Girls. All three of us were good students. We loved to read and took our education seriously. My sister was an especially excellent student and an avid reader.

In my mind the study of Torah was a religious requirement. As I advanced in age, I also advanced in my studies, which included the study of Talmud (Mishnah and Gemara). In time I became fascinated with the intricate discussions contained in these sacred texts, and I studied them with pious devotion not only to acquire more knowledge but also to make myself pleasing in the eyes of God. I was fascinated by the wisdom of the great masters of our Jewish tradition and desired to emulate their devotion to God, their love for the study of Torah, and their commitment to the performance of *mitzvoth*.

Children of very religious families usually attended the Talmud Torah school. But there were also schools with more modern philosophies that Jewish children attended. One of those was the Yavneh school, where Hebrew and Polish were the languages of instruction and Zionism was the educational focus. There were also worldly private Jewish schools, which concentrated mostly on general studies and included Judaic studies. Of course, Jewish children could attend the public school, where no Judaic subjects were taught. Mlawa was also proud of its progressive, very successful six-year gymnasium high school. The education there was advanced and focused on progressive general subjects. All classes were conducted in Polish or Hebrew. Judaism, meaning Jewish and Hebrew subjects and Zionism, was included, but it was not considered a religious high school in the accepted meaning of the word. It attracted the finest modern teachers, was supported by the community, and was the envy of the larger cites. It existed for about twenty years and provided an excellent education for young men and women. It is painful to recall how all of it was destroyed with the Nazi Germany attack on Poland, which led to the horrors of World War II and the Holocaust.

Throughout my childhood, I saw myself as a direct link in the chain of my Jewish ancestors. I lived with an awareness of God's presence and with the conviction that I would live to see better times of peace and security if I lived a pious life. The religious studies became for me a linkage of ideas and ideals to the history of the Jewish people, which was hallowed by the prophets and sages, the interpreters of the Jewish faith and tradition.

Sabbaths were particularly special times in our home, and we looked forward to them with great anticipation. For some twenty-five hours each week, Sabbaths were celebrated with our finest clothes, the best food, and a relaxed and joyous atmosphere. The preparations for the Sabbath on Fridays were very much part of the Sabbath experience. The shopping, cooking, and baking actually began on Thursday. My mother would frequently cook extra portions of food and bring them to a needy family early Friday morning, making sure that no one saw her and thus protecting the recipients from embarrassment. The late afternoon hours on Friday were special in that there was always a rush to make sure that all preparations for the Sabbath had been completed, for cleaning, cooking, and baking were not to be done on the Sabbath day.

Before the sun set on Friday, all the rush and hurry would come to an end. Some of my most cherished memories are of the solemn, awe-inspiring moment when, cleaned up and in our best clothes, we would surround the dining room table and watch our mother light the Sabbath candles, never later than eighteen minutes before sunset. She would light the five candles, cover her face with the palms of both hands, recite the blessing over the candles, and meditate quietly, praying for the welfare of her family and her community and for peace in the world.[10] The male members of the family would then leave for the synagogue to welcome the Sabbath with prayer and song. On our return from the synagogue after an hour or so, we would exchange joyous Sabbath greetings, and a spirit of reverence and holiness would permeate our home and our hearts for the following twenty-four hours.

We sat around the dining room table, which was covered with a white tablecloth and set with our finest dishes and the shining candles in their polished silver candlesticks. This special meal would begin with my father reciting the kiddush (sanctification of the Sabbath) over a cup of wine, the symbol of joy. The most delicious foods were prepared for these meals, which were always served and eaten in a leisurely manner. We would sit around the table, singing *zemirot*—poetic songs expressing praises to God for the Sabbath, the Torah, and his commandments.

We usually slept late on Sabbath mornings, for Jewish law prohibited going to work or school on the Sabbath. My brother and I accompanied our father to the synagogue at nine o'clock. We attended services in the Hasidic Radziminer *shtibl*, where the services were held in a joyous atmosphere, with chants and songs. This service would include the reading of a portion from a Torah scroll written on parchment, consisting of the Five Books of Moses. I remember so vividly how proud my father was, walking with his two sons, one on each side, to and from the synagogue. On our return from the synagogue, we would enjoy a special leisurely lunch, sing *zemirot*, and hold interesting conversations.

We children would usually play and visit friends in the afternoon while the parents enjoyed a nap, reading, or studying. In summer months, because of the long Sabbath afternoons, the family always had time to visit with relatives and socialize with friends and neighbors. We would often all go for a walk to the farms and fields that surrounded Mlawa. On our walks we would have interesting conversations with the Polish farmers, who would be busy working their fields. I can still feel the excitement and the great joy that my sister, my brother, and I experienced visiting with friends and talking to neighbors.

Late in the afternoon the male members of my family would return to the synagogue for the *minhah* and *ma'ariv* prayers. As in all Hasidic synagogues, these services were scheduled to allow enough time between the two services to celebrate the end of the Sabbath with *shaloshsudes*—a third Sabbath meal—together with other Hasidim. This was not a real meal in any sense. It was, rather, a symbolic meal with a slice of challah (special Sabbath bread), a piece of herring, and some simple dessert or cake. The camaraderie and the joy of celebrating the concluding moments of the Sabbath together with other Jews was the focus. In Kabalistic-Hasidic literature, the time of the third Sabbath meal is referred to as the time of Ra'ava De'ra'avin—"Favors of Favors"—the time when God is most disposed toward his people, when he most sympathetically receives their efforts toward spiritual growth. At the *shaloshsudes* before the end of the Sabbath, the Hasidim would sing ecstatically, expressing the spiritual inspiration they had attained during the Sabbath. I remember so very well those moments when the Hasidim sat around a long table, swaying back and forth and sideways, with their eyes closed and with full concentration, singing with devotion and happiness:

> Yedid nefesh av harahman, m'shoch avdekha el re'tzonekha . . .
> (Beloved of the soul, compassionate Father,
> Draw your servant to your will . . .)
> Higaleh na ufros Havivi alai et sukat sh'lomekha
> (Please, reveal Yourself, Beloved, for all the world to see.
> And shelter me in peace beneath Your canopy.)

Their singing expressed their heartfelt piety and longing for God's presence. The entire room seemed to be filled with the purity of spirit generated by these simple men with great and beautiful souls. These Hasidim extended these emotions, pure in spirit, far beyond the *shtibl*. The feelings accompanied them wherever they went during the following week, long after the Sabbath was over.

On returning home from the synagogue, we would recite the *havdalah* (separation) prayer, marking the end of the holy Sabbath and the beginning of the ordinary new week. Before reciting the *havdalah*, my mother would sit near the window, look at the sky, and, with pious devotion, recite a prayer in Yiddish:

> Got fun Avrohomen, fun Yitzhoken, un fun Yacoven,
> Bahit dain folk Yisroel fun alem beizen, bashitz zei in zeier noit . . . .
> (God of Abraham, of Isaac, and of Jacob,
> protect your people Israel from all evil
> and grant the tabernacle of peace to the world . . .).[11]

The *havdalah* was recited over a cup of wine, a lighted and colorful braided candle, and spices. The prayer consisted of four short blessings: one over the wine, one over the sweet-smelling spices, one over the light, and one concerning the distinction between the Sabbath and the rest of the week—"Blessed are you God who separates light from darkness . . . between the holy and the ordinary." Before these four blessings we would recite a few biblical verses that expressed hope and dependence on God as our strength and salvation: "He will help us when we call on him. He will bring salvation to human kind."

Throughout the year we would celebrate the Jewish festivals with the same extravagance, relaxation, and joy as we exhibited on the Sabbaths. Each of these special days brought to our attention its unique message, both spiritual and historical. These holy days made us aware of our historical past, gave us a sense of pride in who we were as a people, and provided us with spiritual strength, security, and hope for a better future. We considered the Sabbath and the holidays to be a foretaste of the world to come.

Of course, the Jews in Mlawa were also imbued with the spirit of *haskallah*, enlightenment, which began among Jews during the nineteenth century. Progressive thoughts, revolutionary ideas, and rejection of religious traditions were also prevalent among the Jews in Mlawa. Yet, as I look back to those years, I see the Jewish community in Mlawa as being like a separate nation within a nation. The same was true of practically all the Jewish communities in the cities and towns in Poland. We cherished our heritage, we lived our culture, and we had our schools, synagogues, social and trade organizations, and religious and political movements of all kinds. All these cemented us so that even though we lived physically in the midst of the Polish people, psychologically and spiritually we lived, to a large extent, in a separate world. We spoke Yiddish to one another, read and wrote Hebrew, and spoke to our neighbors in Polish. And for most of us, our traditional religious practices constituted the core of our lives.

Before I close this chapter about my hometown, I want to mention two literary works about Mlawa. *Pinkes Mlawe* (Book [Notebook] of Mlawa), a monumental book about Jewish life in Mlawa, was published in Yiddish by Velt-Farband-Mlawer (World Association of Jews from Mlawa). I consider the volume to be a memorial book for the Jews of Mlawa who perished in the Holocaust.

The idea for this book was formulated at a meeting of prominent Jewish leaders in Mlawa on April 21, 1939, for the purpose of perpetuating the history of the Jews in Mlawa. Jews from Mlawa who lived in Warsaw and in New York organized committees for that same purpose. Almost all members of the committee in Mlawa involved in the planning of this project perished in the Holocaust, and all the Mlawa historical material was destroyed with them. In his 1950 introduction to the book, Ya'akov Shatzki wrote that the *Pinkes Mlawe* will now have to serve as a memorial for the Jews of Mlawa who perished so tragically in the Holocaust instead of serving as it was intended, to be a literary work of the history of the Jews in Mlawa and a source of pride that would be found in the Jewish homes in Mlawa.[12]

There are still two organizations of people from Mlawa, one in Israel and one in New York. The Irgun Yotzei Mlawa, the Organization of Jews from Mlawa in Tel Aviv, published another book in 1984. This book, titled *Mlawa Hayehudit,* comes in two volumes.[13] Survivors from Mlawa have made significant contributions to these volumes, with articles in Hebrew, English, and Yiddish in memory of the history, development, and destruction of the Jewish community in Mlawa that does not exist anymore.

2

The Rise of the Nazi Party
and the Invasion of Poland

When Adolf Hitler and his Nazi Party came to power in Germany in 1933, I was about ten years old. Although I was young, I was well aware of the drastic political changes going on in this neighboring country west of Poland. From the conversations I heard in our home and from adults everywhere, I learned of the persecution of the Jews in Nazi Germany. Within two months after the Nazi rise to power, a general boycott of Jewish shops and commercial enterprises was proclaimed throughout Germany. The Germans put up signs with the word *Jude* (Jew) painted inside large yellow Stars of David, identifying stores as Jewish owned and therefore the ones to be boycotted. Armed guards picketed Jewish-owned shops, factories, and businesses. The Nazis organized huge rallies to promote the boycott. Soon thereafter, we learned of the public burning of books written by Jewish authors. As far as we could tell, most Germans were acquiescing to the Nazi demands.

The Yiddish newspapers in Poland kept us informed of the latest developments in Nazi Germany. We knew that Jews were being dismissed from public offices and from their positions in the German army and navy. Jewish judges were unseated; professors and teachers were expelled from the universities and public schools. Jews were banned from going to the theater and forbidden to work in the publishing industry, including the press. Nazis terrorized political opponents, Communists, and Jews. The Nuremberg Laws, passed in September 1935, included the Reich Citizenship Law, which decreed that only those people of German blood, Aryans, would be considered citizens of the Third Reich. Persons defined as having "impure blood" now held an inferior status and were subjects of the state without rights.[1]

As the persecution of Jews in Germany became more severe, so, too, did anti-Semitic sentiments spread and intensify in Poland. The aura of Hitler's policies hung over us, and life became more difficult. Every successful act of German defiance of world opinion was making the anti-Semites in Poland more audacious. Poland's reactionary political parties, the Polish National Democrats and the fascist Falangists, had long striven to ride to power on anti-Jewish slogans, and now they had the concrete example of the Nazi Party. The Polish government, comprised at that time by General Józef Pilsudski's followers, also took an anti-Semitic slant, partially to counteract the propaganda that it was a government of "Jew lovers." The anti-Jewish campaigns became more and more venomous. Jewish pedestrians were attacked on the streets. Within a short period of time the anti-Semitic movements were not content with propaganda alone; they translated their words into deeds. In Warsaw they drove Jews from public parks and gardens. On the eves of national holidays, picketers paraded in front of Jewish-owned stores to prevent Poles from entering. The boycott against Jewish merchants was considered legal in Poland, and government officials claimed that targeting Jews economically was not against the law. Of course, the boycott affected the economic situation of Jews in Poland, including those in Mlawa.

The schools of higher education in Warsaw became sources for acts of anti-Semitism. Students were urged not to enter Jewish-owned bookstores. At the University of Warsaw and Warsaw Polytechnic University, Jewish students were barred from sitting with non-Jews. Many Jewish students protested by refusing to sit in their designated places in the lecture halls, choosing instead to remain standing. I remember Noah, the youngest son of the Romaner family, who was a student at the University of Warsaw. On his visit home he told us how all the Jewish students felt discriminated against while standing together in the lecture halls of the university in protest. They also felt a sense of pride by standing together, supporting each other, and not giving in to bigotry.

The Jewish press protested these outrageous anti-Semitic acts as loudly as the state-monitored censors would permit. Jewish representatives appealed to the government, but to no avail. The Polish government, it seemed, closed its eyes to the activities of the anti-Semitic gangs as attacks became more violent and more intense. Acts of physical violence and other excesses against Jews became frequent events. Some of those acts took the form of pogroms, when large groups of Poles attacked Jews physically. When a young, mentally ill Jew from the village of Kalushin shot and killed a sergeant of the Polish army, a pogrom broke out in the neighboring city of Minsk. Although no Jews were killed, many people were badly beaten, the windows of many Jewish homes were smashed, and Jewish homes were burned. The anti-Semitic Endekes (National Democrats) used the slogan "Blood for blood!" calling for all Jews to suffer for the crime of spilling the blood of the higher Slavic race. Nevertheless, the government censor strictly forbade the press from using the word "pogrom" to describe this bloody violence.

In Mlawa, too, there were incidents of Polish youngsters attacking Jew-

ish youngsters. Fights between Polish boys and Jewish boys were not infrequent. I was attacked on numerous occasions, with the assailants calling me
"Christ killer." Sadly, the police response to the complaints was usually one of
indifference. I remember my frustration when I heard Jews describe the reaction of police when they reported anti-Semitic incidents. "You're alive," they
would say. "So what are you complaining about?"

Nevertheless, life in Mlawa proceeded rather "normally." Jews continued
going to their businesses and shops, and children continued going to their
schools. We knew that ours was a history of persecution, and as always, we
hoped for better days. In our days, though, there was a bit of a difference, as
young people began to organize to defend themselves and fight back. Others turned their interest to Zionism, with the intention of leaving Poland and
immigrating to Palestine to help rebuild the long-neglected Jewish homeland. No longer did they wish to wait for the Messiah to bring the Jews to the
land of their ancestors, as they had waited for centuries for this to happen.

After graduating from the Talmud Torah in my town at age thirteen, I attended the local yeshiva, Beis Yosef, for about a year or so until my father decided it was best for me to continue my education in Warsaw. In the fall of
1937, at the age of fourteen, I enrolled in the Mesivta—the yeshiva of the
Ger Hasidim. I enjoyed being in Warsaw, with the countless opportunities to
study under great teachers, develop friendships, and be exposed to new experiences. In the Mesivta, we concentrated primarily on traditional religious
studies of Talmud, the Bible, and Shulchan Arukh. On my own, however, I
studied Jewish and Polish history and the Hebrew language and read Polish
and Hebrew literature, subjects that were neglected in the yeshiva.

While living in Warsaw, Poland's capital city, I became aware of the central position that Polish Jewry held in the life of world Jewry. Poland had the
largest Jewish population in Europe, not only in absolute numbers but also
as a percentage of the general population—before World War II there were
approximately 3,350,000 living in Poland, 10 percent of the total population
of 33,000,000. In 1937, approximately 350,000 Jews were living in Warsaw,
a city with a total population of 1,000,000. Warsaw had the second-largest
Jewish population in the world after New York City. Consequently, Jewish
life in Warsaw was much richer politically, religiously, culturally, and socially
than in any other European city. Jewish merchants, business enterprises, yeshivas, schools, and hundreds of synagogues of all kinds dominated large sections of the city. All the different Hasidic dynasties were represented, as were
countless institutions and organizations. Warsaw was a stronghold of traditional Judaism. It was the center of Yiddish literature and Zionism as well as
the capital of Jewish publishing. Twenty-seven daily Jewish newspapers were

published regularly, as were one hundred Jewish weeklies, twenty-four bi-weeklies, and fifty-eight monthlies. When I was living in Warsaw I felt I was in the center of the Jewish world. Only Vilna, another Polish city with a large Jewish population, could compare as a center of Yiddish literary and cultural activity.

I developed in Warsaw a close attachment to the rebbe of Kuzmir, Rabbi Menachem Dovid Taub, and his family. The headquarters of the Kuzmir rebbe, which included his family's living quarters, was on 39 Nalewki Street, in the heart of Jewish Warsaw. It included a *bet midrash*, where the Hasidim gathered for prayer, study, and celebrations. As I was young and far from my family, I deeply appreciated the loving interest the rebbe and his family extended to me. The rebbe was a tall and strikingly handsome man in his sixties. A pure white beard surrounded his masculine and expressive face, conveying authority, wisdom, and kindness. There was a princely look about him, and he walked with remarkable pride and dignity. People on the streets would stop to admire him. Occasionally, he would call on me to walk with him, which I considered a great honor. His wife, too, was charming and dignified, respected and admired by all who knew her. Their son, Rabbi Levi Yitzchak Taub, and his wife and three children shared the same household. All of them accepted me as if I were a member of the family.

My most memorable experiences with the rebbe were the Sabbath meals, both Friday nights and Saturday noontime, when the Hasidim would join the rebbe's *tish* (table) and take part in the meal. The rebbe would teach Torah, and the Hasidim would hang onto every word of their rebbe's teaching. The gatherings included joyous and fervent singing of Sabbath songs. Our group of young yeshiva students looked forward to joining the rebbe and his Hasidim on the Sabbaths. We loved to sing, and we particularly enjoyed the Hasidic songs at the gatherings at the rebbe's *tish*.

Two remarkable personal experiences stand out in my mind about this rebbe. The first took place on Ta'anit Esther, the fast that takes place on the day before the holiday of Purim. A few yeshiva students and I were in the rebbe's *bet midrash* in the early afternoon when he unexpectedly walked in. Of course, we rose to our feet in the traditional display of respect. I was the only one from out of town. The rebbe looked at me and asked me if I was fasting. He obviously recognized from my face that I was. He ordered us to sit down and told us the following story. His grandfather, Rebbe Yechezkel of Kuzmir, who was known as a great kabbalist (Jewish mystic), once told his Hasidim that the angels in heaven are saddened by the many fast days our sages had established for us to observe every year. The only justification the angels could find for the rabbis' decrees, the rebbe explained, was that the sages did not know that it was going to take so many years for the Messiah to come; in messianic times, all fast days are to be abolished. When the rebbe was finished with this story, he arranged for a tray of breakfast to be brought in for me and ordered me to eat.

The second remarkable experience took place on the festival of Shavuot in June 1939. I had been ill for a few days with some kind of a virus and had not attended services on the first day of the holiday, which was quite unusual for me. On the second day of the holiday, the rebbe inquired about my health and then sent someone to where I was staying with an order instructing me to pack my things immediately and take a train home. I still remember how embarrassed I was to walk to the train with my suitcase on a holiday, when Jewish law forbids traveling. The virus actually turned out to be quite serious, and I spent part of the summer recuperating. By September of that year the war had begun, and I never saw the rebbe and his family again.

This entire family and all the followers of that Hasidic dynasty perished in the Holocaust. Throughout the years I have often thought of them with loving fondness. I was eager to know what exactly happened to this family before they died. Only recently did I find out that Rabbi Menachem Dovid Taub died in the Warsaw ghetto in August 1942 and that his son, Rabbi Levi Yitzchak, was elected by his fellow Hasidim to be the next rebbe. After the Warsaw ghetto uprising in April 1943, he and his entire family were driven to one of the extermination camps, most likely to Treblinka, where most of the Jews from Warsaw perished.[2]

While living in Warsaw, I had more opportunities than I would have had in Mlawa to follow what was happening in Germany. The news that came to us from the radio and the daily newspapers caused increasing concern to the Jews in Poland. The lives of the Jews in Germany were becoming progressively more restricted. The Nazi racial laws aimed to isolate the Jews from the rest of the population. They spread the idea that Jews were inferior and needed to either be constrained in their freedom or leave Germany. Life for Jews in Germany became even more oppressive in 1937 and 1938. Jews were arrested en masse. Jewish-owned shops were pillaged and wrecked, and synagogues were destroyed. All Jews had to register their property as a preliminary step to confiscation. Passports held by Jews were invalidated, and those who needed passports for emigration purposes were issued passports stamped with a capital "J" for *Jude*. Jewish men were ordered to add the name "Israel" to their names, and women were to add "Sarah" to their names.

In April 1938 we learned of the Anschluss, the annexation of Austria to Germany. At that time we did not know whether the Austrians invited Nazi Germany to unite with them and form a larger and stronger Nazi Germany or whether Nazi Germany occupied Austria by force. After the war I learned that both opinions were correct. In the Austro-German agreement of July 11, 1936, Dr. Kurt von Schuschnigg, the chancellor of Austria, acknowledged Austria to be a "German state." He also agreed to provide amnesty to Nazi political prisoners in Austria and to appoint Nazis and Nazi sympathizers to positions of political responsibility.[3] The Nazis in Austria had full freedom for their Nazi activities and were able to organize support for the unification of Germany and Austria. It is also true that Hitler and Goering manipulated and lied to the Austrian chancellor and pressured him to sign the Anschluss agreement, and the German army marched into Austria, amid cheers of welcome, without any opposition. After the annexation the violent treatment of Jews extended to Austria as well.[4]

After the Anschluss, Nazi Germany turned its attention to Czechoslovakia with the aim to destroy the Czechoslovak state and grab its territories and inhabitants for the Third Reich. The pretext was the supposed Czech mistreatment of the German Sudeten population and Germany's desire to protect the Germans living there. They threatened to attack Czechoslovakia and take the country by force. This frightened the British and French governments, and Hitler took notice of this fact and invited the foreign ministers of these powers to Munich for a conference. There, with manipulations and deceit, the Nazi leaders succeeded in persuading and pressuring the British and French governments, allies of Czechoslovakia, to sign their agreement to the German occupation of Sudeten-Czech territory. The two great Western powers agreed to break their pact with Czechoslovakia in order to appease Hitler. By October 1938 the German army occupied Sudeten-German territory without firing a shot. But Hitler was not satisfied. As he confided later to his generals, "It was clear to me from the first moment that I could not be satisfied with the Sudeten-German territory. That was only a partial solution."[5]

Late in October 1938 we in Warsaw knew that seventeen thousand Jews had been expelled from the German Reich. These Jews were immigrants from Poland and had lived in Germany for many years before the Nazi Party came to power. Yet Poland refused to accept the Jewish refugees, and they were forced to live in a no-man's-land in crowded, unsanitary barracks in Zbanszyn, near the Polish border. The Jews in Warsaw were alerted to the appalling plight of the Jewish refugees, who were driven out of their homes with only their clothes on their backs. I remember the collections for money, blankets, and clothing that were collected on the streets of Warsaw for the refugees. This deportation ultimately became a turning point for mass violence in the Nazi persecution of Jews, for this act led seventeen-year-old Hershel Grynspan, a Polish immigrant living in Paris, to shoot Ernst vam

Rath, the third secretary of the German embassy, in Paris on November 7, 1938. The boy's Polish-born parents were among the Jews who had been deported from Germany, and he hoped his act would bring their plight to the world's attention. But when the Nazi official died on the afternoon of November 9, the Nazis used the killing of a German as a reason to punish all German Jews. Five years of discriminatory policies toward the Jews officially changed to wholesale violence on the night of November 9–10, 1938.

Years later I learned that this pogrom was not spontaneous, as the Germans wanted the world to believe. The German Nazis had already planned it in detail; they were only waiting for the ideal pretext for carrying it out. The assassination of vam Rath was the perfect excuse. The pogrom against Jewish citizens took place all over Germany and became known as Kristallnacht, the "Night of Broken Glass." According to a preliminary report on November 11, 1938, about 191 synagogues were set ablaze and another 76 completely destroyed. A total of 7,500 Jewish businesses were demolished. The value of the destruction came to RM 10 million (U.S. $4 million). Ninety-one Jews were reported killed, and thirty-six were severely injured. Thirty thousand Jews were incarcerated in the Dachau, Buchenwald, and Sachsenhausan concentration camps.[6]

The instructions for the pogrom reached Austria a day later, and the action started on the morning of November 10, 1938. My cousin Kitty Goldberg was nine years old and lived with her parents and brother in Vienna then. She told me that the noise of people yelling awakened the family early that morning. From the second floor they looked down from the window and saw Jews being beaten and driven onto trucks. They got dressed immediately, and before long they heard knocking on the door. Her brother opened the door, and five men forced themselves into the apartment, yelling and beating her father and driving him to go down the stairs to the waiting truck. He went down to the cellar instead and was in hiding there for two months. Of course, the family made him as comfortable as possible and prepared food for him daily. He remained in hiding until he, together with his sister and brother-in-law, ran to Germany, and from there they crossed the border into Belgium. On that day of the pogrom, forty-two synagogues were destroyed in Vienna. Some 7,800 Jews in Vienna and 4,600 men from all parts of Austria were sent to the Dachau concentration camp (4,000 of them who were able to guarantee their emigration were subsequently released), 4,083 shops in Vienna were closed, and 1,950 apartments were forcibly vacated in one section of the city alone. In one area of Jewish concentration, twenty-seven Jews were killed, and eighty-eight were seriously wounded. The Austrian population did not interfere, except to participate in the looting.[7]

Hitler was now turning his attention to the part of Czechoslovakia that had remained independent after the German occupation of Sudentenland. By the beginning of 1939 the German Nazi leaders had manipulated the Nazis of Slovakia to request from Germany their independence from the Czechs. This status was granted to them immediately. Slovakia became independent of the Czechs but made an alliance with Nazi Germany. It was now easy for Germany to manipulate and threaten the Czechs so that they signed an agreement for unification with Germany. The prime ministers of Great Britain and France met with Hitler in Munich and gave the consent for this unification.

On March 15, 1939, at 4:00 a.m., the aging and ailing president of Czechoslovakia, Emil Hacha, after an all-night meeting with Hitler in Berlin, finally yielded to Hitler's threats and signed a statement requesting the German leaders to "rescue" his country from ruin. By 6:00 a.m. the German army had crossed the Czech border and was streaming toward Prague. By noon the army had occupied that country without a battle or a protest. Nazi Germany was now getting ready to take on Poland.

Meanwhile, Jews in Germany, Austria, and Czechoslovakia were in a panic and seeking to emigrate, but it was difficult for Jews to get visas to enter other countries. Great Britain held the mandate of Palestine and restricted immigration of Jews to Palestine. Those who managed to leave Germany without permits of entry to other countries remained refugees. President Roosevelt called for a conference to deal specifically with the issue of the Jewish refugees. Representatives of thirty-two countries gathered in Evian, Switzerland, to solve this problem. Nevertheless, the Evian Conference, which lasted five days and which had many people delivering great speeches, ended without any of the countries willing to open their gates for the Jewish refugees. They gave all kinds of excuses.[8]

The German liner *Saint Louis* was another big disappointment for the refugees who attempted to save themselves from the Nazi onslaught. The *Saint Louis*, with 937 Jewish passengers, left Hamburg for Havana on May 14, 1939. Only thirty passengers were allowed to disembark at Havana on May 30. The others were told that their visas were worthless. America, too, refused refuge for the unfortunate. The *Saint Louis* cruised slowly off the American coast for three days, hoping for an offer of permission to land in any country of safety. For thirty-five days the *Saint Louis* continued its aimless cruising until the governments of England, France, Holland, and Belgium agreed to permit entry to some of the human cargo. A spokesman for the League of Nations found it important to announce that the acts of these governments did not constitute a precedent for other refugees. The Jewish refugees were left knocking at closed doors.[9]

By the time I returned home in the summer of 1939, Nazi Germany had demanded the return of the free city of Danzig, which had been a source of dispute between Germany and Poland for years. It had been under the mandate of the League of Nations. In their demands Germany included the corridor of Pomerania, which linked East Prussia to the mainland of Germany. Germany was threatening war, and the response of the Polish government was not to give even an inch. It was a very tense summer, filled with trepidation at the possibility of Germany attacking Poland. Mlawa's location of being only about ten kilometers (six miles) from the East Prussian border placed us in a particularly precarious position. Civil defense groups were organized in cities throughout Poland. I, too, joined a civil defense group in our neighborhood, even though I planned to return to Warsaw to continue my studies. The last meeting of our neighborhood defense organization took place on Thursday evening, August 31. The following morning, Germany attacked Poland with its full military might. This was the beginning of World War II, and for me, my family, and my people, life was never the same.

Indeed, the attack on Poland was not unexpected, but Poland's army was ill prepared to challenge Germany's mechanized military power and had no chance of stopping the invading army. The crushing strength of the German panzers was even greater than the military strategists or popular opinion had imagined. It took the German army only days to break through Poland's western border. Three days after the initial attack, the Germans marched into Mlawa. So swift was the advance of the German army into Polish territory that within a few weeks after the invasion, Warsaw was completely surrounded by the German army.[10] The German Luftwaffe (air force) bombed the city day and night. There were many thousands of civilian casualties in addition to the heavy military losses. A great many homes were destroyed, and the people suffered severely from a serious shortage of water, food, and shelter. The Polish army fought valiantly in the defense of Warsaw, but they were no match against the Germans' powerful army and their superior air force. Moreover, no help was forthcoming from the Western powers. After weeks of heroic fighting, Warsaw fell on the twenty-eighth of September 1939. The Germans occupied all of western Poland, and Soviet Russia, through a secret pact signed before the war, moved its army westward and occupied the eastern half of Poland. German-occupied Poland was further divided into two parts. The western part of the country and some sections of the north were annexed to Germany, and the central part of Poland, including Warsaw, was designated as the Polish General Government under German occupation. Mlawa, located in northern Poland near the border with East Prussia, officially became part of the Third Reich.[11]

From the first day of the German occupation, Polish citizens, soldiers and civilians alike, were exposed to destruction and death. Unarmed citizens were fired on indiscriminately in the streets and in their homes. That was the beginning of a dreadful six years for millions of people in Europe. For the Jews of Europe those six years were a holocaust. By the end of the war in May 1945, the Germans and their collaborators had murdered six million Jews. No one could have imagined the extent of the catastrophe that was beginning to unfold. Murder and brutality and the arrest and abuse of Jews were daily events. At first the Germans charged the Jews with resisting authority, or concealing arms, or violating currency regulations. Then, after a short time, no explanations were given. Jews were rounded up for forced labor in every city and town. Some were sent to Germany and never returned. It is estimated that by December 1939, 250,000 Jews had been killed in German-occupied Poland by such methods as shootings, beatings, and starvation.[12]

From the beginning of the occupation of Poland, Jews were particularly singled out for persecution and murder. Massacres of Jews occurred in the communities of Chelmnik, Konskie, Kutno, Lowicz, Lujov, Zdunska Wola, and Przemiszl. In Ostrowe many male Jews were shot after being forced to dig their own graves. Massacres of Jews also took place in Lask, Sueradz, Czestochowa, Nowe Miasto, and Lodz. Hundreds of synagogues were destroyed in the first three months of occupation. The Nazi press announced the formation of fire brigades devoted to burning synagogues, sacred Torah scrolls, and books of Jewish content.

Some of this horror had been anticipated. After Hitler came to power and began to put his racist theories into practice, some political writers and Jewish leaders warned of the possible attempt to annihilate the Jewish people. I remember Vladimir (Ze'ev) Jabotinsky, the founder of Betar and the Zionist-Revisionist movement, who traveled across the cities and towns of Poland in 1936–37 and, with his great oratory talents, urged Jews to leave Poland and immigrate to Palestine. But no one could have believed that the near future would become so tragically devastating, a holocaust. In reality few options were available at that time for Polish Jews to emigrate. Only some of the younger generation, imbued with the pioneering spirit of Zionism, managed to immigrate to Palestine in spite of the difficulties connected with that move. Most of us continued with our daily struggle for existence and our individual pursuits, in fear, hoping that somehow we would be saved from the potential wickedness surrounding us.

3
Mlawa under German Occupation

My memories of the day the Germans invaded Poland are still clear to me. It was early Friday morning, September 1, 1939, and my mother woke us suddenly, at about 5:30. Practically shaking, she informed us that Germany had invaded Poland. Naturally, we were terrified. The sound of gunfire and shelling at the East Prussian border could be heard in the distance. We sensed that a terrible time lay ahead. Indeed, the war that had threatened us for months had actually begun.

During the morning hours that followed, our city was bombed, and a number of people were killed. Several houses in the center of Mlawa were destroyed, and people began to flee. Some left their belongings behind, taking only what they could carry. Those with means hired horses and buggies to carry more of their belongings, and the roads became crowded with people running in all directions. Because Mlawa was a border city, close to the battlefield, many reasoned that they would be safer farther inland. People ran to surrounding cities, but primarily to Warsaw. The German air force, however, dropped bombs on the roads crowded with running and defenseless civilians, causing many casualties. On realizing that the dangers on the road were just as great as those in the city, some returned home. There was much confusion among the people in the city. The authorities had either fled or gone into hiding. Ironically, those who reached Warsaw hoping to escape the bombing did not find safety because Warsaw was bombarded mercilessly until the Germans occupied it, and thousands of people were killed.

Despite the masses of people leaving Mlawa, my father decided that we would stay. During World War I, he explained, the people of Mlawa had also attempted to escape the invading German and Russian armies. (Mlawa had been the site of heavy battles between the Germans and Russians during the Great War.) People had fled when Mlawa was threatened with occupation by the Russians. The Germans at that time were actually kinder to the Jews than the Russians. Then, after the Russians occupied the city for a time, the Germans returned. The people who had fled the Russians came back, only to run away again when the city was about to be recaptured by the Russians. Who knew what was ahead? my father reasoned. And running from the city caused serious problems for many families. My father was convinced that if the German army broke through the border near our city, no city in Poland would be safe. He also knew that he would have no means to provide for his family in a new and unfamiliar place. He believed that we would be safer in our own city and that we would have a better chance of surviving the war in the place we all knew. His logic seemed sound, and so we stayed where we were. Who among us could have envisioned the impending Nazi "final solution of the Jewish problem"?

My father's store was located in the center of the city, an area that had been bombed, and as fire spread, my father managed to save the merchandise from his store. It became our source of income for as long as the Germans permitted us to remain in the city. Meanwhile, our cellar became our home and shelter from the bombs. We spent that first weekend in hiding, making occasional contact with neighbors, friends, and relatives. Terrible fear gripped us all, and we worried that the Polish army at the nearby border would not be strong enough to withstand the German onslaught. We hoped that the world powers would not permit Nazi Germany to get away with this unprovoked attack. We did not want to believe that the Western democratic nations would permit Germany to occupy Poland as they had permitted the occupation of Czechoslovakia.

Throughout the weekend we heard the shelling, and the bursts of machine-gun fire become more frequent and loud, but by Sunday, September 3, the shelling became less frequent, and by evening we discovered that the Polish army was retreating. Not knowing what to expect, we spent Sunday night hiding in the cellar. It was extremely quiet throughout the night. On Monday morning, we emerged from our hiding place and settled in our home with the hope that the occupation would not last long. A group of us, young people from our neighborhood, watched fearfully as the powerful German army occupied our city. A mass of trucks with German soldiers drove through the center of town. Long columns of well-equipped soldiers with machine guns marched and rolled through the city center, all of them heading toward Warszawska Street, which led toward Warsaw. It was terrifying to watch, and we felt as if the very ground we stood on and the buildings around us were trembling with fear. We understood now that the Polish army would not be able to stop the advance of this powerful force. We certainly did not know what exactly was ahead of us, but we feared that our lives would never be the same. Only a miracle could help us. But that miracle did not come.

On Monday, September 4, 1939, the German army officially occupied

Mlawa, and Nazi rule was immediately established in the city. We had no choice but to accept the reality, so we began making some sort of order in our lives, fearful but hopeful for some semblance of normalcy. Within days of the occupation the Germans, assisted by Polish collaborators, began the persecution of Jews. They rounded up Jews and ordered them to clean up the charred buildings in the city. They robbed and confiscated stores and warehouses owned by Jews. They ordered many families to vacate their homes if those particular houses, buildings, or apartments were to their liking. They confiscated furniture and valuables owned by Jews. Soldiers rounded up Jews for free labor, and some never returned. They abused us and beat us when it seemed to them that we were working too slowly.

One day soon after their arrival, the Germans arrested the prominent Jewish leaders, including the rabbi of the city, Rabbi Yechiel Moshe Segalowitz, an elderly sage of great intellect and prominence. He had led the Jewish community of Mlawa with distinction for more than four decades. Rabbi Segalowitz was a recognized scholar and author and was well respected and admired by all. After a number of days the Germans released the leaders and ordered them to set up a Judenrat (Jewish council). The Judenrat would be responsible to the German authorities for the behavior of all Jews in the city, including fulfilling all the orders and decrees that would be forthcoming for Mlawa's Jewish community. This was consistent with instructions issued by Reinhard Heydrich, second-in-command in the German intelligence service (the SS [Schutzstaffel]) and one of the architects of the "Final Solution," to the chiefs of the Einsatzgruppen (the SS death squads) on September 21, 1939.[1]

In accordance with those instructions the Germans established Judenrats in most of the cities and towns they occupied. The Judenrats were vehicles for transmitting and realizing the Germans' orders. They usually selected for the Judenrats members of the prewar *gemainde,* or *kehillah,* the elected council of Jewish community leaders that commonly existed in Jewish communities throughout Poland. The Jews who formed the Judenrat also regarded their group as the successor to the *kehillah* and continued the custom of serving the Jewish community and defend its interests to the authorities. In Mlawa, too, they tried to find former *kehillah* members to serve on the Judenrat. On his release from prison, Rabbi Segalowitz, with the approval of the Germans, appointed honorable people with fine reputations to serve on the council: Zisza Maizlitz, Aizhe Rotchild, Itzik Alter, Paltiel Ceglo, Noson Mordechai Kolnierz, and Elazar Winograd. Butche Katz was appointed the secretary.

Traditionally, the function of the *kehillah* or *gemainde* in the prewar period was to maintain the religious institutions—synagogues, schools and yeshivas, *mikvehs* (ritual baths), and burial societies. It supported the community's functionaries—the rabbis, cantors, teachers of the Jewish community religious schools, and ritual slaughterers. The members also cared for the community's aged, the destitute, and the sick. The Judenrat hoped to perform these functions, too, but the Germans imposed other, more onerous tasks on it. Immediately after the council was established, the Germans made the Judenrat "fully responsible (in the literal sense of the word) for the exact execution according to terms of all instructions released or yet to be released."[2] The members were threatened with severe collective punishment of the Jews if their directives were disobeyed. The first order the Judenrat had to follow was to register all Jews sixteen years of age and older living in the city. We certainly knew that the Germans would have inflicted massive reprisals for disobedience or resistance.

Ultimately, the Judenrat was assigned tasks that were to serve German ends. These tasks completely subverted the traditional objectives of the *kehillah*. In their systematic approach to the destruction of the Jews, the Germans demanded of the Judenrat first the money and possessions of the Jews, then their labor, and then, in time, their lives. No Judenrat could reconcile the contradictory German and Jewish conceptions of its role. Therein lay the tragic dilemma of the Jewish communal leaders who served in the Judenrats in all the cities and towns under German occupation.

Shortly after the appointment of the Judenrat, the Germans ordered it to register all Jews in the city, not just those sixteen years of age and older, and to demand that all Jews wear a round piece of white cloth ten centimeters (about four inches) wide on the front and back of their upper garments so that every Jew could be easily identified. Later, the Germans changed the color of the cloth to yellow. Jews, under German order, were forbidden to walk on the sidewalk when a German was coming in their direction. The Germans also required us to take off our hats when approached by a German and to stand at attention and respond quickly when addressed by one.

The Germans prohibited the opening of Jewish schools or the conducting of public meetings. Yet teachers organized classes of small groups and taught children secretly. I joined a group of yeshiva students who met clandestinely whenever possible to study the Torah and have conversations. We discussed the possibilities of getting out of our situation by leaving the city. In the beginning it was possible to run to the Soviet-occupied eastern part of Poland. At the pain of separation from family and despite the risk involved, many young Jews left the city and crossed the border into Soviet-occupied Poland. My cousin Jacob Goldberg, too, took the risk and managed to make it across the border, but he returned because life under the Russian was also very difficult, at times even life threatening. The Russians drove some of these refugees to the harsh camps in Siberia, where conditions were extremely dire, and many did not survive. My cousin Yerma Berko and his girlfriend fled to the Russian side also. We never heard from them again. Obviously, they did not survive the Russian treatment of the refugees from the west. I remained with my family in Mlawa with the hope of better times to come.

Soon after the occupation began, our apartment became home for some of our other relatives. My two grandmothers and one of my cousins, Shifra Berko, came to live with us because their homes had been destroyed during the bombing of the city. We all recognized that challenging days were ahead of us, and we each did our best to make life at home as normal as possible. We learned to accept living in fear, not knowing what to expect and what the next day would bring. Feelings of frustration and of being trapped often overtook us. Yet we rationalized that just as wars have beginnings, they also have endings. This war, too, would come to an end, and we hoped that the end would come soon. We were incapable of imagining what was really ahead of us. My family feared particularly for my safety because the Germans often sent young people of my age off to forced labor. I therefore spent many days and nights in cellars and in fields among overgrown weeds and plants. I would usually take along a number of books to read and study. The cellars where I hid were cold and damp and windowless, and I would read and study by candlelight. Yet, despite all the precautions, I was often rounded up for forced labor.

My first personal encounter with brutality was during the early days of German occupation when I and other young Jews were rounded up for one of those forced-labor situations. We were ordered to clean up the remains of the buildings that had been damaged by the German bombardment during the first three days of the air attacks. The SS guards ordered some of us to break down the standing brick walls. Others were ordered to clean the bricks. Eventually, they assigned me to another group to pile up the bricks for further use. At one point, as if out of nowhere, a German supervisor in a black SS uniform ran over to me, yelling in German. I felt perplexed and frightened and did not understand a word he was saying. Then he started slapping me until I fell to the ground, and he continued to yell at me with anger and brutality. I was humiliated beyond words.

Later, my coworkers explained to me that I had been attacked because I had not piled the bricks properly. How was I to know the art of piling up bricks? I was a sensitive sixteen-year-old boy with no work experience who had never been abused or mistreated. Only when I returned home after the day's work did I burst into tears. I could not accept this new reality, that I could be physically assaulted for no reason at any time. We quickly learned just how vulnerable we were. We had no recourse, no protection. We were reminded constantly, in many different ways, that we had no rights and no way to seek justice or register a complaint. The Germans treated us as subhumans to be abused and tortured.

The first experience that terrified the Mlawa Jews as a community took place on the last day of the Sukkot festival in October 1939, just a few weeks after the occupation began. The Germans notified us through a messenger of the Judenrat that morning that every Jew must appear in the marketplace by 1:00 p.m. that same day. They ordered us to bring along only what we could carry by hand. Like any subsequent order, it included the threat that anyone who disobeyed the order would be killed on the spot.

My mother arranged for each of us to carry a little bundle of belongings, and we marched together to the marketplace in the center of the city. It was a pitiful sight, a whole large community of Jews—men, women, and children—each carrying a bundle with the most basic possessions and heading toward an unknown destination. Some walked quietly and with dignity, as if going of their own free will. Others cried and walked with terrified looks on their faces even though at that time we did not know of the evil the Germans were capable of committing, especially against Jews.

In the long line of marchers was Rabbi Segalowitz, along with his wife and his daughter. We later found out that he and his family had been offered the option of returning home, but the elderly and frail rabbi refused, saying that he wanted to stay with his people and go with them wherever they would go. We were all gathered in the center of the city, a mass of Jews huddled together and surrounded by armed Germans; we were puzzled and frightened, not knowing the meaning of it all.

After a while, trucks arrived, and the Germans ordered us to board them. In shock, the people followed the orders, amid an outburst of heartbreaking cries. At one point I looked up and saw my father, terribly frightened, wiping his tears, wishing to hide his inner pain at being unable to protect his family. All of us burst out crying with him and held onto each other tightly. Suddenly, the Germans stopped forcing us onto the trucks and ordered us to return to our homes. No explanation was given. Some speculated that it was just an exercise to humiliate and frighten us. Perhaps the Germans just wanted to let us know how vulnerable we were. It was certainly terrifying to realize that at their will the Germans could drive us from our homes at any time. Others recalled that a high-ranking officer of the Wehrmacht (the regular armed forces) just happened to be passing through the city just then, stopped, and inquired about the meaning of what he saw. He was seen arguing, and it was his order that reversed the atrocity.[3]

In any event, that was the most terrible experience for our community until one Friday night in November, only a couple of months after the occupation began. We looked out our windows and noticed heavy smoke coming from Shul Gass. Our synagogues, the center of our Jewish life, were on fire. A terrible sadness engulfed our home as we watched the awful smoke rise heavenward. The strict dusk-to-dawn curfew prevented us from running to the street. We were told later that Jews who lived in the immediate vicinity had watched from their windows in horror as the Germans poured gasoline and set the holy places aflame. The Germans entertained themselves while these holy places burned. Some Mlawa residents who lived nearby defied the curfew and gathered around the burning synagogues. Their pleas to permit them to save the Torah scrolls and sacred books were met with laughter and mockery. Yet two young men managed to avoid the German guards' surveillance and risked their lives to save two Torah scrolls. Ultimately, the Germans permitted the Jewish bystanders to help extinguish the fire only when the fire threatened the nearby buildings.[4]

The Mlawa Jews were gripped with mourning when they learned that the Germans destroyed their sacred center. That sadness stayed with us for a very long time. A few days later, the Germans rounded up Jews and forced them to clean up the destroyed buildings and to clear the area. No sign remained to mark that synagogues had ever stood there. The Germans also forced the Judenrat to sign a statement that the Jews themselves had burned down their synagogues.[5]

In spite of our depression and the risks involved, we organized secret places for prayer services. A neighbor of ours, Mr. Purzitzky, who owned a mill in our neighborhood, set up the cellar of his mill as one of these prayer places. My father, brother, and I attended services there on Sabbath mornings whenever it was safe to do so. One Sabbath morning a Polish policeman, a collaborator with the Germans, discovered us praying together in the cellar when he was looking for young people to round up to harvest potatoes on a farm. I was the only young person there, and he insisted that I go with him to join the other young people who were rounded up for the same purpose. He assured us that I would return home after the day's work. Luckily, the worshippers were able to bribe him not to tell the authorities about our meeting place. We stopped the prayer services in the Purzitzky cellar for a while until we felt safe enough to resume. I was emotionally distressed all that day. It was the first Sabbath of my life that I spent working. I was also fasting all day because the only food we were offered was not kosher. We worked hard until nightfall, under heavy pressure to produce the maximum. I returned home very tired and depressed.

The random rounding up of Jews for free labor continued and made it difficult to maintain any sort of normal living, for so many people were rounded up daily that we all became fearful to walk the streets. The Judenrat convinced the German authorities to accept a plan whereby it would supply them with free workers daily so that life could become a bit more "normal." Shaiah Krzeslo and Shlomo Tick were appointed to direct the labor department of the Judenrat. It was their responsibility to provide the Germans with as many laborers as they requested—a complex and difficult assignment. They organized a system of rotation so that every male age sixteen and older would be obligated to serve a free day's work, as often as the rotation system demanded, to supply the labor quotas. The Germans would come to the marketplace where we gathered every morning and select as many free workers as they wanted. This system created an opportunity for some Jews to earn for their livelihood by substituting for someone who would rather pay and be free of his obligation to work on the day designated to him. To our disappointment the random roundup of Jews for free labor did not stop completely.

Mlawa was one of the cities to which Jews from the surrounding smaller towns and villages were driven. The Judenrat was ordered to find homes and to organize the absorption of these families into our city. This was also in accordance with the instructions issued by Heydrich in September 1939.[6]

The role of the Judenrat had been difficult from the beginning, but it intensified as the treatment of the Jews in Mlawa became harsher. The Judenrat attempted to create a kind of balance between fear and normalcy at a stressful and traumatic time. Underlying the complex task of leadership was the hope that we would survive the war and that our lives would return one day to the way they once had been.

The Germans regularly picked up Jews with beards and forced them to cut off their beards. Occasionally, the Germans themselves would cut the beards, causing pain in the process. Some shaved off their beards as a preventive measure, and in time a decree was issued prohibiting Jews from growing beards.

Occasionally, the German local authorities made exceptions to their own rules. For some unexplained reason, Itzik Alter, a member of the Judenrat, was the only one permitted to keep his well-groomed beard. He spoke German well and had a pleasant personality, and he succeeded in developing a personal relationship with the local German authorities. He was in constant contact with them and was quite helpful to many people for a period of time. He would intervene whenever he believed he could wield influence for the better and was successful in releasing many who had been arrested. He was truly devoted to this cause, often at risk to his own life. The Nazis' "kindness" was short lived, however. Alter was arrested later for arranging to smuggle a wagon full of potatoes and was sent to prison in Koenigsberg, East Prussia. After ten months of imprisonment, he was sent to Auschwitz and perished there within days of his arrival.[7]

The Germans would often assemble Jews just for the purpose of abuse and humiliation. I was once rounded up and ordered to join a group of Jews, including some elderly people. The Germans led us to an area outside the city and ordered us to exercise. This was particularly hard for the older Jews. The Nazis amused themselves by beating those who failed to keep up. At one point an elderly Jew stepped forward and, in excellent German, pleaded with the Nazis for mercy, but he was severely beaten instead.

One day, my father disappeared. We had no idea what had happened to him or under what circumstances he was taken away. Naturally, we were terribly worried for his safety, for often people were sent to labor camps and never heard from again. The Judenrat attempted to inquire, but no one was able to find out anything. My mother, at great risk to her own safety, went to the German authorities at city hall daily to ask about him, and all she would get were promises that he would return safely. Our worries increased daily, for we knew not to rely on German promises. About one month after his disappearance, my father returned home. He never shared with us any details of his experiences except that he had been "working hard on a farm."

As I mentioned earlier, from the beginning of the occupation of our city, a few of us yeshiva students met as often as possible for secret Torah study. Later on we studied secretly with Rabbi Segalowitz. When rumors circulated about a possible expulsion of the Jews from Mlawa, Rabbi Segalowitz reviewed with us the story of Rabbi Yohanan Ben Zakai. In the year 70 CE, when the Romans had laid siege around Jerusalem and the destruction of the city was imminent, Rabbi Yohanan was determined to leave. He was given permission by the Roman General Vespasian to establish a Torah study school, and at great risk and with great difficulty, he left the city. He gathered a few students in the small town of Yavneh. The students of Yavneh later spread Torah in Israel and in Babylonia, thereby securing the survival of the Jewish people even after the destruction of Jerusalem.[8] Rabbi Segalowitz then ordained us as rabbis, with the condition that we would continue to study and teach Torah whenever possible. I did not take this ordination seriously. I was a seventeen-year-old student who desired study, and becoming a rabbi was not my intention at that time. Certainly no one could predict our futures. It was nevertheless prophetic on the part of Rabbi Segalowitz.

Meanwhile, we continued living in Mlawa in constant fear. It was not safe to walk the streets or to stay at home. The Germans had the right to force Jews out of their homes for free labor or to send anyone off to a distant place for forced labor. We never knew what a new day might bring; there might be a beating or an arrest, often without any explanation. The Germans had complete control over our lives and did not need to justify their behavior. Jews had no rights, and there was no authority we could turn to for any assistance or complaint.

Yet despite what we considered to be oppressive conditions, during the first fifteen months of Nazi occupation, the Jews of Mlawa were more fortunate than Jews in other cities under German occupation. The city remained open, and no ghetto was established as had been done in many cities of occupied Poland. For the most part, we were permitted to continue living in our homes. Although Jews were not permitted to own businesses, those who owned merchandise were able to do business secretly. Farms surrounding our city continued to produce plentiful supplies of food, which the farmers frequently brought to the city and made available to us. Secretly, my father would personally make contact with the visiting farmers and let them know that he had merchandise for sale. He would invite those who showed interest to come to our house to complete a sale. He did so at great risk, because such transactions were strictly forbidden and could cause the confiscation of his merchandise and his imprisonment. My sister, my brother, and I would frequently help by standing guard to warn him of an approaching German or a Polish policeman while trading was taking place in our home.

While in Mlawa, those Jews who survived the first three days of the bombing, even those who had run away from Mlawa to seek safety in other cities and then returned to Mlawa, would find employment and somehow earn a livelihood, some more and some less. There was enough food available in Mlawa during that period. Given the situations in other cities and towns of Poland, we were just grateful to be a family together. The same was true with my extended family. With love and encouragement, we found strength in each other and were supportive of each other. We were grateful for not having suffered any casualties. We were convinced that God would not forsake us. We could not have imagined what lay ahead of us.

4

The First Expulsion of Jews from Mlawa
and the Creation of a Ghetto

We did not know then all the details of the order that Reinhard Heydrich
had issued to the chiefs of the Einsatzgruppen on September 21, 1939. Only
after the war did we learn that the Einsatzgruppen were to concentrate all
Jews from the countryside into the larger cities. Only cities with rail junctions
were to be selected as concentration points. Jewish communities of less than
five hundred persons were to be dissolved and transferred to the nearest concentration center. Furthermore, as we saw in Mlawa, in each Jewish community a council of Jewish elders was to be set up. The council was to be made
fully responsible for the exact and prompt implementation of directives already issued and those to be issued.[1]

By Heydrich's order, accordingly, ghettoes and Judenrats were formed in
many cities of Poland soon after the German occupation of Poland was completed. Some ghettos remained open for many months, whereas others were
closed immediately. Although we still had no ghetto in Mlawa, we did have
the Judenrat, and they did try to absorb all the Jews from the nearby towns
and villages and provide for their immediate needs. Only later did we realize that the Germans wanted to have us concentrated and close to railway stations to facilitate transporting us to camps for free labor and to death
camps to murder us. All we knew then was that we were better off than the
Jews in the cities, so we continued to hope.

That hope was shattered in the fall of 1940 when rumors circulated that
the Germans planned to evacuate the Jews from Mlawa. The German authorities reassured the Judenrat that no evacuation was being planned. In ret-
rospect it appears that the Germans had intentionally sent out conflicting
messages to frustrate and frighten us. They certainly succeeded in making us
feel like we were living on a volcano about to erupt.

On Friday, December 6, 1940, my mother got up early, as she usually did
on Fridays, to prepare for the Sabbath. She went out to do her shopping
but returned immediately. Shaking with fear and in a trembling voice, she
told us that German police, storm troopers, and soldiers crowded the streets.

We dressed quickly in several layers of clothes, including our warm topcoats. Everyone in my family had a little bundle ready in case we were forced to leave our home suddenly. It included only the items we thought most necessary.

We hoped that the Germans would not reach us, because we were the only Jews who lived on the second floor of a building that was a good distance away from the city center. I kept looking out the window from behind the shades. At one point I saw a group of Germans coming toward our building and a young Polish man pointing to the second floor. Soon the Germans stormed into our home, screaming, shoving, and pushing us, ordering us to get out. My sister, brother, cousin, and I ran out first. My father and mother remained behind to help my elderly grandmothers. We reached the streets and found other Jews being driven out of their homes; they were coming from all sections of the city, and Germans were directing us where to go.

At one point I looked back and saw my mother and father each helping my grandmothers walk as quickly as possible and the Germans yelling at them, ordering them to walk faster. When I looked back a second time I was shocked to see that my paternal grandmother had fallen and that my father was bent over her, trying to help her to her feet. The Germans surrounded them and yelled at them, but my dad would not let go of my grandma. He argued with them until they started whipping him and let loose a dog that ripped his coat. Eventually they forced my father to leave his mother lying on the ground. When Father joined us, he told us, with tears running down his cheeks, that they promised they would transport my grandmother on a cart and bring her to the same place we were all being sent. He had to believe them, for the alternative may have been more tragic.

A group of SS men directed us to the gymnasium field, a large enclosed area. It was heartbreaking to see our dad in tears, and we all cried with him. He looked at us, his family, with pity and pain at being unable to protect us and at having to leave his mother. We calmed down a bit when we saw our grandmother being wheeled to us on a cart while we were still waiting for the next order. It was heartbreaking to look around and see hundreds of Jewish men, women, and children surrounded by Germans with weapons, ready to shoot at any provocation. I felt imprisoned, helpless, and frightened, not knowing what it was they wanted to do with us.

That morning the Germans drove half of the six thousand Mlawa Jews out of their homes. They allowed us only the clothing on our backs and small bundles of belongings. We left our homes, where we had grown up in loving relationships. Among the evacuees were my mother's brother Yitche Kleinbard, his wife, Rose, and their four-year-old daughter, Braina. Also in the group were my father's brother, Aaron, his wife, Bailche, and their four children, Sheindel, Shmuel Noson, Alter, and Zisel. The rest of my relatives remained in the city among the three thousand who were permitted to stay.

The three thousand men, women, and children who were expelled from the city were ordered on trucks and driven to Dzialdowo, about ten or twelve kilometers (six or seven miles) from Mlawa. There we found a fenced-off area with three large prefabricated barracks. About a thousand people were crowded into each of the barracks. The barracks contained only straw scattered on the floor. This was to be our place to sit and to sleep.

We were provided with food—soup and bread—once a day but not with utensils to hold the soup. Those of us who had brought some containers managed to get some food some of the time. Others used their hats or anything that could hold soup and water. The distribution of bread was done with cruelty. The German guards would throw a loaf of bread in the air, and whoever was lucky enough or strong enough to push and shove would get some for himself and his family. Many people, including my family, were left without food or water for days. There were no lavatories. The facilities to relieve oneself consisted of just a few holes dug in the ground, with a pole in the middle of the space to hold on to for balance. It was easy to fall into the pit, and some did, an extremely humiliating and disgusting fall.

The Germans would enter the barracks at will, yelling and screaming, and used their pistols and whips to hit the people indiscriminately and for no reason. Often they selected a group of people and ordered them outside to do physical exercise to the point of exhaustion as they yelled and beat them. They selected young women and men for humiliation and abuse. Once an SS man attacked me. In the middle of the night, the Nazi entered the barracks where my family and I were lying near the door. I raised my head, half asleep, and looked at him in fear. He obviously did not like the way I looked at him. He started yelling and kicking me and then pulled out his pistol and aimed it at me. I was sure this was my end. Instead, he hit me on the head with the handle of the pistol and left. My father and mother helped me to stop the bleeding. We were terribly frightened that he might come back and brutalize me again or do something even worse. In this camp some Jews were tortured and then killed in cold blood.

The Germans particularly looked for our revered rabbi. Rabbi Segalowitz and his family had also been driven out of Mlawa and were with us in the Dzialdowo camp. Germans came into his barracks every so often looking for them and humiliated them for all to observe. Rabbi David Kristal, a friend of mine who was then a rabbinical student and studied with Rabbi Segalowitz, stayed near the rabbi in his barracks to assist him whenever he could. Rabbi Kristal gave the following account of one of these incidents:

[A] German officer entered the barracks and saw the rabbi with his long white beard, lying in the corner. The officer yelled at the rabbi and ordered him to rise and proclaim insults against the "God of the Jews" in a loud, clear voice. The rabbi looked him straight in the eyes and said, "No, I will not say this. On the contrary, I proclaim for all to hear that the Lord, the God of Israel, exists and will live forever!"

The officer looked at him and shouted angrily, "I will kill you on this spot if you do not say what I have ordered you to say."

The rabbi looked him in the face and repeated what he had said before: "The Lord, the God of Israel, exists and will live forever!"

At this point the officer pulled out his revolver, pointed it at the rabbi, and shouted with great anger, "Either you do what I order you to or you die here like a dog."

A terrifying silence spread over the barracks. But the rabbi responded in a calm and convincing voice, "You can do with my body whatever you wish, but I am saying the truth, and I proclaim for all to hear and to know that the Lord, the God of Israel, exists and will live forever and ever!"

Then the incredible happened. The officer lowered the revolver, turned around and hurriedly left the barracks.[2]

Much of the horror and brutality in Dzialdowo is buried so deeply that I cannot, or do not wish to, remember. I did recall one incredible barbaric act after reading about it in an excerpt of a book by M. Tzanin. Eleven young people suffered from nervous breakdowns. They ran around the camp yelling and screaming endlessly. The families and friends of these ill people tied them so that they could hide them from the Germans. One of them managed to free himself and ran around again, screaming and yelling. Other Jews tried very hard to control him, but without success. The Germans let a truck run over him and killed him.[3]

After ten or eleven days of barbaric treatment in the Dzialdowo camp, on December 16 or 17, 1940, the three thousand Jews, depressed, exhausted, and confused, were forced on trains and driven to three different cities in the Polish General Government region: Lublin, Lubartów, and Międzyrzec. Our family, including my two grandmothers and my cousin Shifra Berko, were among a thousand people driven by train to the city of Lubartów, near Lub-

Map 1: Poland, 1939, after the division into the German and Soviet spheres. In December 1940 the Germans drove three thousand Jews from Mlawa, half of the town's Jewish population, to the cities of Międzyrzec, Lubartów, and Lublin, most of whom were later sent to concentration camps. The rest of the Jewish population of Mlawa were sent to the death camps of Treblinka and Auschwitz-Birkenau in November 1942.

lin, about 250 miles south of Mlawa. We were driven to a city where we knew no one and no one knew us, and we were left only with the clothes on our backs.

We later learned that those who remained in Mlawa were given forty-eight hours to move out of their homes and find living quarters in a specially designated area—a ghetto—where the housing quality was the worst and most neglected in the city. The Judenrat was helpful in making this move as orderly as possible. I also learned that sometime after our expulsion the Germans forced Jews from several surrounding towns into the ghetto of Mlawa, making the ghetto even more crowded.[4]

The ghettoes were usually set up in haste, and the people often experienced Nazi brutality. Apartments and rooms were overcrowded, and within time people suffered from hunger and despair. By the end of 1941, all the Jews of Poland and the German-controlled territories were either confined to ghettos or labor camps or were in hiding, in partisan groups, or on the run. The ghettos existed until the policy of annihilation was firmly in place and the instruments of the killing centers were established and ready to "solve the Jewish problem."

Yet, as bad as the situation in the Mlawa ghetto was, the Jews there were much better off than those of us who had been driven out into strange cities and unfamiliar environments. We instantly became homeless refugees and ultimately depended on the kindness of others, on strangers, for food and shelter.

5
Refugees in Lubartów

Before World War II, the city of Lubartów, located about twenty miles north of Lublin, had a Jewish population of approximately 3,500 among a total population of more than 8,000. The Germans entered Lubartów on September 19, 1939, and on October 12, 1939, carried out the first persecution of Jews and major plunder of Jewish property. At the beginning of November, most of the Jewish community of Lubartów were ordered to leave the town. Only 818 Jews were permitted to remain; they were ordered to establish a Judenrat and work for the Germans.

In September 1940 the exiled Jews from Lubartów were permitted to return to their town. The Judenrat organized a community kitchen because those who returned were thoroughly impoverished. It was mid-December of that same year when the one thousand Jews from Mlawa, including my family and me, were driven to Lubartów.

My memory of Lubartów is very limited. I do remember that it appeared to be much smaller than Mlawa. It seems that before the Mlawa Jews were deported to Lubartów, the Germans had informed the local Judenrat that we were being sent to their city. When we arrived there exhausted, depressed, and famished, we were served a hot meal in the synagogue, the first hot meal we had eaten after eleven days in the Dzialdowo camp. We found the Judenrat well organized and the Jewish community well prepared to accept our group of helpless men, women, and children. We were registered and then assigned to families who would share their homes with us. Although they were living under difficult conditions themselves, these families accepted us warmly and did their best to accommodate us, even sharing their limited meals with us.

We discovered almost immediately, however, that no home in Lubartów was large enough to accommodate all eight members of my family. To make matters worse, both of my grandmothers had fallen ill during our forced relocations, and they required continuous care. Under the circumstances, we had no choice but to split up. My mother and her mother were assigned lodgings in one home, my father stayed with his mother in another home, and the four children—my sister, my brother, my cousin, and myself—were placed with another family.

After receiving our housing assignments, we decided that all of us would meet the following morning at the home where my mother and grandmother were staying. When we arrived the next morning, we were met with the news that Grandmother Malka had died. She had expired while spending the night on a sofa in the home of good-hearted people, her head in my mother's lap. It was Wednesday morning, December 18, 1940—18 Kislev 5701—a sad day for us, a day that I remember every year and mark by reciting the Kaddish (memorial prayer), lighting a candle, and giving *tzedakah* (charity) in her memory.

My grandmother's death was our family's first loss, our first victim of German atrocities. Bube (grandmother) Malka was a kind, hard-working woman. After my grandfather Hayim Kleinbard had died years earlier, my grandmother continued to run the bakery they had owned together. She was the mother of a son and a daughter and two grandchildren in America and had three daughters, two sons, and ten grandchildren in Mlawa. She had dreamed of going to America after her retirement, where her son Mordekha and her daughter Sonia lived. She died as quietly as she lived, without disturbing or burdening anyone. My father saw to it that Grandma Malka was given a traditional burial. Because of our circumstances, my mother, the only one of her eight children near her, my father, and just four of her twelve grandchildren were able to attend the funeral service.

Two days later, before we could recover from the loss of Grandmother Malka, my paternal grandmother, Toba, died. It was Friday, December 20, 1940—20 Kislev 5701, another sad day, and my father made all the arrangements for a traditional burial. We thus experienced our second victim of the Nazi horror. For me it became another day to observe with the recitation of the Kaddish in the synagogue, the giving of charity, and the lighting of a Yahrzeit (memorial) candle in her memory. I do this every year on the anniversary of her death. She was the mother of a son and a daughter and six grandchildren in Mexico; one son and four grandchildren in Makowa, Poland; one daughter and one granddaughter in Prushnitz; and two sons, one daughter, and sixteen grandchildren in Mlawa.

How my cousins and I had loved to visit our grandmother Toba! My grandfather Shmuel Alter Goldstein died at a young age, and she remained widowed for the rest of her life. She was very religious. Often when I visited her, she would be in the middle of reciting her prayers. She would not speak to anyone until she had completed her prayers. When we were young children, we had the tradition of visiting her on every Pesach to help her grind matzoh into matzoh meal. She would always treat us with nuts. Again, because of the war, my father was the only one of her seven children able to attend her funeral, and my siblings and I were the only grandchildren who attended. Little did we know then that a proper burial would later be considered a privilege. From that point on, no other member of my family—immediate or extended—received a traditional burial.

A terrible period began for my family with the expulsion from Mlawa. Like all the Jews who had been driven from Mlawa, we tried desperately to adjust to our new surroundings and settle down into some routine, but this was practically impossible. There were no jobs to be found, and whatever money my family had saved was soon gone. My father had a particularly difficult time adjusting to this new and troubling situation. His main concern had always been to protect and provide for his family, and now he found himself unable to do either. My siblings and I wanted very much to help. As the oldest, now a "mature" seventeen-year-old, I felt a strong obligation to provide for our family, but work was simply not available. The people in Lubartów themselves had limited incomes, and my family found it emotionally difficult to live off the charity of others and to depend on the daily meal provided by the community kitchen for the destitute.

As time passed, we began to hear of Mlawa refugees joining their relatives or friends in other cities where their chances of survival seemed better. Almost all of the three thousand driven from their homes in Mlawa were in the same predicament as we were—lacking money and no employment, no source of income, and no hope for the situation to improve. Naturally, many chose to return to our hometown, although such a move was prohibited by law and involved great risks. But for most of us it was the only option. In the Mlawa ghetto it was easy to find employment, and there were friends and relatives there who were spared the expulsion and who might be in a position to help.

For weeks I tried to find employment in Lubartów, but without success. The situation was terribly frustrating. My cousin Shifra was in the same position. Shifra and I decided to risk returning to our hometown. With friends and family there, we reasoned, it would be easier to find work and perhaps even help our family join us. But such a plan meant leaving my family behind, something I was not eager to do. Yet, traveling with my cousin was a bit reassuring. She was about two or three years older than I and mature and confident. For reasons I never knew, she and her brother, Yermo, and their mother, Berakha, my mother's sister, lived with Grandma Malka. As I was growing up, I used to see her quite frequently on my visits to my grandmother's home.

She was like an older sister to me, and my cousin Yermo was like an older brother. I was very fond of both of them.

On Saturday, January 31, 1941, Shifra informed me that a group of refugees from Mlawa were planning to leave early the following morning, before dawn, for Międzyrzec (Mezericz) and from there to Mlawa. She had decided to join them and suggested that I join them, too. That evening, as soon as the Sabbath was over, the family gathered to discuss the plan. At first, my father and mother were frightened by the thought of the family splitting up, but Shifra and I convinced them that this was the only possible way for us to improve our miserable situation. After a long discussion, they agreed reluctantly and gave us their blessings.

We did not go to sleep that night but instead waited together until it was time to leave. In the early hours of Sunday morning, February 1, 1941, Shifra and I parted from our family. We hugged and kissed my parents and siblings, and we left with prayers and hope in our hearts that we would make it to our destination safely. We were also hopeful that the family would follow us and that we would be reunited in the near future as so many other families had succeeded in doing. We said good-bye with silent tears. This was the last time I saw my father and my sister.

Over the years I have attempted to find out what exactly happened to them. When and where were they murdered? What exactly happened to the Jews of Lubartów? After the liberation I learned that my father and sister were alive in September 1942; my sister had sent a postcard to my aunt Sonia in Los Angeles that month. In the postcard she mentions that our father was ill and that life was very hard for them. She also wrote that the "days are cloudy." Thinking of that period, I have interpreted that phrase to mean that they were facing dark days ahead of them.

I have asked everyone who came from that area to tell me anything they knew about the end of the Jews of Lubartów. It was obvious to me that they met death like most of the Polish Jews, but I have wanted to know more details about their last days and the circumstances of their deaths.

From information I received recently through the Internet, I know that on April 9, 1942, the last day of Passover, the SS selected eight hundred Jews and drove them to the death camp of Belzec. Three days later the Germans started the deportation of Jews from Slovakia and drove them to Lubartów. By the beginning of May 1942, 2,421 Slovakian Jews had been driven to Lubartów. On October 11, 1942, the Germans drove to Lubartów all the Jews from the Polish towns of Kamionka, Tarlo, Firlei, and Ostrow Lubelski. The total number of Jews at that time in Lubartów reached ten thousand men, women, and children. The Germans selected a small group of men and sent them to the Majdaneck camp. All the others were marched to the train station. Only a few people managed to hide or escape during that march. On reaching the train station, the Germans ordered them into the cattle cars in which fresh lime had been spread on the floors to try to suffocate the Jews in the wagons. After the cattle cars became overcrowded and no space remained, the Germans opened fire and shot those standing on the steps of the train and on the platform. The Germans then shut the doors of the train and sent the Jews to their death in Treblinka.

If my father and sister were in that transport, they were perhaps either shot to death at the railway station in Lubartów or suffocated on the train. I also wonder whether they might have died around the same time as my mother and brother, in November 1942. How terribly depressed I become whenever I think that the four people dearest to me were possibly murdered about the same time by the same brutality. You see, my father and mother were only in their midforties when I saw them for the last time. My sister and my brother were in their teens the last time I saw them. They never got old. They remain in my memory young, vibrant, loving, and lovable, and I still miss them. I will always miss them.

6

On the Way Back Home to Mlawa

Mlawa was almost 250 miles from Lubartów, so the journey back to my hometown would be a long one. Jews were not allowed to travel by train, so our journey was to be done by horse and buggy. The coachman, with his horse and buggy, took us to the town of Międzyrzec, where we intended to spend the night. We welcomed this opportunity, because that was where our uncle, my mother's brother Yitche Kleinbard, with his wife and daughter were driven to from Mlawa through Dzialdowo at the same time we were driven to Lubartów. We very much wanted to see them before we continued to our destination.

I had always been fond of Yitche. While I was growing up, Yitche had not been married, and he worked in my grandmother's bakery. I saw him often when we visited Bubbe Malka. He was a good-natured and intelligent man who had always shown me much friendship and love. He later married Rose Figott from Mlawa, and they later became the parents of Braina.

There was no way for us to inform Yitche that we were coming to Między-zyrzec. It was a chaotic period in our lives, and we did not even know his address. After our arrival, we searched and found Yitche and his family living in a small, crowded apartment with a family who had opened their modest home to them and shared their food as well. Yitche and Rose were surprised and delighted to see us. We could soon see that they were despondent, as there was little chance of improving their situation in the foreseeable future, and they felt guilty about imposing on another family. Unfortunately, we had to tell them the news of Grandma Malka's death. They were saddened, of course, and we all shared our sorrow at the loss and the circumstances of her death.

My uncle and his family were among the more fortunate of the Mlawa refugees in Międzyrzec. They told us of the horrible sufferings of the Mlawa Jews who were sent from Dzialdowo to this town. More than ten thousand Jews lived in Międzyrzec's Jewish quarter before the war, mostly in poverty. After the German occupation, a ghetto was established in the city for the

Jews. Thousands of Jews from the smaller towns were driven into the city's ghetto. By the time the Jews from Mlawa were taken to Międzyrzec in mid-December 1940, twelve thousand Jews were already living in the very crowded ghetto under horrible conditions. Many families in Międzyrzec shared their crowded living quarters with the new refugees, but hundreds of Jews from Mlawa were forced to live in the city synagogues. According to Rabbi David Kristal, a survivor from Mlawa whose family was also driven to Międzyrzec, the Jewish population in the Międzyrzec ghetto reached sixty thousand. In his writings Rabbi Kristal has described how he saw Jews suffering from the cold and from hunger and starvation in the streets of the Międzyrzec ghetto. In comparison, life in Mlawa at that time was one of affluence.[1]

Another individual, a man named Israel Goldstein (not related to me), has also written about the suffering of the Mlawa Jews in Międzyrzec. Goldstein had been driven from Rupin to the Mlawa ghetto, and from there he was driven to Międzyrzec with the Jews from Mlawa. He survived many atrocities, including the death camp of Treblinka. He describes the arrival of Mlawa Jews at Międzyrzec:: "As soon as their train arrived at the station in Mezericz [Międzyrzec], they were driven with whips and sticks to the synagogue. Many died within a few days of their arrival. Soon a typhus epidemic broke out and took the lives of many. The synagogue was then isolated from the rest of the ghetto. The dead bodies were carried out for burial during the night so that the disease would not affect the people in the ghetto. Whatever meager food was available for them was delivered to them through the windows in order to avoid contact with them."[2]

The suffering of the Mlawa Jews in Międzyrzec was described in a song composed by an unknown Jew from Mlawa trapped in that synagogue in the midst of death and hopelessness. Everyone in that place, even those affected by typhus, found inspiration in this song. Their voices, we were told, could be heard coming from the windows of the synagogue, and others in the ghetto would join in.

Ven shney fun himl falt un regn
ven frost oifn fenster tut zich kleybn.
In a tsayt fun elent un laydn
Tut men mentshn fun shtot traybn.

Mlawe tut dos shtetl klingen,
Men hot dort Yidn getsvingen
Tsu farlozn zayere heymen
naket, borves, on kleydung.

Tates, mames, kinder shrayen,
Vu hin zoln mir geyn?
Mit nagaykes tut men shlogn
un of oytos aroyfyogn.

Nokh Dzhaldova hot men unds gefirt,
Yidishe tekhter mit umreyns oysgeshmirt.
Yiddish blut iz dort fargosn
oysgematert, oysgeshosn.

Fun Dzhaldova tut men vayter traybn,
azoy tsien zikh undzere laydn,
Noch Mezritch arayngetribn
in di enge fremde shtibn.

In di Mezritche shul, di sheyene,
Tates, mames, kinder kleyne,
Lign of di pritches harte
un der iker—oysgedarte.

In der Mezritche shul, di groyse—
yeden tog frishe toyte
yeden tog frishe toyte,
Azoy tut men far undz zorgn:

Of mitog a bisl shvartse gritse,
Dos iz undzer eintizge shtitse.
A bisl vaser shvartse zupe,
Dos iz undzer eintzike tsdoke.

Mlawe Yidn zait gemutikt,
nisht shtendig vet ir zain geblutikt,
kumen vet a tzait a naye
Un vider veln mir zain freye.
....
When snow and rain fall from the heavens
When frost sticks to the window
In a time of pain and loneliness
People driven out of town

The town of Mlawa resounds
with the clamor of Jews forced
From their homes
Naked, barefoot, without clothing

Fathers, mothers, children bitterly weep
Wherever are we going
Beaten with leather knots
Driven onto trucks

To Dzialdova we were brought
Jewish daughters defiled and raped
The blood of Jews was spilled depleted
When so many were shot there

From Dzialdova further driven
How our pain continues on
Herded into Mezericz
Crowded into strangers' houses

In the beautiful Mezericz synagogue
Fathers mothers little children
All are lying on the hard floorboards
Bony and emaciated

In the big Mezericz synagogue
Every day new dead appear
Every day new dead appear
That's how we are taken care of

A little black grits for dinner
This is our only sustenance
A little water and black soup
Our only charity

Jews of Mlawa take courage
A new time will come to pass
Not always will you be so bloodied
And we will again be free.[3]

Very striking are the last words: *"Jews of Mlawa, take courage / A new time will come to pass / Not always will you be so bloodied / And we will again be free."* Unfortunately, that hope came true for only a very few of those who were driven from Mlawa to Międzyrzec. Most of them died of starvation and disease. And those from Mlawa who survived the ghetto in Międzyrzec were driven to Treblinka together with the Jews who had already occupied the Międzyrzec ghetto.

We stayed with Uncle Yitche for the night. Despite the dire living conditions, the family that was hosting my uncle and his family welcomed us as well. We spent the night on the floor and shared their meal of bread and tea. The plan was to continue the next day to Yablonna. We left Uncle Yitche and his family with tears in our eyes and pain in our hearts—their situation was so pitiful. Some months later they succeeded in returning to Mlawa themselves.

That morning Shifra suggested that she continue to travel alone under the guise of a Polish girl. She had blond hair and spoke perfect Polish, she explained, and with her looks and her perfect Polish she could easily pass as Polish. She had many Polish friends in Mlawa and hoped they would provide the protection and safety she needed. As a Polish woman she would be able to travel by train. I supported her idea with my blessings. It seemed to both of us practical and safer. I wished her good luck, and we each went our own way. I never saw my cousin Shifra again. I do not know what happened to her and under what circumstances she perished. I wish so very much to know. She was a very intelligent and very kind young woman. What a painful loss!

I continued to travel with the group headed toward the town of Yablonna, near Warsaw, where the Vistula River became the border between the Polish General Government and the Third Reich. We had to cross the Vistula River to be on the German side and be on the way to Mlawa. When we arrived in Yablonna, we were advised by locals to hire a Polish guide who knew the area well and would help us cross the border without being noticed by the German border police. That night was extremely dark, which was preferable, and we followed the smuggler in a long, single-file line. He led us through deep snow and across the frozen Vistula River.

After crossing the river, the smuggler guided us to the train station. There we were discovered by two German border guards; perhaps we were led to them by our guide. The guards surrounded us and demanded money. Those who gave them money were released and free to go. But nine of us, including myself, had no money to give. My pockets were empty. What was I to do?

We had been caught about an hour before dawn and were detained in the train station and guarded until the train arrived. Those who bribed the guards boarded the train. The nine of us who remained were forced to do hard labor all of the following day, without food or water. It was a cold and nasty day, with steady, heavy rain. Our job was to move construction material from one place to the other. In the evening, the guards led the nine of us to the border police station and ordered us to wait in the front room until we were called into the offices one by one. From the waiting room we could hear the beatings—and the yelling and crying of the victims. I doubted we would be let out alive. Then my turn came.

I entered the room. The screaming and whipping began immediately, with no explanation or questions. When our tormentors had their fill, they threw me into a room with the others from my group whose turns had come before mine. We had no idea what they would do with us, and we were petrified. After a while, they came in yelling, warning us that we would be shot to death if we tried to cross the border another time. Again, they whipped us and then, with barking dogs accompanying them, chased us back to the river.

The nine of us stepped into the cold waters of the Vistula, which was now high with melting snow as a result of the day's continuous rain. After crossing the river, all of us were freezing, soaking wet, and terribly tired. We now found ourselves back on the other side, exactly where we had come from. I was completely exhausted, both physically and emotionally. I persuaded the group to rest for a while on a pile of rocks. After a short rest, the other group members insisted on continuing, for border guards might be patrolling the area. This reasoning made sense, but I was still exhausted. I tried to follow them for a while, but I was too tired to keep up for very long. I remember wondering how they found the stamina to continue walking after thirty hours of a terrible ordeal without food or water. For a while, I walked at my own pace until I could walk no longer. I collapsed on a pile of snow at the side of the road and fell asleep.

I do not know how long I slept there, but the wheels of a horse and buggy awakened me. I felt a bit refreshed, and I found the strength to get up and ask the driver to take me to Yablonna, which was not very far from where we were. He refused, claiming that he was only headed in that direction for a short distance and that he would then be turning in the exact opposite direction. Nevertheless, I was willing to take the ride for as long as I could. I persuaded him to let me come with him in spite of the possibility that he might turn me in to the German authorities. After a brief ride we came to a fork in the road, where he was to turn. As I got off, he warned me not to walk on the road because the area was full of border police but to walk instead through the nearby forest. He pointed me in the direction of Yablonna and then turned in the opposite direction, and I headed off toward Yablonna.

I followed his advice and continued through the forest. What followed was one of the longest, darkest, and loneliest nights of my life up to that time. I was shivering in my wet clothes, my feet were cold, and I was drained as I had never been before. As I walked through the woods, I thought of the patriarch Jacob, who had been forced to leave his parents and flee into the wilderness for fear of his brother, Esau, who sought to kill him. I thought of how he had spent twenty years away from his parents' home and of the preparations he had made to meet with his brother after all that time. At one point, as he was heading with his family for the meeting with his brother, he suddenly found himself alone, separated from his family. "And Jacob was left alone," I remembered from Genesis 32:25. He was overtaken by loneliness and great fear. He was afraid to confront his brother, who might try to kill him. He also feared that if it should come to a fight, he might have to kill his brother in self-defense. Above all, he was worried about his family's safety and his future. He wanted to live. He wanted to survive

I remembered how a mysterious man, an angel, appeared from nowhere. The angel wrestled with Jacob all that night but could not overpower him. And when dawn was about to come, the angel was in a hurry to leave. He hurt Jacob's thigh and changed Jacob's name to Yisrael. He said, "Your name will be Israel (Yisrael), for you have striven with beings divine and human and have prevailed." The angel blessed him and disappeared. The morning came, and Jacob, now limping, joined his family, and they continued on their journey safely and successfully.[4] The preparation for his meeting with his brother, his enemy, was filled with much tension and fear, but the meeting of the two brothers brought reconciliation. I wondered, would there be an angel in this forest to bless me and guide me to safety, or would I now encounter the enemy who conspired to kill me? Would my family ever know what happened to me if my enemy had it his way?

I continued walking, unsure if I was headed in the right direction. Suddenly, from afar, I saw light coming from a building. I could not tell whether it was a border-police station or a private home and possibly a safe spot. In my desperation for a place to rest, I headed toward the house. I treaded slowly and cautiously, hoping that as I came closer I would be better able to determine whether it was a threat or a refuge.

As I approached the house, I discovered that it was a private home. I looked in the window and saw a man sitting at a table and writing or drawing. He could have been an enemy, someone who would hand me over to the border police, but I desperately needed the guidance of a person who knew the area to be sure I was going in the right direction. I was so unbearably exhausted and overcome with fear that I permitted my wishful thinking to make the decision for me. I knocked on the door with trepidation.

After one knock, a tall, bearded, strikingly handsome man appeared. I explained that I had gotten lost on my way to Yablonna and that I was hoping he could point me in the right direction. I was going the right way, he said, and my confidence was restored. I mustered up my courage and made a second request: would he be so kind as to give me space on his floor to rest for a few hours before I continued on my way? He thought for a moment and then told me that the area was full of border police and that it was extremely dangerous for strangers to be there. Yet he must have recognized how tired I was and how tearful I was, barely able to talk. Miraculously, he allowed me to come in, but I had to promise to leave by six o'clock the next morning. I entered, and he pointed to a soft, cushioned armchair, where he said I could rest. I fell asleep immediately. I knew that I was taking a very serious risk that could turn out disastrously for me. This man could easily have handed me over to the police. But the only alternative for me was to continue walking, which was risky in its own way, too.

I do not know how long I slept there. It seemed that only a short time had passed when the man woke me up and told me that I had to leave immediately, while it was still dark. He gave me a cup of coffee and a slice of bread with applesauce. This was the first thing I had eaten in two days, and it tasted delicious. He pointed me again in the right direction, and I left. I do not know how long I walked, but eventually I met a group of Polish women collecting firewood. They reassured me that I was headed in the right direction and that I was not far from my destination. For the rest of my journey I kept wondering, who was this man? Was he a Polish man? Was he a Volksdeutsche, Polish but ethnically German? Was he perhaps a German? The best answer for me was that he was indeed an angel, perhaps a human being with the heart of an angel. Yes, I believe that there are human beings with angelic hearts of goodness. Any person, Polish, German, or whatever, may develop a soul of an angel, a heart filled with goodness and compassion. To me that man was indeed an angel.

I arrived in Yablonna safely at dawn, exhausted and with no money. I asked someone on the street to show me the Jewish section of the town. I walked aimlessly through the ghetto, trying to read people's faces and decide who seemed most approachable. I finally stopped a young man whose name I no longer remember and shared my story. He invited me to have breakfast with him and to stay with him and his family until I decided on my next move. He and his wife and three children lived in a small, crowded apartment. The family took a personal interest in me, which was extremely comforting. For food, I took advantage of the ghetto's community kitchen, which provided a hot meal once a day for the poor. In addition, the man offered to advise me about my next move. One thing I was convinced of, I told him, was that I did not want to return to Lubartów. The only reasonable option left for me, we concluded, was to try crossing the border again. The problem, though, was that I needed money to pay a trustworthy smuggler who knew how to avoid the border police.

In the meantime, I met two young people from Mlawa in the same predicament. One of them was Gedalya Goldblat, a contemporary of mine whom I knew well. Within a week or so, the man who had taken me in somehow arranged for the three of us to join a group that was planning to cross the border. He most likely collected money and made arrangements for the smuggler. I regret very much that I do not recall the name of this man who took a personal interest in me. One of the only things I do remember about him was that he was a Hasid, a follower of the rebbe of Gur, who was the most popular of the Hasidic rabbis in Poland because of his personality, scholarship, and wisdom.

On the night of February 27, 1941, our small group of three succeeded in crossing the border, guided by a man who knew the area well enough to take us across undisturbed. Four long weeks had passed since I had left my family. I had overcome one hurdle, the border crossing, but many more were ahead of me. Our group was now faced with the dilemma of how to reach Mlawa. As I said earlier, Jews were forbidden to travel by train, but Mlawa was about sixty miles away, far too long and dangerous a distance to walk. We had no other choice but to risk taking the train. We took off our white armbands marked with a Jewish star (Jews in the General Government of Poland had to wear white armbands with a blue star instead of the yellow star in the Third Reich) and boarded the train. The good people of Yablonna had given us a little money to pay for transportation.

By this time, however, the German authorities were aware that many Jews were heading back to Mlawa, and they had started guarding the train station, looking out for returning Jews. We contemplated getting off the train at Szczegova, one station before Mlawa, and walking a little over six miles to the city, but we saw this as too risky. We stayed on the train, hoping that we would not be recognized as Jews and that no police were guarding the Mlawa train station. As the train approached our station, we became more nervous. When it finally pulled in and we got off, German gendarmes approached us as if they knew who we were. Quite possibly, the Polish passengers who had gotten off earlier had recognized us as Jews and had betrayed us. We were arrested and driven to the police station. There, we were beaten and thrown into the Mlawa prison, which the Germans were now using as a labor camp. It was Friday, February 28, 1941. I was not yet eighteen, and I was a prisoner in the Mlawa jail, a place for criminals in the prewar years.

A Prisoner in the Labor Camps

The Mlawa prison was close to the center of the city in an area I would pass by on the way to visit my Grandma Toba or to go other places. As a child I used to get an awkward feeling whenever I passed by, thinking that it was a place of punishment for criminals. The building evoked fear and made me determined never to break the law or to step foot in that fearful place.

Now I passed over its threshold, sent there for coming back to my hometown, my birthplace, where I had been forced out because I was a Jew. Two policemen led our group to the doors of the prison. They rang the bell, and the commandant of the labor camp greeted us with his screams and ordered us to follow him. He assigned each of us a cell and told us which hours we were to appear for roll call, which would be twice each day, once before leaving for work and once when we returned.

The prison was surrounded by a brick wall and had a small yard in the front, near the gate. This was where roll call took place. The building was a small one-story structure, with corridors and cells inside and a large backyard outside, where our exercises took place twice daily. In the Mlawa prison, we found Polish prisoners who had been arrested for various reasons. We also found prisoners who had been arrested for no reason at all, just suspicion, and had been detained without trial. The thought of being incarcerated was difficult for me to handle emotionally, and equally difficult was the disappointment I felt, thinking I had come so close to my destination but ended up in prison. I thought constantly of my family back in Lubartów, with whom I had no communication for four long weeks. They surely did not know what had happened to me, and this painful thought was uppermost in my mind as the traumatic events of my imprisonment unfolded. But then, in the late afternoon of the first day of my imprisonment, a guard called me to the prison gates. Standing at the gate was my aunt Tzerko. I was relieved to see her, knowing now that I was not completely alone.

Tzerko Sokolover was my mother's younger sister, an attractive and intelligent woman. Her husband, Zalman Sokolover, had immigrated to America in the early thirties, leaving Tzerko and their two sons, Hayim and Simha, in Mlawa. His intention, of course, had been to bring his wife and children to America as soon as he was settled in New York. For reasons unknown to me, however, this never happened, and Tzerko and her sons remained in Mlawa, hoping constantly for their immigration to America. After the German occupation of Poland and with the passage of time, that hope became an illusion, as it became too late for the dream to be realized.

Aunt Tzerko told me that the German authorities had notified the Judenrat of my imprisonment, and the Judenrat had notified my aunt Tzerko. Arranging this visit certainly took much initiative and effort on her part. She probably appealed to influential members of the Judenrat, and the Judenrat used its influence with the local German authorities. Some members of the Judenrat knew me and my family well, and I am sure they all helped in arranging that visit for my aunt.

Aunt Tzerko had always been a loving aunt to my siblings and me, and we always enjoyed visiting with her and my cousins. I especially remember our visits to her house on Hanukkah, when we would all have a great time playing dreidel and eating latkes. My aunt and cousins were always talking about going to America. Even after the war started, they were convinced that Uncle Zalman would surely send their visas soon. But the days and the months passed, and nothing arrived. When my family was evacuated from Mlawa, my aunt and cousins remained in Mlawa, but they were forced to relocate to the ghetto.

As soon as I saw my aunt at the gates, I broke down in tears. After weeks of wandering—alone, in danger, and separated from family—here was my aunt, who cared enough about me to make immediate arrangements to see me. Here I was in my hometown, so close to the house where I had grown up, yet so far from where I wanted to be. My aunt reassured me that she had already been in contact with some influential members of the Judenrat who promised to inquire about my status and to do everything possible to free me. Her warm, motherly words touched my innermost feelings. Someone cared about me. It was a short visit, but one that left me with a feeling of hope and less loneliness.

Before she left the prison that day, Aunt Tzerko handed me a package. I still remember the tears streaming uncontrollably from my eyes as I opened the bundle in my cell. There was a loaf of challah and pieces of gefilte fish, the traditional Sabbath foods enjoyed by Jews on Friday nights. It took quite a while before I calmed down. I was almost eighteen, but I felt like a frightened eight-year-old boy. After a period of controlled silence, I recited the traditional prayers of Kabbalat Shabbat, the welcoming of the Sabbath, and then I recited kiddush over the challah. The kiddush is usually recited over a cup of wine, but in lieu of wine, which I certainly did not have, it is permissible to recite it over bread. As I ate the challah and fish that night, as tears rolled down my face, I thought of the Friday night celebrations I had had with my family every Friday night not far from the prison cell where I now found myself.

It took some time, but I slowly adjusted to my new situation and learned to accept a reality that I could not change. In this labor camp I learned to work hard and tried to follow all the rules and regulations. We went out to work every day. We exercised, marched, worked hard, and were abused. It was in this camp that I began to eat nonkosher food.

The commandant of the camp was an obsessive man. He liked to yell and had us march in military formation. He trained us for hours to march properly. This gave him a chance to yell at us at the top of his lungs, in Polish and in German, "One, two, three, four . . . *Eins, Zwei, Drei, Fier* . . . Right, left, right, left . . . *Rechts, Links, Rechts, Links* . . . Hats on, hats off . . . *Mitzen Auf* . . . *Mitzen Runter* . . . Shovels high! . . . Shovels low! . . . *Spaden Auf* . . . *Spaden runter!*" He drove us with his constant shouting and yelling as he forced us to march in perfect military order.

Within a few days, Aunt Tzerko visited me again and brought another food package. More important, she informed me that the president of the Judenrat, Eliezer Perlmutter, had intervened on my behalf with the local German authorities and had promised her that I would be held for one month only. By the first of April, I would be allowed to enter the ghetto. This was great news, and I started to dream about the time when our family would be reunited. I would be "free" in the ghetto before Passover, which was extremely important to me. I had something joyful to look forward to.

However, this was not to be. A new labor camp was to be opened in Czechanow, about twelve miles south of Mlawa, and our camp was ordered to supply fifteen inmates for transfer. On March 17, after the morning roll call and marching exercises concluded, fifteen inmates were ordered by name to step forward. My name was one of them. We were needed in the new camp, the commandant told us, and we were immediately ordered onto a truck that drove us, under guard, to the newly established labor camp. I do not have the words to describe my disappointment.

Ninety inmates from different prisons were gathered in the new camp, and only six were Jews. The rest were Poles who had been arrested in several towns in the area. The camp was to be a source of free labor for the various needs of the Germans in the region. We were not given an explanation as to why we had been chosen or how long we would be there.

The camp consisted of one large building surrounded by a wire fence, and it was guarded by armed Volksdeutsche. The room where the prisoners were guarded contained enough straw sacks for ninety people to sleep on. The sacks were the only furnishings in the room. There were also a number of rooms for the guards, as well as an administrative office consisting of a few connecting rooms for the SS officers.

The events of my first night in that new camp troubled me deeply. On that night I was reminded once again that the Nazis we faced enjoyed cruelty for its own sake. They derived a certain unexplainable satisfaction by causing suffering and pain to other human beings, and they would, therefore, not hesitate to create situations to provide them with such gratification. On that night, after we had had our first meal and as we were getting ready to sleep, the six Jewish inmates were singled out for "special treatment." Our names were called, and we were ordered to march into the front office where the guards' rooms were located. They asked us first to be seated and then called us one at a time into the SS offices. The first one to be called in was a man named Kaplan, who claimed that an error had been made and that he was not a Jew. From our room we could hear them questioning and beating him. When they were done, they led him through our waiting room. We could see the bruises on his face, and by the way he walked we understood just how badly he had been beaten. I remember thinking that maybe he was beaten because he had lied about his identity and denied his Jewishness. Maybe that would not happen to the rest of us, I thought. How wrong I was!

One by one the others were called in, and we could hear the yelling and shouting and the beatings. By the time I was called into the inner office, I was already terribly frightened. Beatings were not only physically painful for me but also a painfully humiliating abuse that hurt me more emotionally.

When I entered the office, I found a number of high-ranking SS officers, some sitting and others standing. They immediately began to yell and push and shove me. Then they started throwing out questions: "What is your name!? ... Where do you live!? ... Why were you arrested!?" My answers did not matter to them. They continued shoving and pushing me. "You are lying!" they screamed, and slapped me across the face as I continued to answer their questions as honestly as I could. After they had enough of that treatment, they placed me facedown on a bench, with my chest across its width. One of the guards held my head between his legs and another guard held me by my feet. Now that I was properly restrained, two other guards stood on either side of me and whipped me all over my body, mercilessly, until I passed out. Then they poured water over me, carried me back to the barracks—I could not walk on my own—and threw me in my place for the night. That night I could not sleep; every part of my body ached. In addition to the physical pain, there was the emotional anguish. I was petrified that they would do this to the Jewish inmates every day. I knew I could not survive this kind of treatment for very long. The following day we were taken out to work, and I was overwhelmed and filled with anxiety by the fear of being beaten again when we returned to the camp.

Something very helpful happened on the first day at work there. A group of us were assigned to clear the snow and ice on the streets, which was making travel difficult. My group was assigned to clear the ice on a square near a private home where a family lived. As I was standing and clearing the ice I saw a man come out of the house and make contact with one of the guards. A short while later, the guard called me over and said that I should go into the house for a while. It turned out that a Jewish family lived there, and the man had recognized me as a Jew and observed my distress and anxiety. The man convinced the guard to give me the time to come into his house and have lunch with his family. I assume that he was an official of some kind in the city or had bribed the guard for me to receive such kindness. I ate very little, but I shared with the family all that had happened to me, especially my terrible fear of more daily beatings and humiliation.

The husband, wife, and daughter tried to calm me down. After lunch, they promised that they would try to get information from the guard. I rejoined the other prisoners at work, and the man talked with the guard. After a while, the family invited me into their home again. They informed me that the guard had assured them that the beatings were the result of the regional Gestapo chief's visit to the camp on opening day and that the local officers had no intention of repeating such beatings. This allayed my fears, but I was not totally convinced. As the days passed and there was no repeat of the beatings, I realized they had been told the truth. I learned to adjust to a routine of working hard labor, eating nonkosher food, and looking forward to be freed by April 1, as I had been promised in Mlawa.

With Passover approaching, I longed to be released before the holiday and to celebrate the Festival of Freedom with my relatives in the Mlawa ghetto. But April 1 came and went, and there was no sign of release. None of the prisoners knew how long we were to stay there. Still, I continued to believe that I would be freed imminently and permitted to enter the Mlawa ghetto. I did not want to accept the possibility of spending Passover without a seder, without matzoh, in prison and alone. The upcoming holiday now preoccupied my thoughts. Meanwhile, I worked hard and avoided doing anything that would give the guards reason to beat me, which remained my greatest fear. And I kept up my hope that soon I would be free.

One day as we were marching back to camp after work in the middle of the street, I noticed a woman walking on the sidewalk, keeping up with our pace and looking directly at us. I then noticed her motioning furtively to me, as if she was afraid of being noticed by the guards, yet wanted my attention. I was pleasantly surprised when I recognized her to be my aunt Tzvikah Eichler, my father's youngest sister. She had lived in Prushnitz, about twenty miles from Mlawa, and was at that time living with her husband and daughter in Makowa. I was overwhelmed with emotion. I motioned back to her, but I knew that I would not be permitted to leave the line to speak to her. I could tell how relieved she was that I recognized her. Clearly, she had discovered what had happened to me. She must have been trying to see what she could do to help me or at least be able to notify my parents that I was alive.

My aunt Tzvikah, who was single when I was growing up in the twenties and thirties, was a beautiful young woman. We all loved her for her wisdom, intelligence, and kindness. She lived with my grandmother, who had been widowed for some years, and worked as a saleslady in one of the large businesses in the center of the city. My father had made it a tradition, probably after the passing of his father years earlier, to stop at their home every Friday evening on our way home from the synagogue. He would recite the Sabbath kiddush for them, as is traditionally required. On those occasions we would spend time chatting with them before returning home. My aunt, like my grandmother, would show my brother and me much attention. I used to enjoy those occasions and always looked forward to them. A few years before the war, Aunt Tzvikah married Moshe Eichler from Prushnitz, and after the wedding they moved to his hometown, where he and his father owned a successful grain business. They had a daughter named Rachel, who was probably three or four years old when Tzvikah came to Czechanow to try to find me.

Seeing my aunt was reassuring and lifted my spirits. It was an antidote to the long weeks of loneliness and fear. My Aunt Tzerko must have notified her where I was, and she had cared for me so much as to risk her safety for my sake. With sadness I also became aware of what my family in Lubartów must be going through, not knowing whether I was alive or dead.

Aunt Tzvikah continued walking on the sidewalk and making eye contact with me for about ten minutes but was unable to communicate with me except by making signs of caring. As my group turned the corner toward the camp, she continued on her way. It was a short encounter, but I found it very encouraging. Regrettably, though, that was the last time I saw my aunt Tzvikah. I do not know where and when she and her family perished.

Passover was to be celebrated soon by Jewish families the world over, but I was still imprisoned. How was I going to observe the many strict dietary rules and regulations? I had had to compromise the daily kashrut laws because I could not have survived otherwise. But this was Passover, and eating bread during Passover was out of the question for me. Refraining from eating leavened bread had been a law strictly observed by the Jewish people over the centuries. Of course, there was no way I could celebrate the holiday in a festive mood. One needed to be with family to celebrate this holiday appropriately. One needed matzoh and wine and specially prepared Passover food. In the midst of these worries, I recalled the joy with which I had celebrated the holiday in the past, especially the togetherness with my family, the spirituality of that season in our home, and the preparations that took place several weeks before the holiday.

On the day before Passover, soon after we returned to the camp from the day's work, I was called to the gate. There stood two women waiting for me with Passover food for the first seder night. The two women lived in Czechanow and had been contacted by my aunt Tzvikah. It again seemed to me that Tzvikah and Tzerko had somehow been in contact with each other. They arranged for these two women, obviously good friends, to take an interest in my well-being and to do whatever they could for me.

My aunts' efforts on my behalf were a much-needed message of love and caring. Furthermore, my aunts' friends told me that attempts were being made for my release. I am sure their contact with me was not easily arranged, and it may have involved many risks. Bribery was also dangerous and at times backfired.

And so I spent Passover in the Czechanow labor camp. I was grateful for the matzoh and the kosher-for-Passover food. On the first night of Passover I recited whatever parts of the *Haggadah* I remembered by heart, including the answer to the traditional four questions: *"Avadim hayinu l'Pharoh B'Mitzrayim* (We were once slaves to Pharaoh in Egypt) *va'yoitzieinu Hashem Elokeinu misham b'yad hazaka uvizro'a n'tuya* (and God saved us from there with a strong hand and an outstretched arm)." Saying these words brought tears to my eyes.[1]

It is difficult for me to describe fully my emotions on the first seder night in the Czechanow labor camp in the year 1941. It was my first seder without family, and I was incarcerated! Yes, I had matzoh and a kosher meal, but I was alone, without my dear family, my father and mother and sister and brother, and without the usual joyous family celebration at this season of the year. I also missed the inspirational recitation of the *Haggadah*, which had always brought renewed spiritual joy to our hearts. There were no four cups of wine, no *afikoman*, no singing of the Hallel, no recitation of the Four Questions.[2] But there were more than four questions in my heart: Why, O God? How was all this possible? Was this a nightmarish dream, or was it real? Above all, where was Elijah the prophet, who was supposed to bring a message of redemption on Passover night? *Where was he?* This would have been the most appropriate time for him to appear, to be the harbinger of freedom and peace for us! Where was he now, when the redemption of the enslaved was so much needed? I asked the question, *"Ma nishtana halaila hazeh mikol haleilos* (How is this night different from all other nights)?" in a way I had never asked before: *"Why is this Passover night different from all other Passover nights I have celebrated before?"* I had so many more questions, but no answers.

My aunts' friends (regrettably, I do not remember their names) came to see me a few times during the week of Passover with more kosher-for-Passover food. Then, suddenly, they stopped coming. I worried about their safety, but there was nothing I could do to obtain information on their whereabouts. I do not know what happened to them, regrettably.

I remained in the labor camp until May 25, 1941. I had been imprisoned for a full three months and had marked my eighteenth birthday there. I had not seen or been in contact with my family for four long and lonely months, and I had by now been living under Nazi rule for almost two years.

I was then released and permitted to go to the Mlawa ghetto, which had been my intense yearning for five long months. I was overwhelmed with inner joy. It was almost hard for me to believe that my "dream" had come true. I hoped that this would be the beginning of good things to happen for my family and me. Above all, I longed to be reunited with my family in the Mlawa ghetto so we could hope together for the end of the war and begin a normal life together again.

8
Life in the Mlawa Ghetto

Now that I had finally arrived in the Mlawa ghetto, I learned about the three thousand Jews who were permitted to remain in Mlawa after the expulsion of the other half. After that evacuation, the local German Landrat (chief officer) invited the members of the Judenrat to his offices and told them that the evacuation had been necessary. Those who remained should feel safe and secure, he said, but they would have to move into a specially designated area for Jews only. The Jews were given forty-eight hours to gather their belongings and move out of their homes into the assigned area. The Poles who lived in the assigned area vacated their homes and were allowed to select new dwellings from the thousands of homes the Jews had left empty.

The Landrat also found it important to report that the evacuation of the three thousand Jews from Mlawa had gone very well and that there were no casualties. Eliezer Perlmutter was obviously very annoyed by this remark and responded, "I would like to know what you would say if this would have been done to Germans." Those present were astonished at the daring response from the Judenrat president and feared the consequences, but none seemed forthcoming.

The Judenrat was also instructed to register all the Jews and to be sure that all registering was done in accordance with the prescribed order. Thus, the ghetto in Mlawa became a reality.[1]

When I was released from the labor camp on May 25, 1941, and was permitted to enter the Mlawa ghetto legally, my relatives and family friends welcomed me warmly. Moshe Romaner, a family friend who was a member of the Judenrat, gave me new clothes, which I desperately needed. I had been wearing the same rags for about four months.

When the Germans confined the Jews in the ghetto, they ordered the Judenrat to provide for the basic needs of the community as well, including services that would normally fall under the responsibility of a municipality: housing, utilities, food supply, police and fire protection, a judiciary system, public health and sanitation, and many other functions. When I arrived, I found the ghetto community to be well organized. The people who served on the Judenrat, as well as those who served as Jewish policemen, were almost all prominent, respectable individuals who were known to all from the prewar years. I knew some of them personally: Hayim Soldansky, Mr. Liberberg, Shmuel Leib Frankel, Hayim Laska, Shmulik Boimgold, Mr. Zweighaft, Leibel Romaner (Moshe's brother), Mr. Korzenny, Butche Shapiro, Mr. Klein, Mr. Solarsky, Haskel Alter, Shlomo Tik, and Shayah Krzeslo. There were others, too, whose names I do not remember anymore.

The Judenrat utilized every structure, even every shack, regardless of its condition, and made it livable, so everyone had a roof over his head. The Jewish police force, which had been organized to keep order in the ghetto, was also helpful in making life more tolerable. Menashe Davidson, who was the secretary of the *kehillah* during the prewar years, was appointed as the chief of police.[2]

In the beginning of the ghetto period in Mlawa, the Judenrat, under the leadership of Perlmutter, had a positive influence on the local German authorities. The group was able to gain favors and privileges for the people in the ghetto, most likely using bribery. People left the ghetto daily to serve as free labor, and the Germans employed some as well. Outside the ghetto, Jews managed to do business with or work for Poles and thus earn a livelihood. Illegal business activities were going on in the ghetto with people as far away as Warsaw and Lodz. One family even had an illegal radio in its cellar, which supplied news to those in the ghetto who were trusted.

The Judenrat was permitted to run a store, which became a source of food, clothes, and other necessities. The German authorities rationed some of the supplies; others were purchased from the Polish farmers illegally. The Judenrat also organized a small hospital. It was limited in space and equipment, yet it maintained the highest degree of cleanliness and hygiene. Even the German authorities admired it. Polish doctors from outside the ghetto were given permission to look after the sick. Fela Ceitag, the daughter of a prominent Jewish family in Mlawa, was the official nurse. She dedicated herself to this task and excelled in her devotion to the sick. She risked her life to illegally obtain medication to save lives and to ease pain and suffering. She was also credited with helping and saving the lives of many women in Auschwitz.[3] The Judenrat also managed to acquire a cow and a goat, which supplied milk for the sick. The group also organized a community kitchen where the needy could have a hot meal daily. An internal post office was connected to the city post office.

I quickly started working and earned enough money to provide for my basic needs. Because I was alone, I was not given living quarters. I was expected to find sleeping places with relatives and friends. I did not want to burden families that were struggling with limited space, so I slept in cellars and attics. Soon I made contact with my family in Lubartów. Understandably, they had gone through a terrible period of worrying about me. In the interim, my family's situation had seriously deteriorated, so much so that they were forced to depend on the kindness of the community to sustain themselves. The situation in the Mlawa ghetto was indeed much better than that in Lubartów. Those able to work could find jobs and earn enough to hold on to life and not die of starvation as was happening in other ghettos.

After my release from the labor camp, relatives and friends in the Judenrat arranged for my mother and my brother to take the risk of returning to Mlawa. They arrived safely in the ghetto within a month in the summer of 1941. My father was not well enough to travel, and my sister did not want to leave him alone. By the time my mother and brother joined me in Mlawa, the ghetto had become extremely crowded. Over time, more expelled Jews had returned and had been absorbed into this area. In addition, the Germans evacuated more Jews from the smaller towns and ordered the Mlawa Judenrat to take them in and provide lodging for them. Eliezer Perlmutter was appointed commissar of the ghetto, and he accepted the appointment readily, hoping to make the influx safer and less painful for all involved. He succeeded in completing the transfer in an orderly and timely fashion and without casualties. Perlmutter took advantage of his position and convinced the authorities to expand the boundaries of the ghetto to allow for more housing to accommodate the incoming Jews. Still, even with these additional dwellings, the Mlawa ghetto was extremely short of living space. Under these circumstances, my mother, brother, and I were assigned first to live in the town's *mikveh*, which had been converted into living quarters. The *mikveh* space was partitioned with thin pieces of fabric and cardboard and afforded very little privacy.

Living in the *mikveh* became progressively more difficult as the ghetto became more crowded and more people moved in. The winter was approaching, and we knew that the heating system was inadequate to handle the winter's cold. Luckily, our family's influential friends intervened on our behalf. We were assigned living space in one room of a four-room apartment. The room was tiny; it had space for only one single bed, a small table, one chair, and a tiny built-in oven. To get to our room we had to walk through the front room, where a family of four lived. Behind our room were two more rooms. Each one housed a married couple. They had to go through our room to enter theirs. My brother and I insisted that Mother sleep in the bed, and we slept on a straw mattress that we put on the floor each night. We stored the mattress in a corner each morning to give us room to move in the daytime. We also had to coordinate with the people living behind our room to ensure that they had settled in for the night before we set the mattress on the floor. Otherwise, they would be stepping on us when getting in or out of their room.

The Judenrat supplied hundreds of free laborers for the Germans daily. Every Jew in the ghetto had to appear on a given day each week to be taken out of the ghetto for work. As happened in the period before the ghetto was created, this system became a source of income for many people because others were willing to pay not to work. My brother and I, like so many other people, became dependent on that income. The Judenrat coordinated the system well.

My brother and I worked daily in different places. My mother did not work. We each earned DM 1.50 per day, barely enough to purchase survival food. From a construction site where I worked frequently, I managed to bring home scraps of wood that we used for cooking and heating. Now that my brother and I were working and had found a place for our family to live, our main concern became finding a way for my father and sister to join us. Communication between us was infrequent, and we did not know what was going on with them. We learned to live with this concern, to adjust. We sustained ourselves with our daily dream that the war would end and that we would become united. Our suffering was also made more bearable by the knowledge that we were much better off than people in other ghettos. I constantly thought about my father and sister. They, like the hundreds of other families who were forced out of Mlawa earlier, were now living as refugees in poverty and hunger. They were longing to have our situation.

The Mlawa ghetto was so well organized that it could have been a model for other ghettos. Even the Germans were impressed with our strong community ties and our love for life in spite of the limitations and restrictions with which we were forced to live. They could not understand how we endured such limited rights and such restrictions on our freedom of movement. Indeed, most of the individuals who served in the Judenrat and on the Jewish police force worked tirelessly to ease people's suffering to the greatest extent possible. Some of them risked their lives, and many paid with their lives.

The people in the ghetto for the most part recognized the hard work of the Judenrat. In particular Eliezer Perlmutter was recognized by all for his devotion to the Jews in the ghetto and for his daring actions to do all that was humanly possible to make our lives somewhat easier. Because of his ability to make friends with the local German authorities, he obtained favors from them. Eliezer Perlmutter deserves the credit for the adequate amount of food and many other privileges that were found in our ghetto. He arranged for Polish suppliers to deliver heating material during the winter, and at the same time they brought in potatoes and other food products, which helped feed the people.

One incident particularly demonstrates the daring actions of the Judenrat under Eliezer Perlmutter's leadership. When the Gestapo in Mlawa realized that many Jews who had been driven out of Mlawa had managed to return and integrate into the ghetto without their notice, they wanted to verify the rumors and take action. They decided to have all Jews gather in one place one Sunday morning when no one went out to work except with special permission and then check everyone's registration papers. Luckily for us, my mother and brother had obtained legal papers after they had arrived in the ghetto through family friends who were members of the Judenrat.

Perlmutter learned about the Germans' intention and devised a plan. The night before the inspection, the Judenrat arranged for hundreds of people without residency papers to be taken out of the city by trucks in the darkness of night. In the morning, when the German policemen gathered us and checked our papers, they counted far fewer people than actually lived in the ghetto. Still, although hundreds had been taken out, a large number of people were without residency papers. Risking their lives, the Judenrat members and the Jewish ghetto police transferred papers from those who had already been checked to some of those who were without papers.

With all that, the German police still found a number of people without papers. They also searched the houses and found some "illegal" residents in hiding. About a hundred people were arrested. Because the Germans had expected to find a thousand illegal residents but discovered only a hundred, they issued registration papers to those who had been found and then set them free in the ghetto. Most likely, Mr. Perlmutter was involved in convincing them of this decision. I think that heavy bribery was behind his success, as well as his charisma, wisdom, and selfless devotion to his people.

Yet, Eliezer Perlmutter ultimately became a victim of German brutality. On one of the last days of January 1942, this courageous leader was called to the Gestapo headquarters. He had been called many times before, but this time he did not return. The following morning, the Judenrat was notified of his death and was ordered to remove his body. The authorities gave no explanation. Some believed that the chief of the local Gestapo, with whom he had established a unique personal relationship, shot him. Rumor had it that he had refused to fulfill one of his orders or that the local Gestapo chief wanted to cover up his relationship with him because his superiors in Berlin were looking into their activities.

The date of that brutal murder is significant, I think. At the time it was un-known to us, but it is well-known today that on January 20, 1942, the Wann-see Conference was convened in the resort town of Wannsee near Berlin, at which time the detailed plans for "the final solution of the Jewish question" were officially approved.[4] The leaders of the Gestapo in Mlawa may have been moved to act immediately and eliminate what might become problems for them later. Regardless of the reasons, this indeed was a sad day in the Mlawa ghetto. We all felt suddenly orphaned. Our protector had been taken from us, and we feared the changes that might follow. Perlmutter had made us feel assured of a certain degree of safety and had always been ready to put his own life at stake for the sake of his community.

Because of his prominence and with the permission of the Gestapo, Perl-mutter was given a funeral and then buried in the Jewish cemetery, which was outside the ghetto. Only his immediate relatives were permitted to attend. Nevertheless, many others risked leaving the ghetto to attend the funeral of their beloved leader and friend. All those who did not have permission to at-tend the funeral were arrested. Most of them were released after a few days of detention, but twenty-five were kept in prison, including Menashe Davidson. All twenty-five were later sent to Auschwitz, where they perished within a short time. Their families were notified that they could obtain their ashes for the price of 150 German marks.

After the murder of Eliezer Perlmutter, the attacks against the Jews in the ghetto increased, and the quality of life began to deteriorate. The Ger-man authorities appointed Paltiel Ceglo, a respected businessman, as the new commissar of the ghetto. Sholom Gutman, whom every Mlawa Jew feared and hated, was appointed chief of police. He collaborated with the Germans from the first day of occupation, and the Jewish people felt disgraced.

Our activities were now watched more closely. Permission to leave the ghetto became more restricted, and the food supply began to decrease. Ger-man guards were placed at the gate of the ghetto and frequently searched people as they returned after work. Those found smuggling in food or any ar-ticles of value were severely beaten, and the articles were confiscated. Never-theless, the smuggling continued. The people in the ghetto had a strong sur-vival instinct, as well as a great deal of resilience. For a time, it was possible to bribe the local guards to close their eyes to this activity. The Jewish policemen, too, would help in the smuggling activities. As time passed, however, the situation in the ghetto continued to worsen. The authorities became stricter and more relentless in their cruelty as they increased their watch.

One day a group of the Gestapo appeared at the gate when people were returning from work. They searched everyone entering the ghetto and found potatoes, flour, sugar, and butter in a number of people's pockets or hidden under their clothes. Most were beaten and their articles confiscated, but three were arrested and sent to prison. The leaders of the Judenrat attempted to intervene on their behalf, but without success.

A few weeks after this arrest, we were notified that no one was to leave the ghetto that day. Around midmorning we were ordered to gather at the empty lot where the three synagogues had once stood. When we arrived, we found that four gallows had been constructed, and German police with machine guns surrounded the entire area. Before long, four young people were marched in, including one who had been imprisoned separately some time before the arrest of the other three. All were ordered to stand on wooden boxes under the gallows.

Four people were selected from the crowd and ordered to stand next to the gallows and place the ropes around the necks of those on the boxes. The German chief officer then read the decree from the court in Berlin that these people were to be hanged because they had broken German law and had smuggled food into the ghetto. The hanging was done publicly so that it would serve as a warning for all of us to strictly obey German rules. Paltiel Ceglo was commanded to translate the order into Yiddish so that everyone would understand. The four people standing next to the gallows were ordered to pull the boxes from under the feet of the condemned. The bodies were left hanging from the gallows for forty-eight hours. It was a shocking experience, and it stayed in my mind, at least until the next, even more horrible, experience and beyond. The Pole who sold food to the smugglers paid a fine of ten marks.

In April 1942, not long after these hangings, the Gestapo arrested all the Jewish policemen in the ghetto and some members of the Judenrat. Attempts were made to free them, and the authorities made promises to do so. Their ultimate response, however, was an order for everyone in the ghetto to gather again in the same place, the empty lot where the synagogues had once stood. This time, seventeen gallows were built, and heavily armed German police and Gestapo again surrounded the area. With hands tied behind their backs, the seventeen ghetto policemen and members of the Judenrat were led to the square and placed on boxes under the gallows. There was a long delay because the chief officer who was to preside over the execution was late with his orders from Berlin. For one long hour, the victims stood with ropes around their necks. Opposite them stood their families and friends, absorbed in their painful and agonized thoughts, while the Germans watched over us and guarded our every move.

During the long wait, someone cried out *"Nekamah!"* (Revenge!) Another was heard saying, "May we be the last victims of the Nazi brutality!" Leibel Romaner suffered a heart attack and died with the rope around his neck. His brother Moshe cried out, "May God avenge the blood of the martyrs." A German officer with an automatic weapon ran over and warned him that if he said another word he would use his weapon on the crowd. Meanwhile, Germans continued to poke fun and laugh at us. My blood was boiling within me as my mother, brother, and I stood holding each other tightly, motionless, frozen in our places. Some of the people on the gallows were family friends whom we had known all our lives. I remember wanting to run over to one of the Nazis and tear his face with my bare hands. I am sure I was not the only one there with such thoughts. But all of us knew well the consequences of such a move. The Germans were armed with machine guns. They had the power and would not hesitate to kill all of us.

When the chief officer finally arrived, he read a decree stating that because the Jewish ghetto policemen had permitted the smuggling of food into the ghetto, they were to be punished as a warning for all to see and remember the consequences of not obeying the German rules. The decree was translated by one of the Jews into Yiddish. Seventeen people were selected from the group and, at one point, ordered to remove the boxes from under the feet of the condemned people. At that moment, all of our pent-up emotions broke loose. The crowd burst out crying and started shouting. Frightened people ran in all directions to the safety of their homes. That same day, two women were caught baking bread from flour that had been smuggled into the ghetto, and they were shot on the spot. It was a day of horror and pain.

Days of mourning followed. Everyone was depressed, and no one was able to talk about what had happened. Soon, a group of young Jews were selected to replace the murdered policemen. The German authorities informed the Judenrat that the punishment had been completed and that everyone should do his and her best to get back to the "normal" routine of life in the ghetto. The Germans assured us that no further action would be taken against the ghetto inhabitants if they lived up to their responsibilities of following the German laws faithfully and keeping order. Some Jews wanted to believe those promises; others were skeptical. Regardless, we had no choice. Whether we believed the Germans made little difference, because we wanted to live—even if it meant in fear.

A few weeks later the Judenrat was ordered, without explanation, to select one hundred young people to be handed over to the German authorities. We wanted to believe that they were needed for some special work either locally or, perhaps worse, somewhere else. It was a very difficult task for the Judenrat, but the order had to be carried out, and the hundred were selected and arrested. We could not have guessed the Germans' barbaric intentions.

After the hundred people had been imprisoned for a few days, the Germans marched fifty of them into the ghetto and ordered them to dig a ditch of prescribed dimensions in the center of the ghetto. After their job was completed, the Germans ordered them back to the prison. The following day, the Germans ordered all Jews to the center of the ghetto, near the ditch. When we arrived there, the area was surrounded with hundreds of uniformed German police. They marched out the hundred arrested Jews; the fifty who had dug the ditch were ordered to stand on one side of the ditch, and the other fifty, with their hands tied behind their backs, were told to stand on the other side.

Then the local Gestapo commandant explained that the Berlin high court had decreed that one hundred ghetto Jews should be executed for the disorderly behavior that occurred when the Jewish policemen were hanged a few weeks earlier and that this would teach us to accept German punishment without emotional outbursts. The Gestapo head also said that although the high court originally decreed that one hundred young people should be punished, the local Gestapo had intervened on their behalf and received permission to kill only fifty Jews if the Jews behaved in an orderly fashion during this execution. He warned that there must be complete silence and order during the execution. If not, the other fifty would be killed as well. He then moved closer and addressed the soldiers who were about to carry out the execution. "You should feel proud and honored to be given the opportunity to fulfill this order for the good of the Third Reich," he told them.

The soldiers then began the executions. The men with their hands bound behind their backs were ordered to approach the grave five at a time and turn their backs to the grave. Five soldiers with their rifles moved to face them. The Gestapo commandant gave the order to aim and shoot the victims between their eyes. As each group made their approach, they turned their backs to the ditch and faced the five officers opposite them. They were not given blindfolds. We watched with horror as each group fell into their common grave. We held our breath in complete silence. One of the victims moved his head away from the bullet coming toward him. He was ordered to stand aside and watch the shootings of the others before they shot him. After this murderous act was completed, the commandant ordered the other fifty who had dug the grave the day before to cover the dead. We stood there during this lengthy ordeal in shock; we were numb, emotionally frozen, as if the blood in our bodies had become ice. Our hearts wept in silence before we were allowed to disperse. We walked back to our rooms in silence, with broken spirits and in deep sadness. I remember feeling a sharp pain between my eyes, as if a bullet was lodged there.

The mood in the ghetto during the days that followed was a kind of collective depression. All the Jews in the ghetto were mourning with no one to console us. It was very difficult to get back to any kind of "normalcy." I felt that we were trapped in the hands of barbarians without human hearts, without human souls. How is this possible? I wondered. But I could not talk, and I did not know what to say anyway. As never before, the people in the ghetto felt enslaved to a life of constant fear without any recourse

But life goes on even in sorrow and in fear. I remember thinking then about my father and sister. I asked myself, How are they doing? What is happening where they live? I was also thinking back to our shocking experiences in the ghetto since the murder of Eliezer Perlmutter. And I felt sad, realizing how the living conditions in the ghetto had continued to worsen rapidly since then. Food supplies continued to shrink, and we began to feel the shortage of food. Often, there was not enough bread for the three of us. I would tell my brother to take a larger slice of bread, for he was growing and I could get by with less. He would argue that I should have a larger slice of bread because I was working harder. And my mother would insist that because she stayed home, she could manage without bread. It was again our love for each other and the hope that we would be reunited as a family that held us together.

News of daily evacuations of thousands of Jews from the Warsaw ghetto began reaching us in August 1942. We had no idea what significance these expulsions had, and we wanted to believe that an end to this situation would come soon, before more harm was done to us. By the fall we heard of the defeats the German army was suffering on the eastern front, and this news encouraged us to hold on to hope just a little bit longer, even under these difficult conditions. We adjusted to a new routine of changing moods of worry and hope. After all, knowing that the powerful German army was now being pursued by the Russians was not something we could ignore when we all needed so desperately to hold on to some rays of hope. Above all, our dreams of our family being reunited reinforced our belief that better times would come. What we did not know and could not have imagined was that there already existed detailed plans for the annihilation of all Jews living under German occupation. We could not have imagined the degree of bestiality of which the "master race" was capable.

9
Liquidation of the Mlawa Ghetto

As time passed, we in the Mlawa ghetto became more and more aware of the thousands of Jews in German-occupied land who were being shot and killed or dying of starvation. We also knew that Jews living in smaller towns had been forced to settle in overcrowded ghettos in larger cities, just like the Jews in our Mlawa ghetto. What we did not know was the extent of the killings committed by the Germans since the September 1939 invasion of Poland. We in our ghetto had no knowledge of the brutal open-air killings committed by the Einsatzgruppen. Above all, we in the Mlawa ghetto were unaware of what the German Nazi government had clandestinely titled "The Final Solution of the Jewish Question." We had no knowledge of the Wannsee Conference, nor did we know of the existence of death camps.[1]

It was thus easier for us than perhaps for others to continue living with the hope that even if some of us might be killed, most of us would survive. We found strength and encouragement in each other. Even those families who had already been separated and scattered in different places or had lost a member of their family lived with the hope that the war would soon come to an end and that families would be reunited. By the end of the summer of 1942, however, the gruesome reality of the Nazi plan became apparent for the Jews in the Mlawa ghetto, too.

In October 1942, rumors began to circulate that the Mlawa ghetto would be evacuated. By the beginning of November 1942 the rumors took on a very serious note when the Germans ordered that the ghetto be closed and that no one leave. We then knew that major changes were in the making and that the changes did not mean an improvement in our situation. Yet, even without knowing all the facts, the Jews of the Mlawa ghetto were enveloped in deep sadness.

Soon after the closing of the ghetto, the Judenrat was told to prepare a plan for an orderly evacuation, which was to be carried out in three transports of two thousand people each. In great sadness the Judenrat met and prepared three lists of two thousand Jews each. The lists of the people and the dates of evacuation were then made known to the rest of the Jews. The first list was composed of Jews over the age of forty and those incapable of work. They were ordered to appear for evacuation on Monday, November 9. No destination for this transport was announced. My mother, who was in her mid-forties, was on this list.

My brother and I parted from our mother that morning in tears and with deep sadness, but with prayer and hope that we would see each other when our transport joined hers a week later. Our names had already appeared on the second list. That was the last time I ever saw my mother. The people on that first transport were kept overnight in a warehouse within the ghetto, and the following morning they were driven to the train station in trucks and ordered to board the trains. No one from that group was ever heard from again. On meeting the historian Raul Hilberg years later, I asked him specifically if he had any knowledge of where that transport from Mlawa was taken. He responded without hesitation that the people in that group were taken to Treblinka. The historian Martin Gilbert has confirmed this fact.[2]

I imagine now, from what we have learned after the war about Treblinka, that after a day or two of travel, the group arrived there and were immediately ordered to undress and then enter a large, tightly sealed room for "showers and disinfections." Moments later, deadly gas was released into the room instead of water, and within minutes two thousand innocent human beings were put to death because they were Jews. Their dead bodies were picked up and thrown into the incinerators of the crematoria and burned to ashes.[3] Among them was my dear, beautiful, loving, and lovable mother, so kind and so gentle. I assume that she expired on November 11, 1942—3 Kislev 5703 in the Hebrew calendar. Every year on the third of Kislev, I light a candle that burns for twenty-four hours, recite the Kaddish in the synagogue, and give *tzedakah* in her loving memory.

My brother and I left Mlawa with the second transport of two thousand Jews on Tuesday, November 17. I was then nineteen years of age, and my brother was sixteen. Like those in my mother's transport, we spent the night in the same warehouse, and in the morning we were marched to the train station and loaded onto a train of freight cars. The Germans gave a loaf of bread for every two people and squeezed about fifty or sixty Jews into each wagon. The doors were locked and guarded throughout the journey. The train traveled and made many lengthy stops, but we did not know where we were headed. At one stop I remember seeing the name Radom, but the name of the city did not give me any sense of our destination. The wagons were so crowded that there was not enough room for all of us to sit on the floor at the same time. In each wagon the Germans had put one or two buckets to be used as toilets, and they were emptied at every stop. The stench was awful. We were silent most of the time, each of us absorbed in our own thoughts. Gloom, sadness, and anxiety permeated the air throughout the journey, with occasional outbursts of sighing, crying, and praying. Finally, on Thursday night, November 19, 1942, after two days in the wagon, our journey came to an end. When the train first pulled into the station, however, we did not know whether this was just another stop along the way or whether it was our final destination. It did not take long for us to find out.

From what I understand, one more transport of two thousand people was driven out of Mlawa on the twenty-fourth of November. This transport was driven to Birkenau, also known as Auschwitz II. After the war we learned that the Jews from Czechanow and other surrounding towns were transferred to Mlawa after we left. They, with some remnants of Jews from Mlawa, then made up the fourth and final transport driven out of Mlawa, which occurred around the middle of December. Thus, after four hundred years of Jewish life, Mlawa had become *Judenrein*—free of Jews.

10

To the Auschwitz Concentration Camp

Nazi Germany established concentration camps as soon as their party seized power in 1933 and retained them as an integral part of the Third Reich until their defeat in May 1945. These concentration camps were at first intended for political and ideological opponents but later included criminals, social misfits, undesirables, and Jews. World War II brought substantial changes to the Nazi concentration camp system. The concentration camp universe expanded rapidly to meet the demands of war production, and large numbers of prisoners flooded the camps from all occupied countries of Europe. The Nazis also imprisoned in these concentration camps Gypsies, vagabonds, prostitutes, homosexuals, Jehovah's Witnesses, and any other people they thought to be unfit for civilian society. Ultimately, the concentration camps were transformed into an empire for the exploitation of slave labor. Within time they also became the arena for mass murder. Thus, the concentration camps served three major purposes. At first they were penal colonies; later large camps were established to supply labor; and, finally, the camps were used for "liquidation" or murder.[1]

When our transport of two thousand Jews from Mlawa finally reached its destination, the wagon doors were thrust open, and guards started yelling and screaming viciously. They shoved us off the train, beating us all the while and yelling, *"Raus!!! Raus!!! Schneller!!! Schneller!!!"* (Out!!! Out!!! Faster!!! Faster!!!). It was nighttime, and there was barely any light. Everywhere around us we heard dogs barking. There was so much chaos and confusion that we barely had a chance to take in our surroundings. We were ordered to put down our belongings and hand over all our valuables. Men were instructed to go in one direction, women in another. One woman was shot to death in front of us, supposedly for not following orders quickly enough. Gunshots were heard from all directions. I do not know whether more people were actually shot or whether the shooting was just a way to frighten us, but it was terrifying either way.

The guards hurried us toward a platform and clobbered us with their rifle butts, ordering us to move faster. Everything looked bizarre and incomprehensible, like nothing I had ever seen before. My brother and I held onto each other as we marched. We were in shock and filled with anxiety and fear. As we approached the well-lit platform, we were ordered into a single file. On the platform were several German officers, with the one seemingly in charge standing in the center of the platform. As each of us approached him and stood in front of him, he instantly motioned with his finger to the right or to the left.

My brother and I followed the line in fear. My turn came, followed by my brother. The German in charge looked me over and quickly motioned me to move in one direction. I managed to linger for a moment and see him look at my brother and send him in the opposite direction. My brother and I looked at each other, and I reached out to embrace him, but the Germans started yelling at us, and we had to move on, each of us in the opposite direction. At the time I did not know the significance of this separation. The only thing I could think of was that we would be going to different labor camps or that we had been assigned to two different work units within the same camp. This was the last time I saw my brother. This separation was forever.

I did not have any time to think about what had just happened except to remain painfully worried. The guards on my side put us in rows of five, and after a while they marched us, under heavy guard, off from this area. After a march of about a mile or so, we came to an open iron gate with the words ARBEIT MACHT FREI—Work Shall Make You Free—posted at the top of the gate. This is surely a labor camp, I thought, but the true nature of this place would become very disturbing to me shortly thereafter. What followed that night was so terrifying that I could hardly believe it was happening. It was the beginning of a very long nightmare that would last for more than two and a half years.

Before I knew it, we were shoved into a large room and ordered to undress. Despite my disbelief, there was no choice but to comply. We were then driven into another room, where all our hair, from everywhere on our body, was shaved. This was but the beginning of our humiliation. We were then sent into another room—a shower room—where the water came down extremely hard and kept changing temperature from one extreme to another. Finally, while we were still naked, we were forced into a room where we each received a tattoo of a serial number on our left arm. Under the number, they tattooed a small triangle to indicate that we were Jews. My number, 76303, and the triangle remain on my left arm to this day. From that point on, it was explained, the number was to replace our names, and we were required to re-member it and respond quickly whenever the number was called.

This was our first encounter with other inmates, for those who cut our hair and moved us along were prisoners in this camp. We began to feel that this place would be like nothing we had imagined, that it would be worse than the labor camps some of us had already experienced. The inmates' faces were expressionless, and as we moved from room to room they all said such things as "You are in Auschwitz now"; "This is the toughest concentration camp"; "You'll be lucky to last a month in this place"; "Remember the number you were given"; "Forgetting your number may mean your death"; and "Learn to move and do your work fast, for this too may bring punishment." They spoke even in the hearing of the German guards. This only contributed further to my sense of confusion and fear.

Now that we had our numbers—our "new names"—we were ordered into the next room, where we were provided with ill-fitting striped uniforms. The uniforms also came with a patch sewn onto the front of the jacket and on the right side of the trousers that displayed the same number as the one tattooed on our arms. Next to this number was a Star of David, made of overlapping yellow and red triangles, which meant that we were Jews. I learned later that the prisoners in Auschwitz included Gypsies, political prisoners, criminals, Jehovah's Witnesses, "asocials," Russian POWs, and homosexuals and that each of these groups wore a different color.

In just a few hours that night, the Germans had taken away from us all our possessions, separated us from our families, stripped us of our names, and fit-ted us with strange-looking and ill-fitting garments. All of this was done in an extreme hurry, as the Germans kept yelling, "*Schneller! Schneller!*" and not giving us a moment to reflect on what was happening to us. We were forced to run from one activity to the other.

It was close to morning when we were sent to the barracks, which was Block Number VI. This block, like all the other blocks, was a two-story brick building with one large room on each floor. The structure held about six hun-dred people. We arrived at our new "home" totally numb and confused. Not only had the Germans changed our names into numbers but also had trans-formed our homes into blocks and our rooms and beds into two long rows of three-tiered bunk beds with thin mattresses made of straw-filled sacks. By checking our tattooed numbers, we learned that about five hundred of us had been assigned to this camp, which meant that fifteen hundred of the original two thousand from the same transport had been sent elsewhere. We now were able to talk to other inmates more freely. We inquired as to where the Germans sent the others who arrived along with us. It was then that I learned the gruesome truth about this place. The inmates pointed toward tall smokestacks almost a mile away. "They have gone through those chimneys," they said. *They have gone through those chimneys?* I was confused, and innocently I asked myself, *how does one go through a chimney?*

The inmates then explained that this was not just a labor camp. Most of the people who arrived here were sent to another area of the camp, Auschwitz II, otherwise known as Birkenau. After the Wannsee Conference, the Auschwitz and Birkenau camps had been designated as death camps. The inmates chosen for death were first sent to undress, and then they were ordered into a large room that looked like a shower room. Instead of water coming through the showerheads, however, a poisonous gas was released that choked them to death. From there the bodies were transported to crematoria and burned to ashes.[2] *But my brother was among those sent that way! . . . And what about my mother?* I thought to myself.

I was shocked and sick to my stomach. It took a while just to internalize what I had learned. Such evil we had not expected, even from the Nazis. We were now faced with a more terrible reality than we could have ever imagined. We understood then that on that very night, while we were being prepared for the miserable life in this labor camp, fifteen hundred of the men, women, and children with whom we had arrived, the people I had lived with in the same city all my life, friends that I had cherished, my uncles, aunts, and cousins, including my only brother, had just been put to death. My brother was sixteen; some of my cousins were older; the youngest cousin was four years old.

It took me many days to process the information of what had happened to our families and friends. I also began to understand just how dangerous the camp would be for us. Life expectancy was very short, the inmates said, and I began to feel fear and sadness, as if I was surrounded by my dead relatives, dead friends, and my mother and brother, all crying out painfully hard questions: *"Why?! O why?! What have we done to the Germans to kill us so brutally?!"* I had no answer, and for a very long time I felt guilty for living.

The Auschwitz concentration camp was surrounded by a double length of barbed wire fencing. An electrified fence was illuminated at night and was dotted with watchtowers where armed guards manned machine guns. All around the camp were miles of empty space patrolled by German guards. We saw no chance to escape because of its extreme difficulty and risk. Yet, after the war we learned of two successful escapes by four inmates, two inmates in each escape. One of them was a young man from Mlawa whom I knew by the name of Czeszek Mordowicz.[3]

The days immediately following my arrival in Auschwitz are not clear to me. I felt like I was in a fog. But I did learn quite quickly that I was now a prisoner in a harsh labor camp. From the very beginning, my imprisonment in Auschwitz was one of continuous fear and hunger. Every day was filled with unbearable tension, emotional turmoil, and terror. I do not remember exactly how soon after our arrival or under which circumstances I was selected to join a group of about 150 young people of the 500 recent arrivals. They chose us to be trained as masons and bricklayers in the Maurer Shule, the construction school. I felt very lucky as I soon learned what a privilege this was. The vast majority of the inmates headed outside the camp daily to do all kinds of hard labor, but my group went to a special barracks, where we would spend the day inside studying the theories of construction. During the following few months, we of the Maurer Shule had a chance to acclimate somewhat to these new and horrible circumstances. It was indeed a blessing not to be exposed immediately to performing hard labor during that harsh Polish winter.

For a long time we were in a daze, not really sure what to make of our situation. While appreciating our "good fortune" in being chosen for this assignment, we continued to feel numb, isolated from anything that could be considered ordinary living or normal human behavior. The feelings of loneliness and apathy gave us no inner peace. We were convinced that the Germans were keeping us alive just to provide them with free labor as long as they needed that but that they would ultimately do away with us as they did with our loved ones.

The instructors at the school, inmates themselves, were relentlessly cruel and showed no trace of human compassion. Any one of us could be punished with painful blows for not copying a certain design quickly enough, for not immediately understanding new material (lessons were in German), or for no reason at all. I recall one of the instructors by the name of Zigi, a Frenchman, also an inmate. We feared him greatly. Zigi had been a professional boxer and enjoyed demonstrating his abilities on us whenever he felt so inspired. On random occasions he would raise his fists to challenge an opponent and throw shadow punches to the left and the right, expecting us to punch back. When someone did, he would show off with his speed and powerful punches. He enjoyed being cruel, a behavior we could not comprehend, especially coming from a fellow inmate.

By the spring of 1943, about four months after our arrival, our "good times" came to an abrupt end. I do not know whether we were considered fully trained masons and bricklayers or whether our keepers had simply decided that we knew enough to assist the civilian professionals who were hired to do work in and around Auschwitz. Whatever the reason, our schooling was finished. We were then sent out to renovate buildings and build new structures for industrial purposes or for private homes. We were assigned to different construction commandos and thus joined the Auschwitz labor force. The special treatment was over. We were now like every other inmate.

After living in this camp for more than four months, our days felt hollow, empty, like we were living in an aura of gloom. We lived with the stress of an ever-present danger. We could never lower our guard. All our attention was focused on maintaining constant vigilance. Orders were shouted at us from morning until night, and we had to carry them out quickly and accurately. One could be beaten for not following orders fast enough. Sometimes we received a collective punishment for the transgression of an individual.

In Auschwitz the day began at 4:30 a.m. with the ringing of a bell. A half hour was allotted for putting the bunk in order, cleaning, and washing. I welcomed that moment of washing my body with the refreshing cold water. This was perhaps the only positive accommodation that was in Auschwitz as compared with many other concentration camps. We could keep ourselves clean if we had the will and the stamina. After that half hour, we had roll call, a humiliating, annoying, and difficult twice-daily activity. We were expected to stand at attention in front of our blocks, in rows of ten, as soon as the ringing of the bell was heard. The German officer would count us and make sure that the numbers matched the official figures and then report that information to Lager Commandant (the camp commandant). After the Lager Commandant received the reports from all the blocks, he would check them all, and if the numbers did not match, we would have to stand there and be counted again until the discrepancy was corrected or explained. After roll call, we would break up into the labor squads—"commandos"—to which we had been assigned. The commandos would then be marched off to work sites either within or outside the camp. Most prisoners were permanently assigned to a specific commando. Perhaps because of my "special training," I was shifted around to different construction companies, where I would work on different building projects and road building. In addition to brick laying, my work included cement mixing; loading and unloading cement or bricks; carrying bricks and mortar up and down scaffolds; laying rails for trolleys that would carry rocks, dirt, or heavy material from one place to another; and other such masonry activities. The construction commandos I was assigned to usually had about twenty or twenty-five inmates working with civilian Polish construction workers. Other commandos could have more or fewer inmates.

Some commandos were better than others, based on the kind of work they had to do and the disposition of the Kapos (the prisoners/trusties who were in charge of other prisoners). Not all Kapos were equally cruel. Of course, those who worked in the kitchen commando had the best job because they never suffered hunger pains; life expectancy among them was high. The kitchen workers were primarily the Poles who had first arrived at the opening days of the Auschwitz camp. Kapos and Stubendienstens (room/hall supervisors) were also as a rule Polish. Other good commandos to work in were the laundry barrack, the warehouses, and the various workshops, because the work done inside was easier. Those playing in the orchestra certainly had it a lot easier, and their food rations were much greater than the rest of us had. Prisoners in such commandos enjoyed a greater opportunity to "organize"— meaning, in camp slang, to "steal." Working inside gave one greater access to extra food, the most precious commodity in the camp. For the most part, only the old-timers and prisoners with connections worked in these commandos. Inmates with special skills—those with training as masons, electricians, and plumbers, for example—were often able to join favored labor squads that worked under better conditions. So did those who were able to speak German, as they could more easily communicate with the German guards or the German Kapos. Of course, such factors were beyond our control. No one could change his ethnic status or physical strength, acquire a skill overnight, learn a new language, or acclimate to a new climate quickly.

My work now almost always took place outside the camp. Every morning we were marched in rows of five through the gate with the ARBEIT MACHT FREI sign to the accompaniment of an orchestra playing German marches. As we passed through the gates, the SS guards at the gate counted each commando. Most work was performed outdoors, both in the summer and in the winter. During summer the workday lasted up to ten or twelve hours, and during winter the workdays were shorter. Hard labor took place under the watchful eyes of the Kapos and the German guards. The work was always difficult, consisting of loading and unloading bags of cement or coal, mixing cement, and similar tasks. We were given a half-hour break at noontime for a quick lunch of a half liter of soup. The German guards and the Kapos exerted absolute control and made sure that the work was done efficiently and speedily. In some commandos a guard would assign a prisoner to latrine duty to be sure that no one took too long to relieve himself.

When we returned to the camp after work, we stopped at the gates to be counted again to be sure that the number of returning inmates matched the number of those who had left in the morning. Marching back into the camp, we were again "entertained" by the camp orchestra playing German marches. We were not allowed to enter the blocks before the second roll call was completed, even in freezing temperatures or heavy rain. Again we stood at attention in rows of ten until the counting was over. The total number of prisoners present in the camp had to match the official counted figures. Failure of the numbers to agree resulted in considerable agony for us. As with the morning roll call, we would remain in our places, standing at attention, regardless of the weather and frequently for hours, until the reason for the discrepancy was discovered.

The evening roll call was often followed by individual or collective punishments. Over the course of the day, the SS would have made note of inmates' numbers for various reasons, usually minor infractions. Numbers would then be called, and inmates would be subjected to a severe beating of a number of lashes. The rest of us had to stand at attention and watch until the punishment was over. Only then were we allowed to return to our blocks.

Finally, after a long day of work and after the camp rituals, the time came to receive our food rations. These consisted of 250 grams of bread (about two slices) and a thin sliver of margarine. This "meal" presented yet another serious dilemma. Because we did not get anything to eat in the morning, we had to decide whether to save a slice of the bread for the morning or to eat it all when we received it, when our hunger was most acute. In the morning we received only a tasteless lukewarm drink of something the Germans called coffee or tea. If we did decide to save a portion for the next day, it was difficult to guard it overnight. Other hungry inmates often stole such treasures. To keep some food for the next day meant tying the slice of bread to one's body somehow. Hiding it under a headrest, made of our rolled-up clothes and shoes, was too risky.

I almost always forced myself to keep a slice of bread for the morning. I just could not accept beginning a day's hard work without any food in my stomach. At some point—I can no longer remember when—the distribution of food rations was changed. The bread and "tea" were distributed in the morning, and soup was given in the evening instead of at noon, thus eliminating the nightly dilemma.

After taking time for eating and a little rest, those of us with enough strength or stamina would leave the block to meet with friends or relatives in other blocks. These moments were much cherished, as we conversed about good times in the past. We discussed events of the day, the current military situation, and our fantasies of the future. It was a chance to see people I knew from Mlawa. These meetings were a source of support, consolation, and encouragement. It helped us in our loneliness and isolation and in times of depression. At curfew, two or three hours later, we were confined to the cold and dark blocks.

Work took place Monday through Saturday. Nevertheless, Sunday was not a day of rest. Cleaning, shaving, showering in groups, and similar activities were compulsory and kept us occupied even on our one "free" day. Often, the Kapo or Blockaltester—the person in charge of the block—would ask for "volunteers." If you were standing near the Blockaltester or a Kapo when he made a request for volunteers, it was impossible to avoid offering your services. One Sunday when a Polish Kapo called for volunteers, I tried to hide. Obviously I did not do a good job at that, and I learned never to do it again. The Kapo noticed me hiding and whipped me, yelling, "You lazy Christ-killer Jew! Sunday is not your holy day!" He then forced me to "volunteer" to unload a truck with cement at one of the construction sites outside the camp. From then on, I learned to hide more carefully, and if I could not hide I would volunteer. I preferred work to being beaten.

In Auschwitz, all the beliefs, values, and norms of behavior of the world outside were abandoned, and we came to accept this situation as reality without a chance for change. Although we were all prisoners of the same regime, we were not all alike. Camp authorities created a powerful caste system of prisoners in positions of authority: Kapos were in charge of the work units; Lageraltesters (inmate camp chiefs) were in charge of the entire population of camp prisoners; Blockaltesters were in charge of the block; and Stubendiensts were in charge of the orderliness and cleanliness in the rooms and the food distribution. Despite their small numbers, German prisoners generally held positions of authority and occupied key posts in the prisoner hierarchy. German prisoners with sadistic dispositions, some of them professional criminals, were singled out to be "block elders." In my block the block elder was a German by the name of Olshewski. He had a green triangle next to his number, which indicated that he was a criminal. He caused great fear in us and called us the *"Milauer farbrecher bande"*—the Mlawer criminal bunch. Rumor had it that he had once boasted of being imprisoned for murder. When criminals held key positions in the camp hierarchy, we were often subjected to additional humiliation, arbitrary punishments, and physical abuse, including torture. They displayed a total disregard for human dignity. Their sole desire was to fulfill the expectations of the Nazi taskmasters.

The abuse carried out by the SS and the Kapos, both during and after work, was constant. One could easily be beaten for the slightest infraction of the rules or at the German's whim. Being beaten was my greatest fear not only because of the physical pain but also because it caused me to become deeply depressed. I could neither accept nor comprehend how a human being could act so cruelly. Many of the beatings were so severe and brutal that the victim became unable to stand and had to be carried back to the barracks by fellow inmates after work. Those who were unable to stand during roll call were placed on the ground near their blocks to be counted, and after roll call was over they would be taken to the infirmary, from where very few returned. Anyone who did not recover quickly was taken to the gas chambers. And every so often, the hospital would be cleared out and the patients sent to the gas chambers, which were only a short distance away.

In Auschwitz pain from hunger was constant, and thoughts and fantasies about food haunted us constantly. Most of our conversations revolved around hunger and ways of appeasing it by "organizing." A red bowl and a tin spoon were the only items of private property we were allowed to have. We carried them with us everywhere just in case we managed to organize some food to exchange for something. The camp developed an entire underground system of obtaining food. Inmates who worked in the warehouses and in the laundry rooms took various items and gave them to inmates who worked outside the camp and came in contact with Polish civilians at the work sites. The items were exchanged for food, which would be brought in under cover and shared with the suppliers. Some of the "luxury" items, such as butter, salami, or fruit, would be exchanged for bread or soup with those who worked in the kitchen and received their fill of the basic camp foods. The continuous hunger pains were so severe that all of us were ready to take risks at least some of the time, even though the punishment if caught was confiscation of the food and a severe beating.

With such sparse food rations, it was extremely difficult to keep up one's strength. Nevertheless, staying strong was of supreme importance. Every so often there would be a *selekzia*—a selection—in the camp. On such occasions, after the evening roll call we would be ordered to undress completely and form a single line inside our block. A Nazi doctor would then come in with a group of German guards and look over each of us. The doctor and the officers would determine who was "too weak to work" and would tell them to step aside. When the doctor and officers were finished, those who had been selected were sent to the hospital and then to the gas chambers. During one of those selections, the SS officer stopped near me, as if deciding what to do. I stood up as straight as I could, put my chest forward, and managed to put half a smile on my face. This was a moment of terrible fear mixed with a deep prayer in my heart. He looked me over again and moved on. Selections always reminded us of how precarious our lives were in Auschwitz. Even if we were spared at a selection, it was only a temporary reprieve. How soon would the SS doctors come back, and in what physical condition would we be then? we wondered.

Malnutrition, inadequate clothing, hard labor, and exposure to the harsh climate lowered the body's resistance to illness. Many suffered high fever, diarrhea, and festering wounds. We were expected to perform hard labor even under these adverse conditions. Many in that condition would sink into apathy and dejection, become lax about self-care, and lose a sense of self-worth. Moribund, their senses dulled, they would hover in a twilight zone between life and death. Before long their bodies lost their shape, becoming little more than skeletons covered with yellowish dry skin. In such a condition one would be identified, in the camp slang, as a "Muzulman." Gazing aimlessly with lifeless eyes, the Muzulman moved slowly, undisturbed even by the savage yelling of the Kapo to move on, even when beaten. This person would soon be severely beaten by the Kapo and then taken to the hospital, or he would die before being taken away. I saw many who reached such a stage of deterioration. The sight of these tragic people always increased my dread at the prospect of deteriorating into that condition.

Every day at Auschwitz required superhuman effort. As long as we could summon enough strength to stand and to move, we avoided reporting sickness, which would place us in the hospital. Instead, we went to work daily without fail. At times I felt sick or suffered severe headaches and high fever. Nevertheless, I pushed myself to go to work and did my best so that the Kapo or German guards would not notice my condition. The risk of going to the hospital was much greater than the risk of collapsing at work. Some, however, found the prospect of several days' rest in bed, with exemption from roll calls, backbreaking work, and physical abuse, very alluring. They reported themselves as sick and either remained in the block for a day or two or were taken to the hospital. I think they hoped that just a few days would help and that they would be able to return, but, as I said, most who were hospitalized did not come back to the camp.

The days passed, and we were constantly in fear, constantly hungry, constantly exhausted, and, during the long winter months, constantly cold. To survive the winters was the most difficult challenge in Auschwitz. We worked in the cold every day, in temperatures often below freezing, wearing only underwear, a shirt, a jacket, and trousers. The summers, too, were difficult. The days were long, and the heat was often unbearable. And there was always, in the summer and in the winter, the continuous pain of hunger and the awareness that the end might not be far off. We were surrounded by death and evil and loneliness. Despite all our efforts to survive, we knew that most of our families and friends had been murdered. I knew that my mother and brother had been killed, and although I did not have specific information about my father and my sister, I was afraid that they might have suffered a similar fate. But I still held hope in my heart that my sister might still be alive. Meanwhile, I was plagued by a sense of isolation and loneliness.

As I look back, however, I realize that I was actually blessed with a close group of people whom I could call friends. Some were contemporaries from Mlawa, others I met at the Maurer Shule, and some I met during my time as a prisoner at Auschwitz. I remember so very well a friendship that began one day at work as I was mixing cement and moving my lips in prayer, as I did daily. A man in my commando obviously noticed me praying and edged toward me. He started the conversation by asking me if I would help him pray. I was a little surprised, but of course I happily consented. I recited a prayer in phrases, he repeated each phrase after me, and I made a point of explaining the essence of the prayers as much as I could. I selected passages from the Shaharit prayers, starting with the Shema Yisrael ("Hear, O Israel," a section of the morning prayers expressing affirmation of faith) and Shemoneh Esrei (eighteen benedictions of supplication). I frequently included the prayer of Asher Yatzar, the blessing recited every morning thanking God for the body functions. I also included at times the prayer of Elokai Neshmah, in which we thank God for the purity of the soul God has planted in every human being and which we are to keep pure, even though it will be taken away from us. These prayers had great meaning for me.

He was a Jew from Berlin by the name of Isaac Fried. He preferred that I call him by his Hebrew name, Yitzhak. After that first meeting, Yitzhak and I frequently sought each other out, mostly after work, and spent time in prayer and conversation. Over time I learned his story. During the early days of the Nazi regime, Yitzhak was arrested and accused of being a Communist, a charge that was very common at that time. He was kept in prison for years without a trial, for they had no evidence of their charge against him. After he had been imprisoned several years, the Nazis sent him to Auschwitz, which was also common if the accused was a Jew. While isolated in prison, Yitzhak naturally became deeply concerned about his future and the well-being of his family, which brought him to thinking about his identity as a Jew. He had received no Jewish education, and now he sensed that there was something very serious missing in his life. Ironically, here in the concentration camp, he received his first lessons in Judaism. During our meetings, I translated and explained certain prayers to him, and we both found spiritual satisfaction in the sessions.

Not long after our first meeting, Yitzhak introduced me to a young friend of his, also from Berlin, by the name of Benny. He, too, preferred me to call him by his Hebrew name, Binyamin. He was a very pleasant and likeable young man of nineteen, just around my age. I was twenty by then. The three of us met as frequently as possible to pray together, to study Torah, or just to talk. We usually met after work, before curfew. Our conversations often led me to recall a quotation from the Bible, the Talmud, or *midrash*, which I would share with them. I frequently translated and explained passages of various prayers. In this way these meetings also became Torah study sessions. They loved it, and I certainly loved it, too. It gave us a small release from our immediate situation and brought us into a world of the spirit, far removed from the surrounding reality and gloom. They were wonderful and loving friends. I was very grateful for those relationships at the time. They had a profound impact on my frame of mind, nourishing my hopes and strengthening my efforts to go on living. It was not always possible to rely on my own strength. After the liquidation of the Auschwitz camp, I never saw them again. I have wondered many times whether they survived. I certainly hope they did.

I recall now the moments of dramatic hopefulness that lifted our spirits on our gloomy days. One such moment was when we heard about the attempted assassination of Hitler on July 20, 1944. Of course we regretted that the assassination was unsuccessful.[4] But it nevertheless left us a message that attempts to do away with the Nazi regime existed, and thus there was the hope that it would ultimately succeed.

Another dramatic event, which was also for us a moment of joy and sadness mixed into one, occurred on October 6, 1944, when the sirens sounded in Auschwitz. We did not know its significance then, but a few days later we learned that members of the Sondercomando, the special commando of inmates who worked around the gas chambers and the crematoria, had attempted to stage a revolt. The effort involved six hundred inmates who had organized to escape. They managed to throw one of the SS men in the fire of the crematorium and cut the wire fence. The alarm sounded, however, and a regimen of SS troops arrived and killed all six hundred escapees. From this incident we learned that there were resistance organizations even in Auschwitz, although it was hard to believe. After the war was over we learned more of the resistance by Jews in the ghettos and concentration camps and the heroic resistance by Jewish partisans in Poland, Belgium, and France.[5] We also heard about the unsuccessful revolt of the Polish underground.

By that time in 1944, we knew that the defeat of Nazi Germany was approaching. The Polish civilians with whom we spoke at work outside the camp informed us that the German army was retreating from both the east and west. Yet even on the threshold of liberation, we felt the shadow of death loom large over us. The Nazis seemed set on torturing us until the very end.

I remember vividly our conflicting emotions and endless discussions during that period. We knew that the Germans' day of reckoning was on its way. The optimists among us argued that it would be illogical for the Germans to continue these atrocities up to the very moment of defeat. At some point they would have to stop and begin to erase the evidence of their brutality. Yet many others were convinced that the Nazis would not permit us to survive to bear witness to their crimes. I did not know what to think; my emotions ran from one extreme to the other. I was indeed happy to know of the beginning of the downfall of Nazi Germany. On the other hand, I was also filled with a strong desire to survive, and we did not know the Germans' intentions. Would they let us free, or would they blow up the camp with all of us in it, leaving no evidence of the horrible crimes they had committed? I did not dare to guess. It was a time of painful uncertainty, but I tried to maintain my hopefulness even if it defied logic.

By January 1945, the Soviet army was nearing the Auschwitz-Birkenau complex, and the Germans began a hasty and chaotic evacuation of the camps. There were then approximately sixty thousand prisoners in Auschwitz, including all the satellite camps around.[6] After roll call on January 18 we were informed that no one was to leave for work and that the entire camp should prepare for evacuation. Our conflicting emotions became even more serious. What fate was awaiting us? Were we being driven somewhere to be freed, or was there some other evil plan in the minds of our oppressors? Did they perhaps have a plan to massacre us all at once? We had no choice but to follow orders. All we could do was hope that liberation would come soon.

II

The Long Road to Liberation

Thus we left the Auschwitz concentration camp on January 18, 1945. The Germans marched us out of the camp in large groups, a couple of hundred prisoners at a time, with the various groups headed for different camps westward.[1] It was a bitterly cold day. The guards surrounding us carried rifles and bayonets and watched over us constantly. It was the middle of the harsh Polish winter, and we were being sent out and onto the freezing roads wearing only our prisoners' uniforms. As we marched in rows of five, the gunfire became more frequent. Those who could not keep up with the pace were shot to death. Some prisoners attempted to escape, and they were shot, too. As we marched in the middle of the roads, I saw dead bodies lying on both sides of the road. They had been shot by the guards.

This "death march," as it became known, was progressively more exhausting, and we began to notice that the bodies of our fellow prisoners lying alongside the road were increasing. This is the beginning of the end, I thought. The Germans obviously intend to kill us all this way. It is still a mystery to me how I kept up my strength and continued to keep up with that exhausting march. I remember thinking that this was no time to give in to my exhaustion and that I had to maintain my will to live. I continued on with all the energy I could muster, desperately hoping that there was indeed some destination to this march and that I would eventually get a chance to lie down and get a little rest. Luckily, two friends from Mlawa, Sol Mitgang and Jacob Beharier, and I stayed together during the march, and we helped support each other. On occasions when one of us felt at the peak of exhaustion, the other two would hold him up by his arms and thus give him a chance to regain some strength for a while.

I do not remember how long this bone-chilling and frightening marching lasted before we arrived in the concentration camp of Gleiwitz, which was used at that time as a temporary assembly center for the driven prisoners. I do not remember much about this camp except for the chaos and confusion and the relief I felt at finally getting a chance to rest. The camp of Gleiwitz was overcrowded, but we were allowed to spend one night there sleeping on the floor. On the following day the march continued. The conditions of this march were much the same as the first, with prisoners constantly being shot and left dead on the sides of the road. At some point during this march, we boarded a train of cattle cars that took us to the Buchenwald concentration camp. Here, too, the atmosphere was pandemonium, and the camp was extremely overcrowded. The following day a group of us were ordered onto trucks and driven to the camp of Ohrdruf and from there to Krawinkel, two of Buchenwald's several satellite camps.[2] We arrived in Krawinkel on January 27 or 28, which means we had been on the road for about ten days, between marching and traveling.

Krawinkel was a very small camp compared to Auschwitz and held just a few hundred inmates. The wooden barracks seemed to have been constructed poorly and hurriedly. Cold air blew in through the doors and windows, making restful sleep practically impossible. In Auschwitz we had slept in brick barracks, protected from the wind. The restrooms, too, were of subhuman standards and unsanitary. Most disturbing, however, was the meager food rations allotted to us. The slice of bread in the morning was much thinner than in Auschwitz. We were given no margarine, but occasionally we would receive a teaspoon of marmalade. After work we received a pint of "soup" that contained little to chew on.

I had not thought it possible for forced labor to be more torturous than what I had already experienced in Auschwitz, but I found the work at Krawinkel to be really backbreaking. I was assigned to a commando that was constructing bunkers in the surrounding Thüringen mountains. German civilian engineers supervised our work, which involved boring holes into the mountains of this rocky region. We had to hold the jackhammers with long drills in different positions—on our shoulders, over our heads, against our stomachs, and in sitting positions. But in my weakened condition, I found the jackhammer to be very heavy to lift. It would be heavy even for a strong person, I imagined. Yet somehow I found the strength to do it. Perhaps the fear of being beaten or censured in some way gave me the strength and the courage to do the seemingly impossible.

After we drilled holes in the rock in front of us and above us, the engineers would fill the holes with dynamite and trigger an explosion. We, the prisoners, had to load the rocks onto carriages and push them outside the bunker, where the debris would be deposited. The engineers and supervisors continuously drove us to work faster and harder. Of course, we knew the reason for the rush: the Allies were closing in on the Germans from the west. What we did not know, however, was the reason the Germans were having bunkers

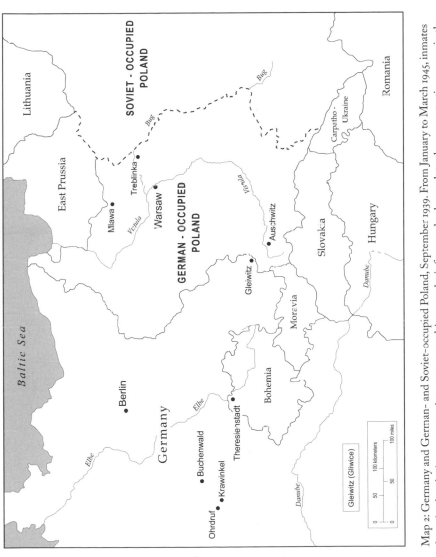

Map 2: Germany and German- and Soviet-occupied Poland, September 1939. From January to March 1945, inmates from the Auschwitz concentration camp were driven on the infamous death march to the concentration camps in the west. I was in a group driven to Buchenwald and its satellite camps, Krawinkel and Ohrdruf. The Germans were attempting to stay ahead of the Soviet army advancing from the east.

built in these mountains. Was there some kind of a plan to surprise the Allied troops as they reached the area, or were these bunkers going to be the place they would kill us? There was no way for us to know.

I was assigned to the afternoon shift, which began at 2:00 p.m. and lasted for ten hours, until midnight. We had to march about a mile or two from the camp to the work site. I used to *daven minhah* (pray the afternoon service) as we were marching to the workplace. By the time I was finished with the *minhah* prayer, I knew that we were close to our destination. After a ten-hour workday and the march back to the camp, I was always completely exhausted as never before. The work was hard and much more intense than what I had done at Auschwitz. And with the food rations being so little, I felt my stamina and strength waning daily. I was beginning to realize that I was in an extremely debilitated physical condition, with my exhaustion creating perhaps a more life-threatening situation than ever before. I could do nothing to improve my circumstances but pray and hope.

I prayed constantly: while marching to work, in the midst of forced labor, and on my way back to camp. I recited every prayer I knew and every passage from the Bible or the Talmud that I could remember by heart. I fervently believed that the angel of death could not strike me while I was engaged in prayer or the study of Torah.

Not only was the labor excruciating at Krawinkel, but the guards were unbelievably cruel. I remember one night, after the work shift had ended, waiting a particularly long time in our usual rows of five as the guards looked for a missing inmate. After a thorough search, they found that this prisoner had fallen asleep. They then beat him to death as some of the inmates watched. I did not witness this beating personally, but I heard how the guards kicked his head and stomach and beat him with sticks until he died. Only afterward were we allowed to return to the barracks. After that incident the guards became even more strict, scrutinizing our every move. We tried to keep our spirits up, knowing that the Allies were closing in on our region. We quietly cheered when we saw American bombers flying low over our heads.

On April 3, 1945, all work at the camp came to a halt because of the Allies' advances, driving the Germans eastward. We were then marched back to Buchenwald, which took a full day. As we were marching, with the guards on both sides of the column, we again noticed dead bodies lying on both sides of the roads—another death march. Yet, we were then convinced that the final collapse of Nazi Germany was imminent. This strengthened our hopes, and I tried to be cheerful. But it was hard for me to continue my cheerfulness because of tiredness and because it was a time of great concern. We did not know what the Germans intended to do with us before they capitulated.

Our emotions became like a roller coaster. When we reached Buchenwald, we found the camp terribly crowded, and everything was in a state of chaos. All I wanted to do was lie down and rest my body. I was not even hungry for food. I managed to find an empty corner to lie down and get some sleep. I have no memory of how long I slept. I do remember that the chaos in Buchenwald continued and that the distribution of food was disorderly for a few days after our arrival.

On April 10, 1945, as the Allied armies advanced toward the camp, a group of us were sent on yet another death march. We were forced on foot for a number of days and passed the nights under guard in warehouses, in farm stables, or at the sides of the roads. We had no idea where we were headed. Several times, when Allied bombers flew over our heads, the guards ordered us to run into the forest. Seeing the Allies continued to increase our hopes a bit and encouraged us to hold onto life with every bit of strength still within us.

One day—I do not know the date—we arrived at a train station and were ordered to board the cattle cars. Our train traveled and stopped and changed direction frequently, as if our guards did not know what to do with us. There seemed to be no purpose to this journey. Perhaps they still intended to finish us off but were waiting for just the right time and place, we thought. Occasionally, soup was distributed, although it was hardly enough to make a dent in our hunger. As I think back on those days, I cannot understand how I found the strength to go on, how I tolerated for so long the uninterrupted physical and mental suffering, the constant threat of torture and death. For five and a half years, while thousands of lives had disappeared before my eyes, I somehow managed to hold onto a glimmer of hope. I wanted so very much to live. I often thought that I might turn out to be the only survivor of the large Goldstein-Kleinbard family. But during the period beginning with the march out of Buchenwald, I remember, the hunger pain was getting to be unbearable, and I began to wonder whether those who had perished earlier and more quickly were not more blessed than I. And I recalled the words of the prophet Jeremiah that he uttered in mourning the destruction of Jerusalem: *"Tovim hayu halelei herev m'halelei ra'av"*—"Better off were those slain by the sword than those who died by famine."[3] I seriously started to doubt my chances of living. I began to feel a sense of resignation, of indifference, as to whether I lived or died. Despite the obvious military defeat, the Germans seemed committed to carrying out their murderous plans until the very end, I told myself. My chances of survival seemed remote by that time, and I accepted this fact with much regret.

I do not remember how many days we traveled by train, for by then my sense of time began to fail me. I do remember that the guards who watched us actually began to treat us a bit more humanely. Because little food was available for us now, the guards permitted us to get off the train at various stops and fetch water from the brooks off the road. They even encouraged us to collect twigs and branches to light fires and boil the water. We added grass and leaves that we found growing nearby, believing they might contain some nutritional value. Occasionally, the guards succeeded in arranging for some food to be brought to us from the villages close to the stations where we stopped. But the hunger was so great and the distribution of food so chaotic that only those who were able to shove and push forward managed to get some. In my state of being, I often remained behind and had to do without food or water.

Luckily, the three of us, Jacob Beharier, Sol Mitgang, and I, were able to continue to stay together. During the various death marches, we kept supporting each other with words and deeds. Still, our physical condition had now reached the low point of having no strength to jump down from the train to fetch food or water. We arranged that each of us would take turns and bring water for the others. In this way we were able to sustain our poor energies a little bit longer.

My physical condition continued to deteriorate rapidly. I became so weak that I stopped feeling hunger or thirst, and I could no longer stand on my feet. I crawled into a corner of the cattle car and lay down in the fetal position. I saw then that people who had died were being thrown off the train, and I thought that my turn would come soon too. I saw myself as just a bundle of bones held together by a thin layer of skin and without vitality or desire for life. I remember thinking then about the prophet Ezekiel's vision of the valley full of dry bones. He prophesied, and the bones stood up and lived.[4] Could this happen to me? Would I ever regain my strength, stand up, and live again? I began breathing heavily and thought my time had come. I was literally at the door of the next world, where the angel of death awaited me. I recited the *vidui* (confession prayer) that Jewish tradition says should be recited before death. I knew some parts by heart—the Ashamnu and the Al Chet—because they are the confessionals we recite every Yom Kippur when we ask forgiveness for our sins. And in my own words, I asked God to forgive me for all the wrongs I had committed, knowingly and unknowingly, against him and against my fellow human beings. I had recited this confession many times before when danger seemed immediate. This time, however, I said the prayer with more seriousness until I lost consciousness. I have no memory of what happened to me during the days or weeks that followed.

My first recollection of self-awareness after that point was when I woke up one day and found myself in a bed. I did not stay conscious long enough to know my surroundings. I dozed on and off several times before I could make sense of anything around me. When I finally was able to stay awake for some extended time, I saw a Russian officer standing near my bed. I was told that I was in a hospital in the Theresienstadt camp, which had been liberated by the Russian army. I was now free to go whenever I wanted, they said. I remember asking myself, *Free to go? What does this mean? Free to go, where?* I was certainly very confused. *I was free to go? What did that mean? To go where?*

The day of liberation I had dreamed of for so long had come, but I did not feel it. I did not know it, and it was not real to me. I felt no joy. I was indifferent to everyone and everything around me. I then saw my friend Jacob Beharier in the bed next to mine, but I do not remember any conversation with him. It seems I was numb and did not know what to say or what to do. Regrettably, after all I had endured, I was even robbed of joy on liberation day.

I found out more details about the days before my liberation only when I was reunited with Cantor Sol Mitgang years later. He told me that the train we were traveling on back and forth for so many days ultimately brought us to Theresienstadt.[5] There the German guards released us and immediately fled. The Jews of Theresienstadt took us in, and we were given showers and food. I was obviously in a condition where I had to be taken to the hospital. We were liberated by the Russians soon afterward, on May 8, 1945. I was in the hospital at that time, but unconscious.

After a few more days in the hospital, I was discharged and assigned to one of the Theresienstadt camp barracks. After the Russian army had liberated Theresienstadt, the ghetto and concentration camp had become a displaced persons (DP) camp, supported by the United Nations Relief and Rehabilitation Agency. Although I was technically free to go, I was not well enough to be discharged and face a life of freedom on my own. I was still extremely weak, physically and emotionally. My physical being needed time to recover, and my mind was numb, like it was empty. I felt no emotional connection to the people around me. After the incredible suffering I had endured, I could not feel the miracle of being alive. All of life's joys had been taken out of me. I was helpless like an infant—and insecure and afraid to be seen or heard.

Much of the time immediately following my liberation is a fog to me. I do not remember how I received the clothes that replaced my prisoner's uniform, but I do recall the terrible fear with which I lived. I remember that my shoes had wooden soles that made noise when I walked and that I was terribly frightened of waking or annoying someone with that sound. I feared that someone would yell at me or that I would even be beaten. So instead of walking normally, I shuffled my feet slowly and carefully so that my shoes would not make any disturbing noise. I lived in fear of being seen or heard and of being harmed. Intellectually, I understood that the war was over and that I was no longer subject to an evil regime, but emotionally I was still a prisoner, as if I was still in a concentration camp.

I depended heavily on the assistance of others, and the only people I trusted were the few fellow survivors about my age from my hometown, those who had shared my experiences in the ghetto and concentration camps. About ten survivors from Mlawa were in the DP camp with me, and they accepted me kindly into their circle. They told me when and where to go for meals and when and where to sit or stand. I was in no condition to take the slightest initiative or make even the most mundane decision, let alone figure out what to do or where to go next.

A postcard image of Mlawa after German occupation in 1915, showing Ulica Plocka (Plotzka Street), a central district of the Jewish population.

My parents, Meyer and Tirtza (Kleinbard) Goldstein, about 1920.

Back row, left to right: My mother's sister Sonia, my parents, and my mother's sister Tzerko; *front row, left to right:* my father's sister Leah and my mother's sister Sarah.

My mother in 1931 with her three children. *Left to right:* Me, Rachel, and Shmulik; in the background is my mother's sister Sonia.

My sister, Rachel, in 1931 in the traditional Crakow region (Krakow-ianka) dress with her aunt Sonia.

Shmuel Alter Goldstein, my paternal grandfather, circa 1918–19. He died shortly after the First World War ended.

Toba Goldstein, my paternal grand-
mother, who died in Lubartów on
December 20, 1940, a victim of the
Holocaust.

I am photographed in 1945 after
liberation.

I wear an Auschwitz uniform borrowed from a friend (taken in Italy at a displaced persons camp, 1945).

Cousin Herbert Kleibard in 1946 with my aunt Yetta and uncle Morris in their New York City apartment, where I was warmly and generously offered a home.

I am finally in America, April 1948.

Mordekhai Golinkin, Riva's father. He served as an Orthodox rabbi in Worcester and head of the rabbinic court in Boston until his death in December 1974.

Haya Freda Golinkin, Riva's mother.

Riva and me at our wedding, July 18, 1948.

Photograph of me in late 1951 in Salem, Massachusetts. *(Photo courtesy of K. S. Melikian.)*

Riva and me, 1971.

I receive the 1984 Brotherhood Award of the Worcester County chapter of the National Conference of Christians and Jews from Sarkis Teshoian.

Riva and me with our son, Meyer, June 1986.

Rabbi Benjamin Kreitman *(left)*, executive director of the World Council of Conservative Judaism, congratulates me on the occasion of my retirement from the Beth Israel Congregation, 1986.

The Goldstein family gathers in October 2005 at the Beth Israel Synagogue for the dedication of the stained glass window *Zachor* ("Remember") in memory and honor of the six million Jews murdered in the Holocaust. *Back row, left to right:* granddaughter Sarah and grandsons Daniel and Jonah; *front row, left to right:* daughter-in-law Sue-Rita, granddaughter Liza, son Meyer, me, cousin Kitty Goldberg, friend Lisa Schachner, and Jonah's wife, Jessica Larko.

With great-grandson Ronan, I celebrate his bris (circumcision), September 27, 2006.

From Slavery to Freedom

The transition from being a prisoner to being a free man was not an easy one for me. I was deeply affected by the six years from age sixteen, when the Nazi horror began, to the age of twenty-two, when I became a "free" man. I continued living with the burden and the pain of the past atrocities and the losses of my dear family. I could not simply switch from being an inmate living with constant fear and in complete servitude known only by a number to being a person with an identity and a will of my own. This change would require a process that would span years.

I continued to be emotionally numb for many months. I had to use all my energy just to get through the day and perform the most mundane activities. Eventually, after weeks in Theresienstadt, I began to internalize the friendships shown to me by the survivors with whom I roomed and had known for years. But I also began to comprehend fully the meaning of having lost my entire family. I was beginning to feel the brutality with which they were murdered. I started to grasp that I had no home to which I could return and that I would have to face my life in loneliness. Yes, I began to experience something I had not been able to do, or not allowed myself to do, for years—I began to feel. Now that I could and allowed myself to feel, there was nothing but sadness and sorrow, and I became entrenched in a period of mourning and depression.

I thought constantly of my mother, who had been deported on that first transport during the liquidation of the Mlawa ghetto two and one-half years earlier. I thought of the moment we separated and how I did not know at the time what that parting meant. I had even been robbed of a proper good-bye. I thought of my brother, who had arrived at Auschwitz with me and who had been sent to the other side. Then, too, I was unaware of the significance of our separation. *He was only sixteen.*

And I thought of my father and my sister. The last time I had seen them was when I left Lubartów in February 1941. At the time, still quite naïve, I had no doubt that we would be reunited sooner or later. By now, I was certain that my father could not have survived the atrocities that followed after our separation. I did have hope, however, that my sister might have made it. She was young, bright, and energetic, and she had a strong will to live. Here in the Theresienstadt DP camp, however, I did not have the physical or the emotional energy to begin the search for her.

When I was not thinking of my immediate family, I remembered my aunts and uncles and cousins. They had all been sent to one death camp or another or had been shot to death or had died of starvation. And I felt the weight of deep loneliness.

At age twenty-two I was now like a lost and confused child. I felt isolated and alienated. Life seemed unreal and trivial. I remember thinking that it really made no difference to anyone whether I lived or died. Ironically, after having spent so many years hoping, praying, and struggling to live, I now felt guilty for being alive. What merits did I have to go on living when all my loved ones had not been given a chance to live?

In addition to dealing with physical and emotional pain, I now had to figure out where to go and what to do next. For weeks after I regained consciousness, I was still not capable of making decisions on my own. Luckily, a group of fellow survivors at the Theresienstadt DP camp befriended me. They had decided to join the movement to immigrate to Palestine. I could not think of any other options available to me, and I had no initiative to do anything by myself anyway. While growing up I had been imbued with the Zionist ideals of the youth movements of those years. I was now easily convinced that the time had come to rebuild the Jewish state and that I should follow the decision of my fellow survivors and make my future there. Non-Jewish survivors of different nationalities returned to their home countries and rejoined their families. A number of Jewish survivors, too, went back to their hometowns in Poland and searched for survivors of their families and friends, but most met with painful disappointments. Most of the Jewish survivors from Poland did not return to the land where three million Jewish citizens, 90 percent of the Jewish population of Poland, had been murdered. Their homes and shops and their schools and synagogues had been destroyed or taken over by Poles. The cemeteries had been vandalized and destroyed beyond recognition. Even the dead were not allowed to rest in peace! Rebuilding a normal life for themselves in Poland seemed impossible and impractical. Some Jewish survivors from Mlawa did return to their hometown and attempted to rebuild a Jewish community there, but they met with the hatred of anti-Semites and had to run away to save their lives.

For most of us in the DP camps, therefore, our future seemed to point toward Palestine. For years before the war, the Zionist movement and ideology had made strong inroads into the younger generation of eastern Europe. As in Mlawa, many young people throughout the eastern European region had been actively involved in Hakhshara. As I mentioned earlier, the greatest obstacles at that time were the policies of Great Britain, which held the mandate over Palestine and would not permit an increase in the Jewish population there. When the war began, the dream of settling in Palestine became a distant possibility. Now, after the Holocaust, most of the survivors believed their only option was to settle in that land and build their future there. The Zionist movement had renewed energy to realize its hope of establishing a Jewish homeland there. The Jewish Agency for Palestine sent representatives to DP camps all over Europe to assist the survivors in their desire to restart their lives in Palestine.

The British government continued to insist on maintaining its policy of restricting immigration to Palestine to a bare minimum. The Jewish survivors of the Holocaust, however, insisted on their rights to immigrate to their historic homeland to which the Jewish people had longed to return since the Romans expelled them in the year 70 CE. The Jewish Agency for Palestine, together with the Jews of Palestine, came to realize that the survivors would be able to reach the Promised Land only via illegal immigration. Part of the agency's work was to direct survivors toward different points in Europe where they could ultimately prepare to sail illegally into Palestine. The movement was aptly titled the Berihah, "The Flight."

At that time, travel throughout Europe was free for displaced persons, so going from place to place was no problem. After about two or three weeks in Theresienstadt, the group that I was attached to decided to aim for Palestine for their future, and I joined them traveling to Prague and from there to Bratislava. We did not spend more than a day or two in any one of these places until we arrived in Budapest. There we met up with a representative of the Jewish Agency for Palestine who was in the city to organize groups and to guide them in their illegal travels to Palestine. We also met up with other survivors headed to Palestine. The representative held a number of meetings to inspire us with Zionist ideals and to provide us with instructions we so desperately needed for our journey to Palestine. After a couple of weeks in Budapest, we were instructed to travel to Gratz, Austria, and from there we continued toward Italy. We arrived in the northern part of Italy in the beginning of August 1945, and we were told by the Jewish Agency representatives there that our next stop would be in Palestine.

After a few days there, however, we were directed to a DP camp in Santa Maria di Bagni, a village in the southernmost part of Italy near the Adriatic Sea. Italy was then under the British occupation, and the United Nations Relief and Rehabilitation Agency supported this camp just as it supported all the other DP camps in Europe. About ten of our group were assigned to a house near the sea that had been abandoned by the owners during the war. We were told to stay there until we received further instructions to sail from there to Palestine. The house was without any furniture except sleeping cots, mattresses, and a stove. Food was provided by the camp kitchen, but we were given the option of receiving a weekly money allowance instead. Our group chose the latter and did our own cooking. We were ten amicable young men, most of us came from the same city, our families knew each other, and we shared the same experiences under Nazi rule. We managed well with food distribution and supported each other in every way possible.

I never learned why, but our journey to Palestine was delayed. I had felt certain when we first arrived in Santa Maria di Bagni that we would be heading toward our final destination immediately, but I was wrong. We ended up staying as displaced persons in Italy for more than two years, first at the DP camp in Santa Maria di Bagni and then a DP camp in Bari. This delay was very disappointing and often frustrating, but admittedly it was also an opportunity for me to begin regaining my health and to strengthen my ability to travel and function better on my own. Most of my physical recovery actually took place during the years in the two camps. The sunny climate of southern Italy and the pleasant natural surroundings helped me in this respect, but most important for me at that time was the fact that there was enough food. I recall this being my major concern on arrival. The pain of hunger was still a fresh memory. In addition to the assurance I received about food when I arrived at the camp, I was also informed that an abundance of grapes was growing in the area, which would serve as an excellent supplement to the rations we were allowed. This information eased my worries, but the constant concern over food remained with me for a long time.

I was now gaining weight and physical energy fairly quickly, but my psychological and spiritual recovery was proving much more difficult. I continued to be frightened and to feel lonely and estranged. The loss of my family was sinking in even more than before and becoming more painful and depressing. I found myself in tears frequently. I longed to have but one member of my own family embrace me and say, *"I am happy you have survived."*

Tormenting questions also plagued me: How had such cruelty and hatred been possible? Why were we so helpless during those many years of horror and destruction? Why were so few people willing to take risks to save human lives? Why did the Western powers take so long to strike at the evil Nazi empire and to come to the rescue of millions?

Furthermore, I was now faced with a religious skepticism. I had been raised in my parents' religious home and educated in yeshivas, where I had been instilled with an unquestionable belief in God and the abundance of his goodness and protective power. Amazingly, I had somehow managed to maintain that faith throughout the years of persecution. But now, when I was beginning to feel the extent of the destruction, I found it impossible to continue in my traditional beliefs and religious observances. Where was God? I kept asking myself. Where had the omniscient and omnipotent God I had grown up believing in been while so many millions of innocent men, women, and children were brutally victimized and murdered? Why had he remained silent?

I became completely indifferent to the observances that had been so much a part of me until then. Torah and mitzvot lost their significance. I could not see or feel any connection between these observances and my existence. My skepticism and doubts also included skepticism and doubts about humankind. Was there any goodness left in the hearts of humans? This led me to question frequently whether there was any meaning or purpose to life in general and to my life in particular. Did anyone really care whether I lived or died? I was unable to deal with these agonizing questions and did not really pursue the answers. I was too tired.

Our journey to Palestine was delayed, but we were still fully intent on immigrating. Meanwhile, three representatives from a large contingent of Jews from Palestine called Hamishlahat Ha-eretz Yisraelit (the Delegation of the Jews from Palestine) arrived at our camp. The organization had actually been established with the support of the British government for the purpose of assisting Jewish refugees in the DP camps with educational, social, religious, and cultural needs. They were actually quite helpful to the refugees during this trying period of waiting. One of the projects they established in our camp that I appreciated very much was the creation of a library and reading room that featured Yiddish and Hebrew newspapers and magazines. For years I had not seen anything printed with Hebrew letters. I was very excited to discover these publications readily available to me. Being able to sit and read in my native tongue was so uplifting that I spent hours at a time reading every word of all the outdated Yiddish and Hebrew articles I could get my hands on.

One of the newspapers in our reading room was the New York Yiddish daily *The Forverts (The Forward)*. One of its features was a listing of announcements of names of survivors from all over Europe who were searching for their relatives in America. This planted an idea in my mind. I knew that my mother had a brother who had immigrated to America before World War I. I knew his name—Mordekhai Kleinbard—but I had no address for him. One of my mother's sisters, Sonia Ulick, lived in California. I did not have her address either. I started writing letters to the editors of the Yiddish newspapers published in New York. Not only did I desire to make contact with my relatives in America, but it also seemed the most logical means of locating my sister. I felt strongly that had my sister survived, she would have certainly made contact with our family in the United States. She had been particularly close to my aunt Sonia.

Meanwhile, many of those who had started their search for living relatives earlier had begun to receive mail from some of these family members. I was naturally envious and anxiously awaited receiving a note from my relatives. Mail was delivered only once or twice a week. At that auspicious time, most of the two hundred people in the camp would gather in front of the offices where mail was distributed. We arrived with the hope that this might be the day our dreams would be realized—perhaps a note from a spouse, a sibling, a parent, another relative, or a friend. One of the clerks would read names aloud. The recipient would run ecstatically when his or her name was called. But those of us who had received nothing would leave disappointed. Life was so painfully lonely, so full of longings to connect with family and friends.

I shall never forget the day my name was called. It was October 26, 1945. I heard my name read. My heart skipped a beat. *Really!? . . . A letter for me!? . . .* With trembling hands, I took the envelope and looked at it with wonder. Yes, it was a letter really addressed to me, with my name, *Baruch Goldstein.* It was from my uncle; he had changed his name from Mordekhai Kleinbard to Morris Kleibard.

My hands still shaking, I opened the letter and started to read. *"Taierer Baruch"* ("Dear Baruch"), it began in Yiddish. As soon as I saw the first two words, I burst into tears and was unable to continue reading until I regained my composure. Eventually, I read on. It turned out that my uncle read *The Forward* every day and never skipped checking the list of names of people being sought by survivors in Europe. My uncle wrote of how overjoyed he was to discover I had survived, and he reassured me that he and his wife, Aunt Yetta, would assist me in any way possible with my future plans. It was a short note, but it touched me deeply. *I found an uncle, and he has written to me! What a miracle! What a blessing!* I read the letter haltingly, holding onto every word as tears ran uncontrollably down my cheeks and wet the paper. I must have read that letter a hundred times in the days that followed, as if to make sure it was real. I practically knew every phrase by heart. One thing was missing; regrettably, there was no mention of my sister, Rachel. When my uncle did not say anything about her, I knew my suspicions about her having died were probably true. I had written to the Red Cross and searched continually through the survivors' lists for her name (and would continue to look for many years), but to no avail. For many years, too, I even dreamed about her appearing one day. I would never stop wishing to know how and when she died.

Soon after my uncle found me, he notified my aunt Sonia, who lived in Los Angeles with her husband, Joe, and their son, Herbert. He also notified another of my uncles, Zalman Sokolover, who lived in New York. He was the husband of my mother's sister Tzerko who had immigrated to America by himself when an opportunity arose in the early thirties.

A steady correspondence developed between my American relatives and me. My aunts and uncles wrote quite frequently. In my letters to them I wrote a bit about my experiences during the war and in the DP camps and about the family members we had lost. To Uncle Zalman I wrote about his family, whom I had seen in the Mlawa ghetto on many occasions until the liquidation. But mostly I wrote of my longing to begin a "normal" life with "normal" problems. I spoke of my loneliness and disappointment in having to live as a stateless wanderer, even after liberation. They wrote back with encouraging words, trying to relay a sense of hope that soon the situation in Palestine would improve and that I would be allowed to immigrate.

They also spoke of the restricted immigration policies of the United States. My aunt Sonia spoke of bringing me to America as soon as the immigration laws changed and about sending me to school. But the immigration laws did not change, and a visa did not materialize. The Polish quota for immigration had been filled for years, and the United States was not allowing any new immigrants. Later on (I believe it was 1950), America did permit one hundred thousand refugees from the DP camps to come to America. My heart was set on going to Palestine anyway, so I was glad that I did not have to make a decision, for the matter was not in my control to decide.

Though I was separated from these people by thousands of miles, the knowledge that I had relatives who cared about me made a big difference in my moods. It gave me a feeling of belonging and connectedness. Yet the feelings of isolation and loneliness also persisted. I was frequently depressed and often thought that anything good happening to me was an illusion. I would not allow myself to feel good for long periods of time. When someone spoke to me in a friendly manner, I would think it was a hallucination. Why would anyone want to speak to me? I wondered. And if I accepted these gestures as genuine, I would feel anxious and hope that the conversation would end soon. I continued to live in fear and mental isolation most of the time. I enjoyed writing to my relatives in America and wrote to them frequently, but I never revealed the depths of my feelings. Still, this correspondence did calm my anxieties somewhat and helped me along the path toward emotional recovery.

Indeed, many people played major roles in my psychological recovery. One of the most important was Zvi Aldouby, one of the three representatives of Hamishlahat Ha-eretz Yisraelit who had arrived soon after our arrival in Santa Maria di Bagni. Zvi was a warm and caring person who loved the Jewish people and their traditions and culture. He loved the Hebrew language and the Land of Israel. As part of his mission he worked at strengthening the commitment of the refugees to these values. Zvi's main interest was creating opportunities for the intellectual and educational growth of the displaced persons. He organized lectures and courses in Zionism and Jewish history. He mimeographed pamphlets for special occasions and started a drama club. (Reluctantly, I even accepted his offer to take a minor part in the production of the famous Yiddish play *The Golem.*) It was his initiative that created the library and reading room that so lifted my spirits and helped me find my family.

But what stands out in my mind when I think of Zvi is how well he understood the survivors in our camp, how he empathized with our loneliness and anxieties. Zvi put effort into getting to know all the people in the camp, and he established personal relationships with as many people as possible. He paid special attention to me after learning of my background and my knowledge of Hebrew. One day, after he had been in the camp for a few months, he approached me with a proposal that I assist him in his work, especially in writing and mimeographing educational material on Jewish history, Zionism, and the festivals. My self-image had been shattered for such a long time and my self-esteem was so low that I considered his proposal a great mistake. How could I be of help to him when I could not help myself? Naturally, I thanked him for the offer and declined. Zvi was persistent, though, and I eventually agreed to work with him, although I remained convinced that as soon as he got to know me better, he would want nothing to do with me. But that is not what happened.

To my surprise, Zvi seemed pleased with my work, and he continued to treat me kindly. He made me feel that I was a great help and that he could not have accomplished as much as he did without my contributions. For me, this experience was the beginning of psychological and spiritual healing. I continued working with him for many months. Ultimately, however, the population in our camp decreased, as some managed to head toward Palestine illegally and others chose to immigrate to other countries, and the camp was closed. Those of us left were then transferred to the camp in Bari. Sadly for me, Zvi was transferred to Rome. A month or two later, however, he requested that I join him there, where he would set up a desk for me in one of the offices of Hamishlahat Ha-eretz Yisraelit. He even arranged for me to receive a salary that was enough to pay for housing (sharing a room with another survivor) and food. I accepted his offer gladly. At age twenty-four, this was my first paid employment, but more important, it provided me with a sense of self-worth. I started making friends in the circle of survivors in Rome. We met daily in the city for lunch in the only kosher restaurant, which was organized and supported by the Joint Distribution Committee for the benefit of the survivors. I began to feel like a respectable person again but was always conscious that I was a refugee, a lost person on a road that led nowhere. Two and one-half years after liberation, even with all the progress I had made, I was still in transit. I longed to know where my future lay.

13
Decision Making

Many have compared a person's life to a book. Jewish tradition, in fact, speaks of *Sefer Hachayim*, the "Book of Life." Every day creates another page in our personal book; a group of days creates a chapter in our book. Some of the pages we write ourselves when we have the freedom to do so. Other pages are written for us when our freedom is limited. In most cases, however, we choose freely but with the limitations put on us by others or by ourselves. We call it destiny, or fate, or a mysterious hand from above, or randomness, or countless other names. Whatever one calls it, it is what guides and directs some chapters in our lives toward a purpose often not known to us. The Rabbi Golinkin family of Worcester, Massachusetts, was part of that mysterious hand for me, through their daughter Rivkah—Riva.

Rabbi Mordekhai Jacob Golinkin and his wife, Haya Freda, were the parents of four children: Eliyahu, Noah, Rachel, and Rivkah Golinkin. In the 1930s, Rabbi M. J. Golinkin was appointed chief rabbi of the Orthodox community in Danzig, a city with a somewhat tumultuous history. It had once been under the control of the kingdom of Poland but had become part of the German empire in the 1870s. As part of the Treaty of Versailles that ended World War I, Germany had to concede the area, and because of the city's history, the Allied powers decided the best recourse was to declare Danzig a free city, an independent quasi-state, and placed it under the protection of the League of Nations. The city was to be accessible to both Polish and German shipping. Nevertheless, it was almost certain that after the Anschluss of Austria in 1938 and the occupation of Czechoslovakia in 1939, Hitler would demand the annexation of Danzig because in Danzig, like in Sudetenland of Czechoslovakia, the majority of the population was ethnically German. Because of the persecution of Jews in Germany, many Danzig Jews were concerned about their future should Germany succeed in occupying the city. Many Jews began to seek refuge by emigration, but the option of coming to America was closed because the Polish quota there had been reached. Noah Golinkin, however, discovered that favorable exceptions were being made for rabbinical students. He applied to and was accepted at Yeshivah College (now Yeshivah University), and he came to America in 1938. By that time his parents, too, recognized the danger looming ahead for the Jews in Poland and especially for the Jews in Danzig. Noah immediately set out to do everything possible to bring his family to the United States. He succeeded in arranging rabbinical visas for his father and mother in 1939 shortly before the outbreak of World War II. His siblings, however, were not included in the visas. They decided to leave Danzig for Vilna, a part of Poland where the family had lived before moving to Danzig.

On their arrival in America, Rabbi and Mrs. Golinkin settled in Worcester, Massachusetts, where Rabbi Golinkin was appointed rabbi of the Orthodox community, and Noah continued his efforts to obtain visas for Eliyahu, Rachel, and Riva. Meanwhile, World War II began on September 1, 1939, and in accordance with the Hitler-Stalin pact, the Russians soon occupied the eastern part of Poland, including Vilna. The Golinkin siblings remained in Vilna, anxiously hoping to join the family in America. They sensed that the pact between Hitler and Stalin might not last.

After many months of extraordinary efforts and political connections, Noah was able to obtain visas for his siblings. The visas were kept for them at the U.S. consulate in Moscow, however, and they had to appear in person to pick them up. Such a task was not simple in those days. After several months Rachel and Rivkah received permission from the Russians to travel to Moscow. Eliyahu decided to stay behind in Vilna because his fiancée, Miriam Kozlovsky, to whom he had become engaged in Vilna, had no visa, and Eliyahu would not leave without her. Rachel and Rivkah did not want to miss this opportunity to join the family in America, so they left Vilna and headed for America without their brother. Eliyahu and Miriam moved deeper into Russia, where they worked as teachers in Russian schools.

The young sisters' trip to America took several weeks. After picking up their visas in Moscow, they traveled across Russia to Vladivostok and then went on to Kobe, Japan. From there they proceeded to San Francisco and then to Chicago. They arrived in Worcester on June 21, 1941, the very day Hitler attacked Russia, occupying Vilna along with large segments of Russian territory. Unfortunately, Eliyahu and Miriam did not fare well. After Germany attacked Russia, they walked hundreds of miles to the far reaches of the Soviet Union to flee the Nazis and ended up in Kazakhstan, where they married. The living conditions there were very difficult, however. Eliyahu took ill, died, and was buried there before the end of the war.

After being reunited with her parents and spending some time with them, Rivkah headed to New York City, where she enrolled for courses of study at

Hunter College and worked as a kindergarten teacher at a Jewish day school. About two years later, her mother suffered a serious stroke, so Riva traveled back and forth to Worcester frequently. But working, studying, and traveling back and forth were exhausting, so at the insistence of her parents, Rivkah took a much-needed vacation. She traveled to California in 1947 to visit her sister, who by that time had married Dr. Max Sherman and lived in Los Angeles.

It was there that Riva met my aunt Sonia Ulick. Sonia and Rivkah quickly became the type of friends who share concerns with each other, and it was during this time that Sonia showed Riva my letters and the photographs I had sent from the DP camp in Italy. Riva, being a sensitive and caring person, identified and empathized with the writer of those letters and resolved to do whatever she could to help this poor refugee still caught in a DP camp.

On her return home to Worcester, Riva lost no time in this new effort. She contacted her brother, who was then rabbi of a congregation in Pittsburgh, Pennsylvania, and asked him to find a way to bring me to America. She also wrote me a note in Yiddish, the one I described earlier, which began with the words "*Tairer Fraind*" ("Dear Friend") and ended with the words "*Aiyer Rivka*" ("Your Rivkah"). In this short note she quickly got to the reason for her writing. After introducing herself as a friend of my aunt Sonia and telling me she had read the letters I wrote to my aunt, she said that she understood how much I longed to start a normal life and that she was moved to help Sonia bring me to America if that was what I wanted.

Needless to say, I was deeply touched by that letter. A total stranger calling me "dear friend"? A heavenly blessing, indeed, I reflected. An American girl writing in Yiddish was also unusual, I thought. Not long after Riva's letter arrived, I received a note from Riva's brother Noah, telling me that he had learned from Riva about my background as a yeshiva student before the war. He wanted me to know that he had submitted an application to the yeshiva school Mesivta Tifereth Yerushalayim in New York to enroll me as a rabbinical student. He assured me that I would be accepted and with this acceptance I would be permitted to enter the United States. The government was still making exceptions to the restrictive immigration quotas and permitting rabbinical students to enter the country. At a time when I was living in a fog of despondency, I began to feel a ray of sunshine breaking through the clouds surrounding my future. I was touched by the friendship and caring extended to me.

I was not quite sure what to do with this offer. By this time I had given up observing religious traditions, and I was not sure I believed in God, which certainly would not make me a good candidate for rabbinical school. Furthermore, I had been planning to go to Palestine, not the United States. Nevertheless, I wrote a warm thank you note to Noah and told him to go ahead with my enrollment and make all the necessary arrangements. I was not sure when, or if, I would make it to Palestine. The United States was certainly a good option to contemplate. Meanwhile, a friendly correspondence developed between Riva and me. I began to seriously anticipate a positive change in my life, a light at the end of a long, dark tunnel.

In December 1947 Riva notified me that I had been accepted as a student at Mesivta Tifereth Yerushalayim. Soon after that, I received formal notification from the American embassy in Italy that a student visa was waiting for me in Rome. I was advised to prepare the necessary documents. Riva and Noah also informed me about assistance I could receive from the Hebrew Immigration Aid Society (HIAS) in arranging the trip from Italy to New York. But something had happened in the interim that presented a dilemma for me. On November 29, 1947, the United Nations voted to partition Palestine and create both a Jewish state and an Arab state. Although the surrounding Arab nations rejected this plan, the Jews of Palestine rejoiced, as did Jews worldwide. By May 15, 1948, there would be a Jewish state. Ironically, now that I had a visa to the United States, I would also finally be free to immigrate to Palestine—the land I had been dreaming of for so long.

I was then confronted with two options, two paths that would lead me in opposite directions, and it was up to me, alone, to make a choice. For the first time since the end of the war, I had to make my own decision. I could not follow a group one way or another. And no one was willing to tell me what to do.

It was an agonizing dilemma. On the one hand, I was thrilled to have obtained a coveted visa to the United States, the place where my only living relatives were waiting for me. On the other hand, this was not my original plan. Since my first days in the DP camp, my intention had been to settle in the Land of Israel. I had been infused with Zionist ideals since the end of the war. The Jews of Palestine had worked so hard and invested so much effort, and so many had given their lives, to re-create a Jewish homeland. My people's dream had become my dream. I longed to live in the land of my ancestors and to build a meaningful life there, in a Jewish environment. I had survived some of the most horrible experiences the world had ever known, and I believed that it was my duty now to help in the rebuilding of a Jewish state. Yet the longing to be near relatives was just as strong. I had no relatives in Palestine. The only family I had in the world was in the United States.

I sought out advice from countless people and spent many sleepless nights thinking and rethinking the issue. The people with whom I shared my dilemma said they would support me in any decision I made, and no one felt it their place to tell me what to do. As I write these words, I recall a lengthy conversation about my dilemma that I had with a woman who worked in the same office as Zvi Aldouby. She was a particularly caring person who had fought as a partisan in the Russian forests and was now an ardent Zionist who worked to help the displaced persons passing through Italy on their way to Palestine. I was certain she would advise me to head to Palestine, but after listening carefully, she advised me to follow the feelings of my heart. And I was left with my dilemma to be resolved by myself.

After agonizing over this decision for many days and nights, I finally decided to head for the U.S. As much as I wanted to be in the Land of Zion, where a Jewish homeland was being rebuilt, my heart longed to be close to family. After having lost all of my dearest and suffered from loneliness for years, I chose not to go to Palestine because I feared a continued loneliness in a country where there was not a single person I could claim as family. And so I began to plan for my trip to America.

The first thing I needed to take care of was to claim the U.S. student visa. For that I had to present a passport. At the time, however, my status was technically "stateless," and I had no passport. I had purposely not applied for a Polish passport after the war, even though I was entitled to one, because I was advised that it could be limiting to me. As a Polish citizen I would fall under the Polish quota of whatever country I applied to enter. As a stateless refugee, I had a better chance of being admitted to one of the several countries that might grant me a visa. Still, the visa I was to receive to enter the United States would be granted outside of the quota system, and therefore a Polish passport would no longer present a problem. So, because I had to provide a passport, obtaining a Polish one seemed the most logical route. Once this was taken care of, I was able, with the help of HIAS, to make all the necessary arrangements for my trip, and on March 16, 1948, I boarded the SS *Sobiesky* in Naples, Italy, bound for New York City.

The boat ride was fairly uneventful, and time passed slowly. A large contingency of survivors was on the ship. Among them was a group of young Hungarian Hasidic Jews dressed in their traditional garb of long black coats and black hats. I remember admiring their strength of faith, how they had held onto their beliefs and lifestyle as if the massacre of our people had not occurred. I also remember wondering how they could continue in their strong commitment to our religion after one-third of our people had been wiped out. But mostly my thoughts focused on memories of my parents, my sister, and my brother—and how they were not there with me to reunite with our family in America.

I also had feelings of excitement and anticipation. As we got closer to our destination, my emotions were heightened, and I often found myself moved to tears. We knew that the end of our journey was near when the Statue of Liberty came within sight. A wave of excitement spread throughout the ship. Finally, after two weeks of sailing, our ship anchored in New York Harbor. It was March 29, 1948. As we docked, we noticed small boats sailing alongside us. We were told that agents of the Immigration Department were on those boats and would be coming aboard. Indeed, the agents boarded our ship. Tables were set up, and lines were formed for us to wait for our documents to be examined. I placed myself in one of the lines, confident that this procedure was routine and that I had nothing to be concerned about. Before the hour is up, I will be in the arms of my uncle Morris and aunt Yetta and cousin Herbert, I thought.

I looked ahead of me and watched the documents being checked. Almost everyone was leaving with his or her papers in hand, but a few were asked to stand aside and wait. I did not anticipate any problems, but when my turn came and I readily presented my documents, the agent looked at my papers, looked at me, examined the papers again, and, without saying anything, scribbled something on the papers and ordered me to step aside. I saw an HIAS representative consult with the agent, and then he came over to me. To my dismay, he informed me that I would be held back for further examination.

Haven't I waited long enough for this moment to arrive? I wondered. All kinds of disturbing thoughts raced through my mind. Might I be sent back? For what reason? Were my papers not in order? If so, what did that mean for my future?

Before long, Uncle Morris found his way onto the ship, using a borrowed press pass. Through his warm embrace I felt his love, but I also sensed his concern. Nevertheless, he assured me I had nothing to worry about. He spoke with the HIAS representative and then informed me that the immigration officials had doubts as to whether I was really a rabbinical student as my documents indicated. I would therefore be held back until the Immigration Department could conduct further examinations and decide on my status. My uncle reassured me that whatever doubts the agent had would be cleared up and that I would be free to go within a few days. Aunt Yetta and Riva were waiting on the pier to welcome me, he said, and he suggested we go to the upper deck and look for them. We headed up, and there, in the distance, we could see them waving. They looked beautiful, dressed in their best. I longed to join them, and I tried to tell myself that I would be released soon. Uncle Morris stayed with me as long as he was permitted to and left me with a warm, reassuring hug and kiss. Still, I sensed he was as disappointed as I was.

I was then taken to Ellis Island. For the next several days, two agents escorted me daily by ferry to what seemed to me then to be a courtroom but was probably the office of the Immigration and Naturalization Service. A Yiddish translator was assigned to me so that I could communicate with the agents. They asked numerous repetitious questions, as if they were trying to find discrepancies in my answers. They wanted to know why I had chosen to study in America instead of in Palestine, where a Jewish state was about to be created. The majority of their questions were actually about any possible connection with Communism. Was I ever affiliated with the Communist Party? Did I know anyone with connections to Communism either at present or in the past? I found myself puzzled, and I feared being accused of a serious crime. After all the atrocities I had lived through during the war, being interrogated now and possibly being accused of something by government officials was particularly worrisome.

Thinking back on those events, I suspect that the official who examined my documents had likely compared me with the other Hasidic rabbinical students traveling with me. They wore traditional black hats and coats, and I went bareheaded. They adhered to the kosher food laws throughout the journey and stayed together as a group. I did not observe the kosher laws and associated with people on the ship who showed no sign of religious observance or any connection to Jewish studies. It now seems logical that the officials might have suspected me of being a Communist or an agent of an enemy state. I did not fit the profile of a rabbinical student when I was compared with the other Hasidic rabbinical students.

During the following days, my aunt Yetta visited me several times and assured me that the immigration officials would ultimately decide in my favor. She was right. After five days I was notified that I would be released, but a bond of $500 had to be posted as an assurance that I would leave the country after I completed my studies. My uncles Morris and Zalman and my aunt Sonia put up the bond money for me.

On Monday, April 5, 1948, I was released from Ellis Island, and Uncle Morris came to bring me to his home. I can still clearly remember the moment I entered my uncle and aunt's home in the Bronx. They, along with my sixteen-year-old cousin Herbert, embraced me with a loving welcome, and I felt a warm family connection instantly. During the days that followed, we had lengthy conversations recalling family events, particularly the details of what had happened to our family during the years of terror. They were shocked into a saddened silence when I spoke of specific members of our family and how they disappeared and perished. I could feel their pain as they listened in horror to my pain.

Within a few days, I began my studies at the yeshiva. Although I still felt conflicted about religion, I also felt obligated to attend the yeshiva that had sponsored my immigration to the United States. I attended classes and lectures and pored over volumes of the Talmud like all the other students. Talmud study came back to me quite easily; after all, I had studied it from the time I was a young boy. To my surprise, few of the students paid attention to me and showed no interest in conversing with me. I was content not to have to answer questions about myself.

I also decided to make the study of English one of my highest priorities. I understood immediately that I needed to do whatever was possible to learn the language spoken in this country where I planned to build a new life. I enrolled in night courses offered in the Bronx for new immigrants, and I listened to the radio and to conversations attentively. With the help of a dictionary, I made efforts to read. My aunt and uncle gave me all the encouragement I needed and complimented me frequently on my ability to learn.

From the beginning, Aunt Yetta and Uncle Morris made me feel welcome in their home and treated me like a member of their immediate family. Although they lived in a one-bedroom apartment, they never made me feel like they were being crowded because of my presence, nor did I feel cramped. To me, their home was comfortable, even palatial. They gave me all the comforts I could have imagined. More important, their genuine, warm feelings toward me provided a healing for the loneliness I had lived with for so many years. Aunt Yetta was a kind, beautiful, and intelligent woman and a wonderful homemaker. All the furnishings in their home were beautiful and tastefully arranged. Never were any of their rooms cluttered, and every corner was sparkling clean. My aunt reminded me much of my own mother. I admired her and loved her very much, and I cherish fond memories of her. Uncle Morris, too, was extremely kind to me, and often, gently, he offered me fatherly advice. He helped me take my first steps in this new and different world and to learn of life in New York City. We often traveled the subway together, and he showed me, with a sense of patriotic pride, the wonders of America. And like his parents, my cousin Herbert too was kind and always very friendly to me.

Both my uncle and aunt loved the Yiddish language and were well versed in Yiddish literature. They loved to discuss Yiddish authors and their writings. They both took part and made great contributions to the organizations of their choosing. Uncle Morris was very active in the Arbeiter Ring (Workmen's Circle) and served on its board of directors. He also served as secretary of the Mlawa branch of the Arbeiter Ring for many years. My Aunt

Yetta served on the school committee of the Bronx Sholom Aleichem Shule (School). They had a wide circle of devoted friends who loved and admired them dearly.

Riva was living in New York at that time and was teaching kindergarten at a Jewish day school. She was also taking courses at Hunter College. Within days of my arrival, she called the Kleibards to inquire about me. They invited her over immediately, and we all spent a very pleasant evening together. Thereafter, the Kleibards invited Riva frequently, and they grew very fond of her. So did I. Her sincere interest in my welfare developed into a genuine friendship between us. I welcomed that friendship very much. It provided much-needed healing for my troubled heart and mind. I found her companionship reassuring and comforting to my soul, and I sought to spend as much time with her as she would allow. Our conversations, which were all in Yiddish or Hebrew, were always interesting and stimulating. I admired her wisdom and maturity and her ethical and moral values. Just being in her company made me feel good. I also kept in touch with friends from Mlawa who had also made it to New York. I enjoyed getting together with them, as we had so much in common.

Between going to yeshiva, studying English, and getting together with friends and with Riva, I found myself quite busy. With all these changes and the loving embrace of the Kleibard family, I finally began to feel that it might be possible for me to live a normal life once again.

14
First Passover in America

Passover was fast approaching, and I had not considered making special plans for the holy days. I felt I was now a member of the Kleibard family and would celebrate Pesach with them, of course. I was looking forward to spending the holiday with family, at last. During the three years since the war had ended, I had marked the holiday only by refraining from eating any *hametz* (leavened foods) and by eating matzoh provided by the DP camps. I had not attended a seder or celebrated the festival in a meaningful joyous spirit for eight years. The last seder I celebrated with my family was in the Mlawa ghetto in 1940.

Now, shortly before the holiday, Riva invited me to join her and her family in Worcester for the Passover festival. At first I hesitated, for I wanted to be with my family, but more than that, Riva's father was an Orthodox rabbi, and I, having been away from religious practices, was not certain how I would be accepted by her family. At that time I identified with the Kleibard family and their practices. The Kleibard family had a strong Jewish cultural identity but did not follow Jewish religious practices like the Golinkins did or the way my parents did.

Yet, Riva thought differently. She wanted me to experience a traditional Passover again. She knew that the Pesach with her parents would be the same as celebrated in my home as I was growing up. She knew of my education and religious background and was aware of just how observant my family had been before the war, and she also knew about my current state of religious nonobservance. In just a short time, our friendship had grown so that she understood me in ways I did not understand myself. I was eager to please my new friend, who was quickly becoming an important presence in my life. My uncle and aunt encouraged me, and I accepted her invitation. In fact, I began to look forward to spending the festival of Pesach with Riva and her family, and I have never regretted it. Subconsciously, I may have welcomed the opportunity to again experience Passover in a religious spirit.

On Erev Pesach, the day before Passover, I boarded the train from New

York to Worcester. Riva was waiting for me at the train station, and we walked together to her home. The Golinkins' apartment was on the east side of the city where most Jews lived, within walking distance of five Orthodox synagogues. From the moment I entered their home, Riva's parents made me feel welcome. Although Mrs. Golinkin could hardly speak because of her stroke, she still managed to convey how happy she was to have me as their guest. The house was ready for the holiday. Naturally, there was no bread to be found; the matzoh was waiting; the dishes had been changed to the special Passover dishes; and the kitchen counters were covered with silver foil so that no crumb of leavened food would touch the Passover food, utensils, or dishes. Everything was just as it had been in my parents' home. And the aroma of Pesach permeated the house, exactly as I remembered. It was all amazingly familiar to me. Worcester was six thousand miles from Mlawa, but in so many ways it seemed to be so much the same.

In the late afternoon, about twenty minutes before sunset, Riva's mother, with Riva's help, kindled the holiday candles, and I joined Rabbi Golinkin on his walk to the synagogue. It was a short distance to the small shul, where I was warmly received as the rabbi's guest. This was probably the first time in eight years that I had joined a congregation for prayer services. I had not been in a synagogue or davened with a *minyan* since 1941. Yet when I entered the synagogue, I felt like I had been in this place many times before. I did not know anyone there, had never met them, but not for a moment did I feel like a stranger there. The synagogue and the people there looked very familiar to me, as if I had known all of them from a distant past. The prayer books, the prayers, and the chants were the same I had grown up with. When I became involved in the familiar prayers, I felt like the years in between had been erased from my memory and that I was continuing from where I had left off the day before. I was pleased to be there participating in holiday prayers.

On returning home we found the table in the dining room beautifully set with the finest dishes. Riva and her mother were dressed in their finest. Her father checked the *k'arah* (seder plate) to be sure that all the symbolic items had been placed in their proper order. He put on a *kittel* (white robe), and the seder celebration began immediately. As is customary, he started with kiddush. He then continued leading us with all the readings and rituals contained in the *Haggadah*. Even though there were just four of us (usually relatives and guests also come), the seder was conducted joyously in accordance with traditional readings and discussion of the *Haggadah*. Rabbi Golinkin would frequently look into his *Haggadah*, which contained commentary on the seder, and would share an idea he found of interest. He would also stop occasionally and share his own comments, highlighting a certain theological or philosophical message. The reading of the *Haggadah* led to some discussion having to do with the celebration of the exodus from Egypt.

At one point during the seder my thoughts brought me back to my own home, to the loving surroundings of my family and to the sedarim I had experienced during my childhood. Those celebrations were remote now, yet they felt so close and so real. I could still see my father dressed in his white *kittel*, sitting at the head of our table in a festive mood. He would read aloud from the *Haggadah*, pose questions, and share commentaries, just like Rabbi Golinkin was doing now. I could also see my mother sitting beside my father, with her broad smile, so very happy to be surrounded by her family. The seder here in Worcester seemed like a direct continuation of that period in my life, and the years in between seemed just a bad dream.

I recalled the last seder I had celebrated with my family. It was the Pesach of 1940, when we had already been living under Nazi rule for about eight months. We were still in our own apartment then, before we were driven out of the city and before the Jews were forced into the ghetto. We had managed to obtain matzoh—not an easy task at the time—and we were still able to observe Pesach according to tradition, although our seder lacked the usual joy of the season. I recalled also the mood of fear that prevailed in our lives and the cloud of uncertainty that was hanging over us. I remembered how we had still managed to be inspired by the words of the *Haggadah*, how we had looked with hope at the symbol of Elijah's cup of wine on the table, symbolizing our hope that the prophet Elijah would appear soon as the harbinger of the coming of the Messiah, who would bring redemption to the world. There were eight of us at that seder, alive and well and hoping, and now I was the only one of them left alive.

I could not linger on my thoughts for very long. I had to come back to the present. We were finishing up the section of the *Haggadah* that focuses on the details of the Exodus story that says, "Each person is obligated to see himself as if he personally has come out of Egypt."[1] This would not be difficult for me, I thought. And we then raised our cup of wine and proclaimed, "Therefore we are obligated to revere, exalt, extol, exclaim, adore, and glorify the One who performed all these miracles for our ancestors and for us."[2] For me, yes, I thought, miracles had been performed, but "for us"? These miracles had been performed for just a small portion of our people—for only one-third of our people in Europe! For most of us the miracles had come too late, I reflected. We then continued reading from the text, "And let us say before Him a new song, Hallelujah!"[3] But what song could I sing when there was so much sadness in my heart?

Of course, the seder included the mitzvah of eating of the first piece of matzoh, the *maror* (bitter herbs), to remind us of the bitter times our ancestors suffered as slaves in Egypt, and the charoset (mixture of apple, nuts, and wine) to remind us of the mortar the slaves used in the building for the pharaoh in Egypt. Finally, an elaborate gourmet festive meal was served. Everything at this seder was exactly the same as I had it in my home every year surrounded by my family.

We continued the evening with the chanting of the Hallel. I had recited these psalms on many occasions in my life. They are traditionally recited on the first day of every Hebrew month and on every festival day, so I practically knew them by heart. But at this time and in this setting, some of the verses raised questions and created theological challenges for me in my mind. "Who is like God, our Lord, enthroned on high, concerned with all, in heaven and on earth? He lifts the poor out of the dust; he raises the needy from despair."[4] Oh, why did he raise so few of us? All of us needed to be raised!

"God had surely chastened me, but He did not doom me to death."[5] True, but why did he doom to death so many innocent men, women, and children, including my father, mother, sister, and brother? Despite the problems I had with the words, I sang along. This was not the time to linger on such thoughts or to raise these difficult questions. I had to put off this dilemma to be dealt with some other time.

The Golinkin seder was lengthy, exactly as it had been in my parents' home. Riva's parents then retired for the night, and Riva and I cleaned up and talked until the early hours of the morning. I managed to wake up early enough to join Rabbi Golinkin on his walk to the synagogue. That morning, for the first time in eight years, I was called to the Torah. It was a moment filled with conflicting emotions. I recited the traditional blessing thanking God for giving us the Torah, and I thought of the words in a way I had not done for years, thanking "the Lord our God Who has chosen us from amongst all the nations and given us His Torah." "Chosen us" for what? I asked myself. *Is* there perhaps really something special about us and the Torah?

The lunch after we returned from the synagogue was elaborate, exactly as it had been in my parents' home on every Shabbat and holiday. After taking a nap in the afternoon, Riva's father invited me to study Talmud with him. I suspected that this might be a test of some sort to see how much Talmud I knew. Either way, I found the experience quite pleasant and uplifting. After a couple of hours, Rabbi Golinkin complimented me on my knowledge of Talmud. Considering that my intensive study of it had been interrupted for some eight years, with the exception of just a few weeks at the yeshiva since my arrival in America, I felt extremely gratified by the praise.

The second night and second day of Passover was much like the first—joyous and filled with memories and troubling questions. And yet despite these memories and religious quandaries, I found the holiday enjoyable, even meaningful. It was the holiday of liberation—a remarkable festival marking the beginning of Jewish history as a nation. We were still a distinct people some thirty-three hundred years later. This was something to think about, indeed. I began to feel something changing inside of me, but I was not quite sure what it was. I felt so much at home there. Everything seemed so peaceful and normal—and I wanted very much for things to become normal even though a large part of me did not feel that things were that way.

Hol hamo'ed (the intermediate days of the holiday) were much less structured, and Riva and I had many more opportunities to be alone with one another. We spent countless hours together in the city parks and at the Golinkin home. We took long walks, where we talked and shared our feelings about life, our values, our families, my experiences during the Nazi period, and her experiences under Russian occupation. She also described how she came to America. Our friendship grew in depth, and I began to dream of possibly spending my life with her.

When Riva had first befriended me, I had not dared to think of her in a romantic way. My emotional state was extremely fragile and unprepared for romance. After everything I had been through, I was just happy to have a real friend. I could not even hope to find anything more. But Riva was so naturally sensitive and so full of understanding and wisdom and confidence. Without exactly articulating my feelings to her, she understood my thoughts. Her kindness allowed me to hope that good things would eventually happen in my life, and it gave me the strength to allow myself to fall in love.

On the last day of *hol hamo'ed,* in the beautiful surroundings of Worcester's Green Hill Park, it became evident to both of us that we were meant to be together, and we expressed these feelings to one another for the first time. We did not speak of marriage, only of our love for each other and our good fortune in having met. On the final day of Pesach, the day before I was to return to New York, Riva and I shared our feelings with her parents, and before I could even begin to understand the ramifications of such a decision, we asked for their consent to consider us engaged.

The Golinkins expressed delight with our request and gave us their blessings. We were now officially engaged, although we were nowhere near ready to set a wedding date. Engagement to be married was good enough for me at that time. I could not expect anything more.

Many times over the years I have asked myself how I was able to make such a major life decision after just a few short weeks of knowing Riva. How could I have taken on the responsibility of becoming a husband when I was at such an uncertain, tenuous point in my life? I had no skills and no plans for my future, and I was penniless. I was educated in Judaism but religiously not observant, and Riva was quite traditional. I have never been able to come up with a satisfactory answer. Perhaps Riva's genuine friendship, selfless caring, and love for me attracted my love for her. It was, perhaps, her complete acceptance of me as I was, and the loving embrace of the Golinkin family, that made this important decision possible for me. Above all else, I sensed that our friendship was the beginning of a true healing for me and that this friendship would provide me with the normalcy I longed to share with one who knew the meaning of sharing.

The following day I returned to New York and shared with my aunt and uncle the news of my engagement. They, too, expressed their delight with our decision, although I read their thoughts that I was perhaps moving too fast, not thinking of any practical considerations. They knew that on my student visa I was not even allowed to seek employment, so out of their love and caring for me, they were concerned. As a married man I would have to be a provider. Meanwhile, I was happy, and they were happy for me, too, and we left it at that.

Also at that time I was undergoing another major change in my life that I ended up cherishing very much. By the time I expressed my love to Riva and told her of my desire to spend my life with her, I knew that my lifestyle would have to undergo a serious change. I understood that I would have to begin observing mitzvot again. In truth, I welcomed this change, for it was really a return to a way of life I had grown up with and loved. I made a decision to observe the laws first and then try to understand them. Actually, this was the way our ancestors responded at Mount Sinai: "Na'aseh v'nishmah—We shall do and then understand."[6]

Spending the holiday with Riva's family was a major factor in making my decision. I felt so well accepted by the Golinkins, who treated me as a member of their family. During Passover, I almost felt as if the previous years of horror had disappeared and that I was picking up my life where I had left off some ten years earlier. I joined Riva's father in going to the synagogue for prayer daily. We studied Talmud together and shared words of the Torah, as well as good conversation. This was in a sense for me the beginning of my own *yetziat Mitzrayim* (exodus from Egypt)—my personal exodus from slavery and oppression.

When I made the conscious decision that all the difficult and serious theological questions that I struggled with would have to wait, I still wanted to know certain things. Why was my dearest family not given the same chance at life as I was? Why could they not be together with me now, when life finally seemed so promising? But I knew and accepted the fact that the answers would not come easily and that I might have to grapple with them my entire life. I was convinced, though, that living with the principles and discipline of Jewish beliefs and tradition would bring spiritual satisfaction and perhaps even more understanding and clarity in my life.

After I returned to New York, I continued my studies at the yeshiva, and Riva resumed her studies at Hunter College and her job teaching kindergarten. We saw each other quite frequently, and as the next few weeks went by, our love and caring for each other grew. Also during this time, even though we had not initially spoken of setting a date, we began to feel some pressure from Riva's parents. Riva's mother continued to ail after suffering several strokes, and her right hand and right leg remained paralyzed. Riva's parents then suggested that we get married within three months so that her mother would be able to see her daughter married before her health condition deteriorated further.

I was not quite ready for marriage either emotionally or practically. Yet, even though I am not quite sure how, I managed to ignore my self-doubts and to bring myself to talk about setting a wedding date. For any doubt and any question I raised with Riva, she found an answer. I realized that Riva agreed with her parents, and I wanted so very much to make Riva happy. Her happiness had become my major consideration in all my decisions. And I began to prepare myself mentally for becoming a husband. It was an overwhelming thought so soon after my arrival in America and with so much insecurity in my life. There were also many practical considerations. Where would we live? How would we support ourselves? The Golinkins then offered to share their apartment in Worcester with us until I finished my studies and set myself up with a career. I would meanwhile continue my studies at the yeshiva along with my general studies and acclimate myself to my new country. They encouraged us not to concern ourselves with financial issues at all while we lived with them and to allow ourselves enough time to examine the options available for our future. All this sounded very reasonable, and our wedding date was set.

On Sunday, July 18, 1948—11 Tammuz 5708—Riva and I were married in her parents' home at 30 Providence Street, Worcester, Massachusetts. The guests included friends of the Golinkin family; Riva's brother, Rabbi Noah; her sister, Rachel, who had come from California with her baby son, Eliyahu; and my uncle Morris, aunt Yetta, and uncle Zalman from New York. My aunt Sonia and uncle Joe and cousin Herbert Ulick from California could not make it because of Sonia's ill health. Riva's parents led her to the *huppah* (wedding canopy), and Uncle Morris and Aunt Yetta led me. Riva's father officiated at the wedding, assisted by Rabbi Noah.

As I stood under the *huppah* I could not hold back my tears. I felt the joy of having Riva at my side, my happiness as we began to share our life together. But these were not only tears of joy. As part of the ceremony, I requested that the memorial prayers of El Maleh Rahamim ("God full of Mercy") be recited for my father and my mother.[7] As this moving prayer was chanted, I could not hold back the pain of their absence. I felt their spiritual presence and the presence of my sister and brother. But this was not the way it was supposed to be. They should have been with me in person so I could see their presence and their joy and to hear their blessings and feel their embrace and kisses. When we broke the glass at the end of ceremony, the guests jumped up in celebration, as was truly intended by the custom, but I was still wiping my tears off my face. It was a bittersweet joy.

Riva and I spent an enjoyable honeymoon week in the White Mountains of New Hampshire at the kosher Maplewood Hotel in Bethlehem. We were treated royally, like newlyweds usually are. As we began our married life, I could feel a rebirth of sorts taking place. A bright light began to shine for me at the end of a long and dark tunnel. It was not just a new marital status I had entered, but for the first time in many years I began to feel happy to be alive.

Husband, Father, Teacher

Now that our honeymoon was over, it was time for Riva and me to settle into a daily routine. As we had decided before our wedding, we moved in with Riva's parents in Worcester. Although the circumstances were not ideal for newlyweds, Riva's parents made our living arrangements as comfortable and as pleasant as possible. They treated us graciously and were very supportive of us. As promised, they encouraged us not to worry about any financial obligations. "Just concentrate on your studies," they would say. Riva's brother, Noah, and sister, Rachel Sherman, also treated me kindly, like a newfound brother. I soon found myself to be a beloved member of the Golinkin family.

When Riva and I were in New York for school and work, we would stay with the Kleibards, who opened their home warmly to us. I did not focus only on my studies at the yeshiva. I also enrolled in English language courses at Worcester Junior College and audited English literature courses. Mastering the English language was of the utmost importance to me. I saw it as a necessary requirement in adjusting to my new country. Between all my classes and commuting between two states, I was extremely busy.

To my delight, everything started coming together, albeit slowly. I started to feel stronger emotionally. I thought frequently of the miraculous developments in my life, of how I had been blessed with a new and loving family after all I had been through. I also began to taste the nourishing and uplifting spirit of living a life according to Jewish tradition. A *ruach hadashah*—a new spirit—was rising in my soul, and I sensed frequently that I was letting go of the weight of Nazi oppression, which I had been carrying within me for so long.

Still, despite these developments, I was very conflicted. On the one hand, I was attending yeshiva, where the studies centered mainly on Talmud and its commentaries. I felt satisfaction in the Torah study, recalling the kind of fulfillment I had experienced as a yeshiva student in Warsaw before the war, but on the inside I was plagued by questions that gave me no real peace of mind. Why had God hidden his face from us when we needed his help? Where was his *yad hazakah*—strong hand—and *zero'ah netu'yah*—his outstretched arm—that he had used to free our ancestors in Egypt? Why had he not used his strength to protect the other members of my family? I missed them and wanted so much to share with them the blessings of my new life. With these questions in my mind, I could not approach my Talmud studies with the same interest and eagerness of my prewar years. I was unable to recapture, or to renew, the unwavering faith with which I had grown up.

I talked to no one about these feelings. I did not think anyone could help me with my doubts or even relate to my dilemmas. I viewed my inability to solve these problems by myself as my weakness, which I was embarrassed to share with others. Practically speaking, though, these doubts made little impact on my daily routine. I was content—I even welcomed—living the traditional lifestyle I had lived with prior to the war. I began to attend services, to put on tallith and tefillin every morning, and to observe the laws of kashrut and the Sabbath, which I had not kept for years. I welcomed this major change, feeling that I had come back to the source of my being. I concerned myself with studying and acclimating to my new world. There was order in my life now, a stability that had not been there for ten years. Ironically, as the events of my life unfolded, I found myself entrenched in the religious world more than I ever could have imagined.

One of the most enjoyable groups Riva and I joined during the first year of our marriage was the Hug Ivri, a Hebrew-speaking circle of fifteen to twenty couples. Once a month we would meet in the homes of the members for discussions, lectures, and socializing, all in Hebrew. It was at one of these meetings that I met Zvi Plich, one of the prominent members of our group. Mr. Plich spoke impeccable Hebrew, but more important, he was the principal at the Hebrew school of one of Worcester's local synagogues, Congregation Beth Israel. We befriended each other after a few meetings, and before long he asked me to consider applying for a teaching position at his school. I was pleasantly surprised and felt highly complimented at the offer but reluctant to even consider it. I thanked Mr. Plich for his confidence in me and explained that I was uncertain about my English and my ability to conduct a class in what was still a foreign language for me. We always conversed in Hebrew, and I thought that perhaps he was unaware of how faulty my spoken English was.

What I did not tell Mr. Plich, however—and what I could not even admit to myself—was the true reason for my hesitation. More than the lack of my language skills, my poor self-image made me reluctant to think about the offer. I simply did not believe I had the talent to be a teacher. Since my childhood, I had viewed teaching as one of the most respected and honorable professions, one that required extensive knowledge and special skill. Although I now understand more fully just how the years of Nazi oppression had destroyed my self-confidence, all I knew then was that I simply could not imagine myself in such an important and challenging position. Furthermore, I was still unsure whether I wanted to be a religious role model. I certainly did not want to inflict my doubts on young children. In addition, I was still unsure in general about my professional goals. Did I want to be a teacher even if I did have a talent for teaching?

Mr. Plich did not take my reluctance seriously and invited me to meet with him to acquaint me with the Beth Israel Hebrew School system. Despite my hesitations, I longed for a normal way of life and wanted to earn a livelihood, so I accepted his invitation. We had a few very enjoyable meetings, and I was pleased to learn that the Beth Israel Hebrew School offered an intensive educational program beginning with a kindergarten class for first-graders that met once a week on Sunday mornings.

The Hebrew school program consisted of a six-year curriculum of study designed for children who attended public school. It began with second grade and ended at seventh. Classes met four days a week, Sunday through Wednesday, for two-hour sessions each day. The curriculum consisted of Hebrew language, *tefillah* (prayer), Jewish history, Humash (Torah), the early prophets, and Jewish holidays and customs. It was an intensive curriculum, indeed, considering that the students met for only eight hours per week. After a few meetings with Mr. Plich, during which I benefited from his professional guidance, I began to feel more confident. Riva, too, was particularly encouraging, and as always she reassured me that I could succeed at anything I set my mind to. Yet she left the decision entirely up to me. With her support I agreed to Mr. Plich's suggestion to present a model lesson.

On a Sunday morning in the spring of 1949, Mr. Plich, in the presence of members of the Beth Israel School Committee, introduced me to a fifth-grade class as a possible teacher for the forthcoming school year. I greeted the students with "Shalom, *talmidim* [my students]," and they responded warmly, "Shalom." I presented a lesson in Humash, a lesson in Jewish history, and a lesson in Hebrew grammar. I conducted the class in Hebrew, but I had to supplement many explanations in English.

I was standing in front of the students, teaching, when I suddenly realized that this was the first time in about ten years that I had seen a group of Jewish children gathered in one room for the study of Judaism without fear of being discovered by German police and the consequences that would follow if discovered. Of course, I could not linger for very long on that thought.

During the five-minute break, I conversed with the children. I looked at the beautiful faces of those boys and girls, and my mind turned to the 1.5 million children who were murdered only because they were Jewish children. Again I drew my thoughts back to the teaching assignment, and I taught for another hour. For the students and the visitors the class was routine, but for me it was an extremely moving experience—both sad and joyful, sadness for the loss of an entire generation of Jewish children in Europe and joy for realizing the failure of the evil Nazi plan. I was grateful to find myself in the midst of a Jewish community in America where a new generation of Jews was growing to continue the chain of our tradition. And I thanked God for America, the land of freedom, a great blessing for our people. Mr. Plich and the school committee observed my lessons and, to my pleasant surprise, seemed pleased.

On my way home my thoughts turned to exactly four years earlier, April and May of 1945, when I was near death and had lost any hope for surviving, and then I thought about the four years following liberation, when I would not have believed it possible for me to even consider an opportunity to teach Torah to a group of Jewish children. And here I was experiencing the incredible. I was in a classroom with about twenty-five young children, and I was teaching Torah. What a miracle! With the excitement of a young child, I shared my thoughts and my feelings of satisfaction with Riva, who was delighted.

A few days later Mr. Plich informed me that the school committee had decided to offer me the available part-time teaching position for one class, which met four days a week for a total of eight hours. I still had my doubts about taking the job, but the classes were elementary and would not require me to confront the theological or philosophical quandaries that concerned me. After discussing everything with Riva, I accepted the offer. About a month later, in June 1949, Rabbi Hershel Fogelman, the principal of the Lubavich Day School in Worcester, approached me with his need of a teacher for the morning hours to teach practically the same subjects I would already be teaching in the afternoons. Having accepted the position at Beth Israel, I now found it much easier to accept an offer from Rabbi Fogelman, too. Soon thereafter, Riva accepted an offer from Rabbi Fogelman to teach a kindergarten class at the Lubavich Day School.

It became clear to me that I could no longer continue commuting to New York. Actually, the frequent traveling was always extremely onerous, but with my new responsibilities it would simply be impossible. My father-in-law, however, still felt strongly that I should continue my yeshiva studies. He urged me to work toward *semichah* (rabbinical ordination) and offered to study with me in Worcester. He was well aware of which subjects I needed to study to earn the title of rabbi, and he discussed the matter with two rabbis he was close to in New York. Together they came up with a course of study for me. In a few years, when I had mastered the required subjects, the rabbis would test me and then grant me an official *semichah* certificate. My father-in-law thus became my teacher and mentor.

I now turned my attention toward preparing for the upcoming school year. I studied pedagogy and read the textbooks I would be using and the lessons I would be preparing. Then, in September 1949, I began my teaching career. By that time I felt a bit more confident in my abilities, and I found myself more able to separate my internal religious doubts from the subjects I was teaching.

The first few months as a teacher were challenging. I had difficulty handling discipline problems and relating to my American Jewish students. I came from a school system in which students stood up in respect when a teacher entered the classroom; the behavior of the students at this school was something I could have never imagined as a child. Yet I was always aware of the special privilege granted me to relate to and to teach Jewish children. I looked at their faces every time I entered the classroom and saw them as a blessing and saw myself as having the responsibility to teach them and to love them.

Ultimately, I learned to understand my students better. These children came to my class after they had already spent an entire day in public school. It was not surprising that they occasionally acted up. Once I learned how to relate to them, I found it easier to manage the class, and my teaching skills began to improve. From the positive feedback I received from students and parents, I was encouraged. Most of all, I felt privileged to teach Jewish children Torah. As the year progressed, I focused with pride on acclimating myself to my new country and to my new roles as husband to my beloved Riva and being a Hebrew teacher.

During the fall of 1949, shortly after I began teaching, Riva informed me happily that she was pregnant. I was thrilled—my hopes and prayers were being realized. The normal life I had dreamed of seemed more than ever to be within my reach. The news gave me even more incentive to excel in my studies and at my job. Riva had difficulties through her pregnancy, yet she always attended to her parents' needs as she had before we were married. I tried to lighten her load by helping more around the house and seeing to it that she had enough rest and received the best medical attention possible.

On May 2, 1950, Riva gave birth to our son. This event was an awesome blessing that brought tears of joy to my eyes and much gratitude to my heart. We named our son Israel Meyer after my father and decided to call him by his middle name, just as my father had been known. My father had been my model throughout my life, and I wanted to be like him. And I now sensed that in some mystical way my father had been "reborn" in the soul of my son. A special joyous feeling began to grow within me. I now had the blessings of a loving wife and a beautiful son—a family of my own—and a job that would perhaps be the direction of my future.

Before the end of the school year, both Mr. Plich and Rabbi Fogelman invited me to continue teaching the following year. Things were falling into place. I felt encouraged by the offers, and Riva, too, felt a sense of satisfaction in seeing me excel. Our newborn son was the focal point of our joy and a source of great *naches* (spiritual satisfaction) to us and to his grandparents. In addition to taking care of our son, Riva continued to help her parents, particularly her mother, who increasingly required special care.

The attention and love surrounding our son came naturally to us. Of course, Meyer was the most beautiful and smartest baby in New England, perhaps in America! He acquired only one "disturbing" habit during his infancy. He decided that sleeping was a waste of time and insisted that we sing to him before he would fall asleep. And he needed a lot of singing. In the early morning, when his mother and I were in need of another hour of sleep, he would start demanding "Hopa! Hopa! Hopa!" This translated into "Free me from this prison. I want to get out of the crib and take care of things around the house." Thus, Riva or I had to give up an hour of much-needed sleep in the morning, but he was happy. Of course, we were delighted to watch him grow while surrounded with much love from his parents, his grandparents, the other Golinkins, and the Kleibards.

My second year of teaching was easier and more enjoyable than the first. I fell into a routine, and it no longer felt strange for me to think of myself as a teacher and as a religious role model. I became more cognizant of the blessings in my life and my *z'khut*—my privilege—to teach Jewish children. I frequently thought that the Jewish children I was teaching were the building blocks of my people's future. I felt good making a vital contribution by teaching children to grow up as knowledgeable Jews and good people. The Nazis had attempted to annihilate us, to destroy our future, but they had not succeeded. A young, beautiful generation of committed Jews was growing up in America, and I was helping it to become a reality.

Riva enjoyed spending the morning hours at the kindergarten and was thrilled to see me make progress in my jobs. She complimented me frequently on how well I was acclimating myself in my new country and thriving in my work. That year she also decided that commuting to Beth Israel by bus from the east side of Worcester, where we lived, to the west side of the city, where the synagogue was, was too onerous and suggested that I take driving lessons. Naturally, I accepted her suggestion. This would be another step in becoming normal. After I received a driver's license, we bought a new Chevrolet with $2,000 that Riva had saved, and I started to feel even more normal and more acclimated to being an American.

I made much progress that year, 1950–51, both professionally and emotionally. I felt more confident in my teaching and settled with my small family. In the spring of 1951, I gladly accepted the offers to continue at Beth Israel and the Lubavich Day School the following year. During the summer of 1951, we had the joy of spending more time with our son, and I continued my studies and preparations for the upcoming school year.

During the last week of August 1951, the three of us took a short vacation to relax a bit before the new school year and its busy schedule began. On our return after the Labor Day weekend, only a few days before the start of the new school year, I received a call from Rabbi Abraham Kazis of Temple Shalom in Salem, Massachusetts, about a ninety-minute drive from Worcester. The temple's Hebrew school needed a new principal, and he suggested that I apply for the position. I declined to even consider this offer, for I felt it wrong to withdraw from my commitment to the schools in Worcester just a few days before the beginning of the school year. But Rabbi Kazis assured me that he had already discussed the matter with Dr. Benjamin Shevach, the director of the Boston Bureau of Jewish Education, who was in charge of staffing for all the Hebrew schools in Massachusetts, and with Mr. Plich. With their approval, I agreed to an interview the following evening with the school committee in Salem. The position, I learned, came with more responsibility than I already held as a teacher, and it would demand much more of my time. In addition to teaching two classes, the principal was to be in charge of the entire educational program and would be required to lead the Junior Congregation services on Saturday mornings.

At the conclusion of the meeting, I was excused and asked to wait outside the committee meeting room. After the committee members had a short discussion, I was invited back into the room and was offered a full-time position, with a salary that tripled my current one. However, housing was extremely tight in Salem, and finding an apartment to rent near the synagogue would be practically impossible. I would have to commute from Worcester, ninety minutes each way, and I would need to be away from home on the Sabbaths to lead the Junior Congregation. Riva and I discussed the offer for many hours, and together we decided that taking on this new challenge would be good for me. It was an opportunity for my growth that I could not turn down.

I reluctantly resigned from the Beth Israel Hebrew School and the Lubavich Day School. I rented a room with a family who lived near the synagogue, and I began my duties at the Salem Hebrew School the Sunday following Labor Day 1951. It involved me commuting from Worcester to Salem twice a week while Riva and the baby would remain with her parents for the school year of 1951–52. I would spend Shabbats in Salem and remain there for Sunday morning classes. On Sunday afternoon I would join the family in Worcester until Monday noon, then return to Salem and stay there until Thursday evening. I then traveled to join the family until Friday afternoon and returned to Salem for the Sabbath. When Sabbath ended early in the wintertime I would also travel to Worcester on Saturday evening and return for classes on Sunday morning.

As I look back, that year in Salem at Temple Shalom was good for my emotional and educational growth. I continued my studies, gained teaching and administrative skills, improved my spoken English, attended conferences and lectures on pedagogy, and developed lasting friendships. My Temple Shalom experience proved to be yet another blessing. Nevertheless, being away from my family so much was just too difficult. The Salem community wanted me to continue in my position, and everybody promised to maximize their efforts to find us an apartment. Again, Riva left the decision entirely up to me. If I wanted to continue at Temple Shalom, she would readily move to Salem. Still, despite her encouragement, I sensed that she would not be happy to leave her parents on their own. I therefore decided to leave the position in Salem and return to Beth Israel in Worcester, where I now had been offered a full-time position to teach two classes. My salary would be less, but the monetary sacrifice seemed worthy for the greater good of the family.

I spent the summer of 1952 studying hard to prepare for my *semicha* exams. By the end of the summer, I had passed the necessary exams and was ordained a rabbi teacher by Rabbi Yitzhak Turets, Rabbi Yosef Weinberger, and Rabbi Mordekhai J. Golinkin.

Congregation Beth Israel was happy to have me back, and I was equally happy to return. I decided then that I would make my future in Jewish education. The last few years had laid the foundation for my calling. I felt more confident in my abilities, and I felt well accepted by students, parents, and fellow teachers alike. At this point, Riva was offered and accepted a teaching job at the Beth Israel kindergarten, a position she enjoyed for a number of years, and we settled into a routine. We purchased a home near the Beth Israel Synagogue, and, five years after having applied for citizenship after my marriage to Riva, I received my citizenship document in June 1953. I now felt truly blessed, with my loving and lovable wife, my beautiful and smart son, and my own home. After a few months of being alone, Riva's parents moved in with us.

Our son was growing amid our love and much joy. At the age of four, he began attending the Beth Israel kindergarten. For the school year 1955–56, we enrolled him in the Lubavich Day School. In third grade, he began attending the Beth Israel Hebrew School in the afternoon to supplement his Hebrew language studies. He continued this schedule for three years and graduated with honors from the Beth Israel Hebrew School at the age of ten when his fellow students were thirteen. We were always delighted with his educational achievements and his intellectual growth.

On the sixth day of Nissan, 1959, Riva's mother, Hana Haya Freda bat Avraham David, died. When Mrs. Golinkin suffered her fist stroke she lost her speech, and her right side remained paralyzed. She suffered from various illnesses over a period of seventeen years before she died. She was a remarkable woman. In spite of her physical limitations, her mind was as sharp as ever, and she was attuned to everything going on around her. With just her facial expressions and the two sounds she could make, she communicated all her wishes, feelings, and needs. Of course, her passing was a painful loss to all of us, including Meyer. She used to sing to him, play with him, and show him affection, and Meyer returned his affection for her generously. She was a perfect mother-in-law, and I respected her very much for her wisdom and her kindness to me. May she rest in peace.

After graduating the Beth Israel Hebrew School, Meyer continued his studies at the Lubavich Day School. In addition, he continued his Hebrew studies at the Prozdor Hebrew High School in Worcester, which was affiliated with the Prozdor of Hebrew College in Boston. At the age of fourteen, Meyer graduated and received a Hebrew High School diploma from the Hebrew College in Boston with honors.[1]

By that time, I had been offered and gladly accepted additional responsibilities to direct the youth activities of Beth Israel's United Synagogue Youth (USY). Under my leadership, Beth Israel USY grew to a membership of 120 teenagers divided in three groups: Kadima, Junior USY, and Senior USY. Shortly after that, I accepted an opportunity to teach a class at Prozdor High School in Worcester.

I loved my Beth Israel students and cared deeply about the youth under my direction. I loved their parents, who were always supportive of my efforts. I became very close to many of the members of the Beth Israel community and developed many friendships. They all accepted me with great warmth. I stayed with this congregation in Worcester for twelve years, until the fall of 1964.

16
I Find My Calling

The year 1964 marked the beginning of more big changes in my life. In the spring of that year, Rabbi Jack Schechter, executive director of the United Synagogues of New England, suggested that I apply for the rabbinic position at Temple Emmanuel in Wakefield, Massachusetts. Rabbi Schechter and I had met a number of times at conferences and conventions, including at conventions of United Synagogue Youth, and he had befriended me. At first I declined even to consider applying, for I was not really interested in seeking the pulpit. I had received such offers before but had always declined. I was content to continue in my position with the Beth Israel Synagogue in Worcester. Again, I felt that my qualifications were not good enough to assume the position of spiritual leader.

Rabbi Schechter was persistent. After several phone calls, I agreed to meet with the board of directors of Temple Emmanuel in Wakefield to be interviewed for the position of rabbi and education director of the congregation and its religious school. I was hoping that I would not be acceptable for the position.

Riva and I traveled to Wakefield for the interview. Before the meeting I conducted the *ma'ariv* service and preached a sermon. The meeting with the board of directors was very pleasant. We all asked many questions and had an exchange of ideas on such issues as Jewish values, the importance of the education of the young, programming for the youth, adult Jewish education, relationships with the non-Jewish community, and so on. I felt good when I left the meeting, and on the way home I shared with Riva my doubts that I would be offered the position and my inclination not to accept the offer even if the board made one. To my surprise, the day after the meeting, Mr. Jack Rubenstein, president of the congregation, informed me that the board of directors voted to offer me a contract to serve the congregation as rabbi and education director. I respectfully declined the offer, giving him no reason for my rejection. Again Rabbi Schechter contacted me and asked me to meet with him in his office in Boston. He wanted to know my reason for not accepting an offer to negotiate a contract with the Wakefield congregation. Trying to come up with an argument that would end the discussion, I told him I objected to the playing of an organ at Sabbath services. I was sure that this would be enough of a reason for the congregation to withdraw their offer and that therefore the subject would be closed for me.

Rabbi Schechter tried to persuade me that the organ was acceptable and that many Conservative synagogues in the Boston area used an organ during Sabbath services. This was true, but I convinced him that I was not going to change my mind on that issue.

He shared this information with the congregation's president. A few days later, Mr. Rubenstein informed me that the temple board had agreed to discontinue using the organ on the Sabbath if I accepted the offer. I then felt bound to agree to begin serving the congregation as rabbi and education director. Following my resignation from the Beth Israel Congregation, Riva and I moved to Wakefield, and I began serving the congregation of Temple Emmanuel of Wakefield effective August 1, 1964.

During the following High Holidays that September, when usually all members of the congregation attend worship services, I was welcomed by all very warmly. Soon after the holy days, I reorganized the Jewish youth of the community and affiliated them with the national and regional organizations of United Synagogue Youth. By the end of the first school year, I had upgraded the curriculum of the religious school. I increased the number of days and hours of instruction to three days, six hours per week, for six years to qualify for bar and bat mitzvah and graduation celebrations. Prior to that time, the program was two days per week for a total of four and one-half hours per week. I also introduced the study of Humash and strengthened the quality of the reading and comprehension of the Hebrew language. I prepared the bar and bat mitzvah students to lead the entire Friday night service and to chant the Friday night kiddush and readied the boys to read from the Torah scroll on Saturday morning. The students who graduated seventh grade were then encouraged to continue their Jewish education for a two-year confirmation program, and most of them did. Over time I introduced adult education programs and established contacts with the non-Jewish community and clergy. I was blessed with the support of the congregation, and I loved the pleasant association with my congregants. Riva, too, enjoyed the friendship of many of the congregants and took much pride in my accomplishments. These warm friendships lasted throughout the seven years of my tenure with the congregation and beyond. Many of the friendships have continued to this day.

When we moved to Wakefield, we were hoping that Riva's father would follow us and live with us there. He decided to remain in Worcester, however, so Riva traveled frequently to take care of his needs. Meyer decided to stay with his *zeide* (grandfather) and continue his education in Worcester. For his high school education he enrolled at Maimonides High School in Boston and commuted daily from Worcester to Boston. Meyer was among the star students of that high school and graduated in 1967 after he had just turned seventeen. For college he chose to attend Yeshiva University in New York. After two years there, he transferred to Brandeis University and graduated magna cum laude in 1971.

During the winter of 1971 I was informed by Congregation Beth Israel that it would be interested in having me back if and when I should decide to leave the congregation in Wakefield. I enjoyed my work and the relationship with the congregation and youth in Wakefield very much, so I considered this possibility with much care. In addition, Riva's father was aging and needed more attention than Riva could provide to him with visits only. Thus, after only seven years of service with the Wakefield synagogue, another change was to take place.

In the spring of 1971, I resigned from Temple Emmanuel and accepted the offer from Beth Israel to serve as associate to Rabbi Abraham Kazis, the synagogue's head rabbi, and as director of education and youth activities. It was a very difficult decision for Riva and me, and the Wakefield congregation attempted to have us reconsider our decision. Our parting was very difficult, but it was necessary.

I returned to Beth Israel in the summer of 1971. I was very pleased to come back to the place where I had started my teaching career. Riva and I also felt good about being able to take better care of her father. Two years later, in March 1973, we were saddened when Rabbi Kazis fell ill. I was asked to take over all his responsibilities temporarily. On October 31, 1973, Rabbi Kazis died at the age of fifty-seven, after having provided eighteen years of distinguished service to the congregation and the community at large. His passing was a heavy blow to the congregation, to the city of Worcester, and to me personally. I had known him and his family for about twenty years, ever since I had served under him as principal of the Salem Hebrew School. He was a good and trusted friend to all and a wise leader. He was particularly credited with the construction of a new, larger, and conveniently located synagogue designed for future expansion, to which the congregation moved during his tenure in 1959. Rabbi Kazis had foresight and worked hard to achieve his goals. His vision proved to be a blessing for the growth and the future of the congregation. He also accomplished a great deal for the general Worcester community. At a December 1973 membership meeting of the Beth Israel congregation, I was elected to take the position of rabbi of Congregation Beth Israel.

One year later, in December 1974—the nineteenth of Kislev 5735—our family suffered the loss of Riva's father, Harav Mordekhai Yaacov ben Reuven v'Rivka Golinkin. Rabbi Golinkin held high rabbinic positions in the cities of Zhitomir and Dokszitz in Russia and in the Free City of Danzig before he immigrated to America. He served as the Orthodox rabbi in Worcester from the time of his arrival in America in 1939 until his passing. For many years he also served with distinction as the *av bet din,* head of the rabbinic court of Massachusetts. He was a devoted husband and a good father and grandfather. He and my son, Meyer, had a very special relationship. They frequently studied classic Jewish texts together, and a special bond developed between them.

After graduating from Brandies University in 1971, Meyer traveled for a year across the United States and then went to France, England, and Israel. In 1972 he continued his education at New York University Law School and earned his law degree three years later. He did his law internship with the Legal Aid Society and worked for them afterward for a number of years. In 1979 he married Sue-Rita Silverman, and they made their home in Teaneck, New Jersey. In 1985 they moved to Mission Viejo, California, and seven years later he and his family moved to Portland, Oregon. They are the parents of four children, Jonah, Liza, Sarah, and Daniel, and they are the grandparents of Ronan, son of Jonah and Jessica.

The Conservative Beth Israel Congregation that I rejoined in 1971 was much larger than the Wakefield congregation, with many more responsibilities and activities. The seventies was a time of heated debates in the Conservative movement. A group of scholarly young women committed to equal rights for women demanded that women be allowed to enter the Jewish Theological Seminary and be ordained as rabbis equal to men. Vigorous debates ensued in many synagogues about full and equal participation of women in synagogue rituals. For example, some asked, why cannot women be counted in a *minyan* at worship services as men are? Why are women not allowed to be honored with *aliyot,* the honor of being called up to read from the Torah scroll? Why are women not allowed to lead congregational services as men are? These issues were discussed among the rabbis and at the conventions of the Rabbinical Assembly. Discussions also took place among the laity and among the clergy at the United Synagogues conventions. These discussions were very heated at times, and they caused tension between those who would not tolerate any changes and those who wanted a policy based on full egalitarian participation of women in all areas of synagogue life.

Beth Israel had been a Conservative synagogue with mixed seating for many years, but it had been traditional in most other areas of synagogue practice. The leadership and general membership consisted of traditionalists who would not tolerate any changes, whereas a younger group demanded that the congregation follow the spirit of the times by adopting a totally egalitarian policy. When I became rabbi of the congregation, I understood the just and sincere arguments of both sides of the issues but wanted to hold onto the status quo as long as I could. I soon realized that the future would lie with those who demanded full participation of women. When the debate became more heated and more serious, I succeeded in leading the congregation into an evolutionary policy of change based on one change at a time. It was not easy, but this was the best way to do it while simultaneously keeping the congregation together and avoiding schism. With the help of good people we succeeded, and by the end of my tenure at Beth Israel, the congregation was almost fully egalitarian.

During my tenure with the congregation I brought innovations to the Beth Israel Hebrew School system, reactivated the USY chapter, taught a class at the local Prozdor Hebrew High School once a week, organized adult education programs, and introduced Sabbath eve and festival celebrations in the synagogue. I also organized *havurot* (circles), groups of friends who would meet regularly in their homes for socializing and educational programs, and together with other rabbis I organized citywide educational programs and weekends with scholars in residence. I promoted and offered financial assistance to young people to attend what I considered to be the finest educational summer-camp programs, Ramah and Yavneh, and I promoted and offered financial assistance to young people to participate in educational programs in Israel. I developed warm associations with all the rabbis in the city, Reform, Orthodox, and Chabad. I also participated with non-Jewish clergy in ecumenical activities and preached in Christian churches. Of course, I officiated at weddings and funerals, made shivah calls, visited the sick, and attended practically all committee meetings of the synagogue. I kept busy and worked very hard to fulfill, to the best of my abilities, all the duties expected of me. I was constantly on the go, and I found much satisfaction and fulfillment in my service to this congregation. Considering where I had been on my arrival in America, I am grateful for having been able to be what I have become and been able to do what I thought to be right and just. Yet, I always thought that I ought to do more, that my congregation deserved the best, and I did not think of myself as being the best.

By the end of 1984, I began to have serious doubts about my leadership and thought that another rabbi would be more successful in leading the congregation and satisfying its many needs. It took me a year and a half of discussion and deliberation with myself and with Riva before I announced, with mixed emotions, my resignation from the Beth Israel Synagogue and my retirement that would begin in the spring of 1986. The congregation accepted my resignation with mixed emotions, too, and honored me with an elaborate retirement banquet attended by about six hundred admirers. In recognition for my devoted leadership the congregation awarded me the title of rabbi emeritus.

After I retired I made myself available to speak frequently on the Holocaust. I have traveled thousands of miles in Massachusetts, Connecticut, New Hampshire, and Maine to lecture and to share my message with students at universities, colleges, high schools, and elementary schools and with members of many organizations and congregations, Jewish and Christian. And whenever I spent time in California and Oregon I continued lecturing there. As I mentioned earlier, as a survivor I felt obliged to bear witness and give honor and a voice to those who could not speak out and allowed a chance to express their pain.

It is often painful for me to reopen again and again the wounds that never healed. But the positive responses of my listeners have made the pain worthwhile, and that has been a source of encouragement for me to continue to speak and to teach the message of the Holocaust. In my lectures I talk not only about the horrors that were committed and the terrible suffering that occurred but also make an effort to leave a message of hope and to inspire my listeners to create a more tolerant and more gentle society. It is my conviction that humans can and must learn how to eradicate bigotry, hatred, racism, and prejudice, the sources of all evil in the world. One of my trips that made my conviction even stronger was my return visit to Mlawa.

17
My Return to Mlawa

The Russian army liberated Mlawa at the beginning of 1945 as it was marching toward Berlin in pursuit of the Germans. After the defeat of Germany, a small number of liberated Jews from the concentration camps returned to Mlawa to search for surviving family and friends. They were joined by a smaller number of young Jews from Mlawa and other cities who survived the war in Russia. The first to return to Mlawa was Joel Rosenberg, who survived miraculously as a Polish Catholic. His wife, Hinda, and their daughter had survived in hiding. They joined him, and then they established a home for themselves in Mlawa. Some of the returnees came only to search for family and, after finding that none were left, departed. Others remained, intending to make their future there. Joel Rosenberg was always very helpful to them. At one point the number of those who remained reached about sixty. Together, this small group attempted to re-create a Jewish community in Mlawa.

One of the first things they did was to exhume the bodies of those who had been killed and buried in different places in the ghetto and then reinterred them in a mass grave and fixed a tombstone on top of that grave. Polish vandals later destroyed the tombstone.[1]

The Russian army that occupied Mlawa established an academy for the training of Russian officers. The Russian in charge of that academy was a Captain Gindzburg; his assistant officer was Lieutenant Feld. Both of them identified themselves as Jews to Joel Rosenberg. Feld sought out returning Jews, and Gindzburg assisted them in finding homes and work in the city. Feld in particular visited with the survivors frequently. One day, as he was walking in the city park with a few of the returning Jews, he pointed to a monument that had been erected in memory of the Russians who fell in the battle around Mlawa. He told them that between 60 and 80 percent of them had been Jews, but their identity as Jews was not mentioned on the monument.

As the number of returning Jewish survivors increased in the cities and towns of Poland, the hatred for Jews increased, even though the total number of Jews was very small. The anti-Semitic slogan *"Polska bez Zydow"* ("Poland without Jews") spread into the cities and towns wherever Jewish survivors had returned. In Mlawa, too, the survivors began to feel the hatred against them. They were advised by Officer Feld to stay home at night and to secure their homes inside. In October 1945, only five months after the Nazi atrocities against the Jews ended, a pogrom took place in the neighboring Polish city of Raczons, which left several Jewish Holocaust survivors dead. A delegation of Mlawans, consisting of Joel Rosenberg, Avraham Shaft, Moshe David Frankel, and Sara Spigel, met with Officer Feld, who informed them that Officer Gindzburg had had Russian soldiers guarding their homes for some time. The Russians had not notified them about it because they did not want to create a panic, but they believed that a pogrom in Mlawa was a possibility.

A few days later, Gindzburg and Feld notified the Jewish returnees that a pogrom against them was actually being planned. They advised them to leave the city and provided them with transportation and military protection to bring them as far as the western border of Poland. Since then, no Jews have resided in Mlawa.[2] Only occasionally have Jewish families or individuals made short visits there in search of signs of the Jewish life that once existed there.

Over the years I have had thoughts of visiting my hometown. I knew that no Jews were living there and that nothing there would bring me joy. Yet, after my retirement, my desire increased. I wanted to see the house in which my parents had raised us, to walk the streets I had walked daily to and from school, and to walk in the parks where my sister and brother and friends used to play. I wanted to see Shul Gass, where the three Jewish synagogues once stood. I wanted to be in my hometown and to recall the hundreds of families I had known who had been murdered by the Germans.

Fifty-three years after the liberation of Mlawa, an opportunity presented itself. The authorities of the city had decided to clear up the Jewish cemetery that had been neglected and to build a monument there in memory of the Jewish people who once lived in the city and had contributed generously to its growth. They turned for financial assistance to the Mlawa Societies in Israel and in America. Not all of the Mlawa survivors were in favor of this project, but enough of us supported it, and the monument was built. By that time Riva and I had moved to Portland, Oregon, to be close to the family. We decided to join Mlawa Jews from both sides of the Atlantic to participate in the dedication of the monument, which was set for July 27, 1998. This trip would also give us an opportunity to honor the memory of my two grandfathers and the members of my extended family who were buried there.

We invited Meyer and Sue-Rita to join us, and the four of us took a flight from New York on Thursday night, July 23, 1998. We arrived in Warsaw the following morning. While walking the streets of Warsaw, I recalled the vibrant Jewish community of pre-Holocaust years. I was hoping to recognize a remnant of the large Jewish section of Warsaw where more than 300,000 Jews had lived. I recalled the thousands of Jewish merchants, along with the shops, the businesses, the markets, and the thousands of Jewish buyers and sellers who filled the streets every day. As I continued walking, I recalled the many Fridays when I had witnessed throngs of people shopping for the Sabbath. Others would be rushing home to begin preparing for the observance of the Sabbath. By candle-lighting time, those streets would be completely transformed. As if by magic the people would disappear, and a spirit of holiness would descend on the streets of the Jewish section of Warsaw. Soon after candle-lighting time, you would see men, dressed now in their Sabbath attire, walking slowly, each one to his favored synagogue, for Kabbalat Shabbat—the welcoming of Sabbath. That peaceful holiness in those streets was felt throughout the Sabbath day. Now all of that had been destroyed, and the people had been murdered. Yes, the city of Warsaw had been rebuilt, but the Jewish people and their spirit were gone. Not a sign was left, as if the Jewish people had never existed there. It was painful to behold.

We prepared for the Sabbath and prepaid for the Sabbath meals in the only kosher restaurant available. Before sunset we walked to the only existing synagogue in all of Warsaw, the Nozik Shul. This shul looked impressive in its structure and architecture, but it conveyed loneliness, emptiness, and neglect of this holy place that used to be filled with worshippers every day. We met the rabbi of Warsaw there, who welcomed us warmly. We waited for a *minyan* to begin the afternoon prayers. Men continued to arrive, one by one, looking sad and broken in spirit. All were survivors of the Holocaust.

In my conversation with one of the worshippers, I learned that the average age of the congregants was around seventy years and that the younger generation was not interested in attending religious services. Therefore, it was difficult having a *minyan*. I recalled that four hundred synagogues existed in Warsaw prior to the war and that each had usually been filled with worshippers each Friday night without fail. The current situation was depressing.

As soon as ten men were present, the rabbi led us in the *minhah* prayers. Before the conclusion of the service, a group of about thirty young Jews visiting from the United States, members of the National Conference of Synagogue Youth (NCSY) and their advisors arrived to join us in prayer. After *minhah*, the rabbi invited one of the leaders of the NCSY contingent to lead the congregation in Kabbalat Shabbat. A new spirit began to reach me as he began chanting the opening verses, "*Lekhu neranena lashem nariah letzur yisheinu*"—"O come, let us sing unto the Lord; let us joyfully acclaim the Rock of our salvation." Hearing the voice of the young man chanting these words with the tune I was used to hearing was uplifting. When we came to "Lekhah Dodi"—"Come, my beloved, with chorus of praise, Welcome Bride Sabbath, the Queen of the Days"—the chanting became stronger and more joyous, and I felt as though I were being lifted heavenward.

At the conclusion of "Lekhah Dodi," the whole NCSY group burst forth in joyous singing and dancing that lasted for a good hour. It reminded me of the festival of Simhat Torah, when Jews get into a mood of ecstasy of song and dance in the synagogue and are completely overtaken with the pure joy of Torah, God, and Israel. My son and I were standing near each other. I became emotional and tearful, and when I looked up at him, I noticed that he was also moved to tears. My immediate reaction was to hug him out of love and a desire to share our feelings, which I knew were the same without talking about them. Meyer and I both cried long and hard. I am sure he identified with my feelings of sadness and loss, as well as my joy at seeing this new generation of Jews—who had grown up in the distant land of America—continuing the impassioned tradition of singing and dancing with the joy of Sabbath, of Torah, and of the People of Israel. They were picking up where the Jews of Warsaw had so tragically been forced to stop this very act of faith, hope, and joy with our tradition. These young people chose to visit the places where our ancestors had built Jewish homes and Jewish communities dedicated to the perpetuation of Jewish life of faith, tradition, and culture. I looked up to the women's gallery and saw that Rivka and Sue-Rita had joined the young women of the NCSY group, also dancing with great joy. It was a moving experience that combined the highest degree of sadness and joy, the essence of Jewish history: joy, sadness, and joy again.

At dinner in the restaurant that night, we met the same NCSY group, and my mood of mixed joy and sadness continued. These young, spirited Jews reminded me that all of us were "orphans," that our parents and grandparents were gone. They had not been given a chance to live and to celebrate their lives with us.

When the group learned of my background and the fact that I was a rabbi, the leaders invited me to address the group, which I gladly did. I gently shared with them my thoughts about how difficult and painful it was to live with the memories of the destruction suffered by our people in Poland. I also assured them that they were the hope and salvation of our future as a people. We cannot bring our martyrs back to life, I said, but you young Jews are bringing our ancestors' spirituality back to life. I assured them that they were making a great contribution to the eternity of the Jewish people, that they and every person living today could help to bring about a better, kinder world for ourselves and for future generations. My message, I thought, was well received, but deep in my heart, while I believed in what I was saying, I remained focused on the result of the Holocaust tragedy, doubting whether humans can be trusted to eliminate hate and evil. The following morning we made another visit to the Nozik Shul for Sabbath morning prayers, and the NCSY group again lifted our spirits with their singing and dancing.

On Sunday we visited the memorials, which continued to remind us of the torment endured by the Jews in the Warsaw ghetto, where tens of thousands suffered and died of starvation. We visited the Umshlagplatz train station, from where hundreds of thousands of Jews were transported in trains of cattle cars to be killed in the death camps of Treblinka and Belzec. We stood at the impressive monument in memory of the Jews of Warsaw who perished. We visited the bunker of Mila 18, the headquarters of the Jewish ghetto uprising. We recalled the heroism of the young martyr Mordekhai Anielewicz, who led the uprising, and his followers, who fell fighting for the honor of our people in the Warsaw ghetto uprising of April 19–May 26, 1943. We stood at the monument to the martyr Janusz Korczak (Henrik Goldszmit), physician, educator, writer, and director of the Jewish Orphans Home in the ghetto. He had refused to accept the offer of his Polish friends outside the ghetto to save his life. He preferred to remain with his orphans as they went to their slaughter at Treblinka. We saw the remnants of the ghetto wall. A plaque on the wall shows a map of the ghetto. At each of these places, we identified with the martyrs and their struggle for life and felt great sadness for their tragic end.

In Warsaw we also met Jews who had grown up as Christians in the homes of Christians who had risked their lives and the lives of their families by hiding these Jews during the Nazi era. After these people discovered their true identities, they organized and created a Jewish Community Center near the Nozik Shul. By the time we visited, they had established Jewish cultural and educational activities there, including a theater that presented classical Yiddish plays in the Polish language. Yes, we did see signs of Jewish revival in Warsaw and in Cracow, and a Jewish revival is still going on in the larger cities of Poland. But remembering Jewish life before the Holocaust in Warsaw and other cities and towns reminds us of the terrible destruction of the Jews living in Europe in 1939: two of every three Jews in European countries under German occupation or under German influence were put to death in the period between 1939 and 1945.

On Monday morning we traveled with a Polish guide to Mlawa and joined the townspeople who had gathered at the cemetery. The cemetery had been totally destroyed by the Nazis and had remained in ruins for a half century. We found that the Polish people of Mlawa had cleared the cemetery and had built a new fence around it. They had collected the broken tombstones that had been scattered in fields around the city, and with those pieces they had erected six huge monuments, each one in the shape of a menorah (candelabra) as a memorial for the six million Jews and the six thousand Jews from Mlawa who were murdered. We listened to speeches by Polish dignitaries crediting the Jewish people who lived there and contributed with their talents and generosity to the growth and welfare of the city. We had the honor of the participation of Mr. Shimon (Sigmunt) Nissenbaum, a survivor of the Warsaw ghetto. After an absence of some forty years, he had returned to Poland and set up the Nissenbaum Foundation for the restoration of the neglected and destroyed Jewish cemeteries in the cities and towns of Poland. In his remarks, Mr. Nissenbaum criticized those Polish people who corroborated with the Nazis in their persecution of the Jews. We lit memorial candles and recited chapters from the book of Psalms. We recited the mourners Kaddish and concluded by chanting the memorial prayer of Malei Rahamim (God full of mercy).

It was also an opportunity for me to memorialize and to recite the Kaddish for my two grandfathers, relatives, and family friends who were buried in Mlawa. I recalled the many families I personally knew who had perished in the Holocaust. They were not given a resting place, and no family members had survived to remember them.

The following day we traveled to the Auschwitz-Birkenau concentration camp complex. Our visit to that place was very traumatic and very difficult for me to describe fully. When we passed over the rail tracks in our car, I felt a pain in my stomach as I realized that those were the same tracks over which I had been taken and over which my brother, relatives, and hundreds of thousands of Jews were driven to their deaths in closed, overcrowded, suffocating cattle cars. A shiver went up my spine as I passed through the iron gate of Auschwitz, with its imposing inscription of ARBEIT MACHT FREI. I recalled the nightmare of the night I first passed through that gate some fifty-six years earlier, November 19, 1942. I had passed through that gate 2000 times to and from work during the two and one-half years I was forced to do hard labor there.

We continued into the camp and into the barracks in which I spent a thousand days and a thousand nights in hunger and in fear. At the start of each day I had feared what might happen to me during that day. Each day I wondered whether I would be strong enough to return to the barrack for the night or whether I would be beaten so badly that I would have to be carried back to the camp by others. At the beginning of each night, I feared not being well enough to get up and be on my feet in the morning—either one of these might have been the beginning of my end.

Seeing in one of the barracks the mountain of shoes worn by the victims, the mountain of suitcases brought by the victims, and the mountain of eyeglasses worn by them, I became mournful and so numb I could not shed a tear. I stood there frozen, thinking of the men, women, and children to whom these articles belonged and whose lives were taken away so tragically. I stood looking at those articles for quite a while, thinking that these objects were permitted to survive but not the people who wore them or carried them. These articles were permitted to remain because they were not Jews. I wished to know which of them belonged to my brother or to my uncles, aunts, or cousins, and kiss them.

I stopped at Block XI, the place of torture and death, where a childhood friend of mine, Shaya Mondry, had been seen being taken there. From that block, no one came out alive. I recalled the fear I would feel just by looking at that building every time I passed by it. And I recalled the heroine Rosa Robota, a woman of twenty-three from the neighboring city of Czechanow. She smuggled dynamite from her place of work to give to the Jewish underground, which blew up the crematoria on October 6, 1944.[3] She was tortured in that building mercilessly but would not give out any names of the co-conspirators. She was hanged in front of the inmates in the women's camp. I was deeply shaken entering the various blocks and recalling the constant fear and hunger I felt there. In fact, every step I took in the Auschwitz barracks brought memories of brutality and horror.[4]

We ended that day by marching to Birkenau (Auschwitz II). We stood in front of the gas chambers and crematoria that were used to kill and then burn or cremate the dead into ashes. There we saw the remains of one of the five crematoria blown up during that October 6, 1944, revolt by the inmates who worked there. All six hundred inmates who took part in that revolt were shot to death during their attempt to escape. Every time I took a step at Birkenau, I felt I was stepping on the ashes of my people and my dear friends and relatives. We recited the Twenty-third Psalm and the Kaddish for all who were murdered there. I was totally drained emotionally and unable to talk for the rest of the day, and I spoke very little during the rest of the trip.

I had intended to visit Treblinka, where my mother's life had been taken. I had also intended to visit Majdanek and Belzec, where my father and sister may have been murdered. I wanted to connect with them in those places and to say Kaddish where they were murdered. But my children, Meyer and Sue-Rita, were concerned about my emotional well-being, so we did not go there. I mourned and said Kaddish for them in my heart, and we continued to Cracow, where we spent the last night of our five-day visit in Poland. In the morning we visited some of the historical places, but my heart was not in those visits. My thoughts were in Auschwitz with my brother and my relatives and my friends who were gassed and burned and went up to the heavens in smoke through the chimneys there.

By the time we left Poland, I felt like I had visited a huge cemetery for five days, and I was filled with sorrow and pain. Three million Polish Jews are buried there, not in the ground but in the air, in the smoke of the crematoria of one death camp or another. For one thousand years Jews lived creatively in Poland, and now they are in a huge cemetery. I left Poland deeply depressed, and that depression lasted for many months.

Was this trip worthwhile? Yes, indeed. I had the opportunity to go to the place where I was born and grew up and to walk in the steps where my parents and siblings had walked. I visited the parks where we used to spend time happily. I recalled precious moments that we spent as a family and with friends and neighbors. I am compelled to reemphasize that Mlawa has been rebuilt but that not a living sign remains of the six thousand Jews who lived there, not a single remnant of the Jewish life that flourished there for hundreds of years.

Did this trip bring about "closure" on that tragic period for me, as some people think a trip like this should do? Most certainly not. Memories of the Holocaust have never left the hearts and minds of the survivors. We are destined to live with these bitter memories of grief and sorrow and to continue mourning over our losses while we go on living with commitment to life and to love and with dedication to serve and to hope for a better and more secure future. We must never forget that humans committed those evils against humans and that it is up to humans to become more humane and not permit this evil to be repeated.

This trip strengthened my resolve to speak and write on the subject of the Holocaust. It is my obligation to do so for those who were not permitted to live and to tell of their sufferings and of the barbarism committed against them by humans.

To Jerusalem

By the time Riva and I had moved to Portland in 1998 to be closer to our family, Meyer had taken an active interest in the Jewish community and began to organize classes for adult Jewish education, including the serious study of Talmud. This led to the introduction to the community of the Melton Adult Jewish Education program, a two-year course of instruction for people serious about their Judaic studies. Meyer was selected to be one of the four teachers because of his excellent Judaic background and teaching skills.

In the year 2000, Meyer's name was brought to the attention of the national office of the Melton program. He was subsequently interviewed and offered a fellowship for a year of studies at Hebrew University in Jerusalem. Riva and I encouraged him and his family to accept the offer, which they did, and we joined them in Jerusalem in the summer of 2000. We spent an enjoyable year there, in spite of the intifada and suicide bombings. Meyer kept busy with his studies. Sue-Rita and Sarah volunteered, visited friends, and studied in an *ulpan* (an institute for the intensive study of the Hebrew language). Daniel enrolled in school there and made new friends. Jonah and Liza had remained in the United States, with Jonah staying in Portland and Liza attending Drew University, but Liza later joined us for her semester abroad at Hebrew University. Riva and I kept busy with our own interests and enjoyed seeing relatives and friends and attending interesting programs and lectures. We had visited Israel many times before. Just being in Israel, with our people in the land of our people, has always been a very special and enjoyable experience for us.

At the end of the academic year 2000–2001, Meyer and his family returned to the United States, and Meyer accepted an offer to work for the Jewish Federation of Rhode Island in Providence. Riva and I remained in Jerusalem, intending to stay there indefinitely. Five months later, in October 2001, we discovered that Riva was suffering from a serious illness. It was very shocking and devastating for me to realize that Riva's life might not last more than a few weeks. I checked with a number of well-known physicians, all of whom supported the diagnostic interpretation of the ultrasounds and X-rays taken.

I then agonized over what to do next. Naturally, my son wanted to be with his mother before she died. With the approval of her physicians, we decided to join Meyer and his family in Providence. We arrived in Rhode Island on October 24, and two weeks later, on November 5, 2001—19 Heshvan 5761—the beautiful and pure soul of Rivka (Riva) Goldstein bat Harav Mordekhai Ya'acov v'Hana Haya Freda Golinkin joined the souls of the righteous with God in heaven.

Riva was buried in Worcester, Massachusetts, near the graves of her parents. Hundreds of Riva's admirers gathered to pay their respects to her at the Beth Israel Synagogue. She was eulogized by the then rabbi of Congregation Beth Israel, Rabbi Jay Rosenbaum; by her brother, Rabbi Noah Golinkin; and by me, her husband, Rabbi Baruch Goldstein.

Life for me without Riva would never be the same. She had first introduced herself to me from a distance of some six thousand miles in a short note beginning with the words *"Taierer Fraind"* ("Dear Friend"). We had remained devoted and loving friends from that moment on until her passing, fifty-four years later.

When I met Riva for the first time in April 1948, the world around me was like a complicated, unsolvable puzzle. I did not want to live with the horrible memories of the past, yet I had no direction and no ambition for my future. The loss of my entire family seemed like a pain that was destined to last forever. I felt empty, drained of all life, and doubted whether I could lead a normal life. I did not believe in my ability to accomplish anything meaningful or worthwhile. Of course, I did not reveal my inner feelings of anguish and inadequacy to anyone.

Yet Riva, after a friendship of only a few short weeks, understood me completely—all my weaknesses, my self-doubts, and my fears. Nothing was hidden from her. She possessed a warm, friendly, and trusting personality that made me feel comfortable confiding in her, including my negative traits. But she also understood well my background and the brutality and horrors I had endured, without me talking to her of the unspeakable. She was wise and recognized my potential better than I did. She was convinced that I had the ability to begin a new and meaningful life, and she agreed to be part of my life and to share her life with me. With wisdom and true love she opened my eyes to see and breathed into my soul a new spirit of hope and inspiration. She gave me the strength to say *yes* to life, *yes* to our faith. And she did it all with kindness, with patience, and with understanding. She was always at my side with kind words of encouragement to do what was good and right for me, for us, for the synagogue, and for the community, and she never expected any reward. She gave me the will and the strength to follow my destiny and become the man I was destined to become.

The following are excerpts from the eulogies delivered at Riva's funeral.

The essence of Riva's life was respect and admiration, love and friendship. Young beautiful Rebecca started her life as "Rivele dem Rov's," lovingly called "Rivele the Rabbi's daughter," the proud daughter of a great, highly respected father. . . . During her formative years she always acted with maturity and understanding. She was always the one of her three siblings to offer assistance to her family whenever needed, always the first whenever help was requested. Her own personal needs were second to the needs of her father and mother. . . . Rebecca climaxed a life of great intensity and caring as the proud wife of a highly beloved husband. . . . Riva did not live for herself. She always lived for others. . . . Through various periods of her parents' sickness, she worked very hard to provide comfort for her mother and father. Through various periods of economic uncertainty, she worked very hard to create economic security.
—Rabbi Noah Golinkin, Riva's brother

Like Rivka Imeinu (our matriarch) our Rivka too was an *ishah tzenuah,* a woman of modesty and grace. She shunned the limelight and preferred to do *tzedakah* and *mitzvot*—good deeds—behind the scenes, in an unassuming way. . . .

The story of Riva and Rabbi Goldstein reminds me of the story of Rachel and Rabbi Akiva. Rachel was the daughter of a prominent father. She discovered Rabbi Akiva before anyone knew him or was aware of his potential, and she dedicated her whole life to make his rise to great leadership possible. It was a story of heroic sacrifice for love. In many ways the story of Riva and Rabbi Goldstein reminds me of that story. . . .

In 1947, Rabbi Goldstein was still in a DP camp in Italy, feeling quite devastated by the losses he had sustained during the Holocaust, exhausted by his own struggle to survive, and beginning to lose hope in the future. . . . Riva was out in California for a vacation, and she was out on a date with a doctor who received an emergency call from a woman who had been in an accident and needed his medical attention. This woman happened to be the aunt of Rabbi Goldstein.

Riva was invited into her house with the doctor. Riva was so kind to the woman in need, and the woman was so impressed with her, that she invited Riva to stay with her as her guest as soon as she recovered. Riva accepted that invitation, and they became dear friends. The woman talked with Riva in glowing terms about her nephew who was still in a camp in Italy and shared his letters with her. Riva would read the letters and was found once in tears upon reading one of the letters. Riva became determined to help him. . . .

After her return home she pressured her brother long and hard enough so that he arranged to get a student visa for Baruch to come to America and enter into the yeshiva of Rabbi Moshe Feinstein, Tiferet Yerushalayim in New York. Riva and Baruch were married four months after he came to America. A year later, Rabbi Goldstein's wonderful influence on our community began to take root and flower and increase daily in strength and depth for the next fifty years. . . .

Knowing Rabbi Goldstein as the source of strength to us that we do, it may be hard to imagine him as having his own doubts—but it doesn't take much of a leap of the imagination to understand what the Holocaust did to a person's feelings of self-worth. Rabbi Goldstein has shared with me that it was Riva that restored to him his faith in God, his faith in humanity, his faith in the power of love, and his faith in his own worthiness. . . .

Add to that the tremendous impact that Rabbi Goldstein himself has had on us—the thousands of people of all ages that he has counseled in distress, inspired, taught Torah, touched in the most profound way—all of the people to whom Rabbi Goldstein has given life, and encouragement, and hope. . . . All of this was made possible, in the most unassuming, behind-the-scenes way, by the strength, wisdom, and compassion of our modern-day Rivka, Riva Goldstein.
—Rabbi Jay Rosenbaum

May the memory of Rivka—Riva—Goldstein, bat Harav Mordekhai Ya'acov v'Hana Haya Freda Golinkin, remain for a blessing to all who knew her and admired her.

19
Faith after the Holocaust

Never shall I forget the little faces of the children, whose bodies I saw
turned into wreaths of smoke beneath a silent blue sky. Never shall I
forget those flames, which consumed my faith forever. Never shall I forget
these things, even if I am condemned to live as long as God Himself.
—Elie Wiesel, *Night*

Like Elie Wiesel, I cannot and will never forget the brutality I have seen and
experienced in the labor camps, the ghettos, and the concentration camps.
Above all, I cannot and never will forget the loss of my family, my friends,
and the six million of my people whose only crime was that they were Jews.
Neither can I, nor will I, forget the torture they were made to suffer before
they died. Degradation and brutality wounded my soul. And my faith, too,
has been scarred and has never been the same as it was before the Shoah.

I was raised in a home where both my father and my mother lived every
day of their lives with unquestionable faith, belief in God and his Torah. I
lived in a community where most of the Jews lived their lives with faith in accordance with our tradition. All the synagogues in my city were well attended
by Jews of faith every day and more so on the Sabbaths. Even the streets in
my community testified every Saturday to the holiness of the Sabbath spirit.
This was true practically of all the Jewish communities in Poland.

Because of what I had seen and experienced in my parents' home, in my
schools, and in my community, I held on to my faith throughout the Holocaust years of suffering. Even under the most difficult conditions, I was conscious of God's presence, and I frequently turned to him with my pleas to
help me and not forsake me. I was particularly keen about reciting the standard traditional prayers daily, as many as I remembered by heart. I held on to
my belief in a "*Shome'ah tefillah*," a "God Who listens to prayer." It gave me
hope and strength to hold on to life in spite of the cruelty that surrounded me
practically every day for a very long time. I also shared words of Torah with
fellow inmates in the ghetto, in the labor camps, and in Auschwitz. When the
Nazi atrocities were being committed against my people, against my family,
and against me, I was preoccupied with surviving, and my mind was not challenged with questions about faith.

I have been trained to think of Jewish destiny as a chain of suffering. I have been taught to interpret our sufferings to be *yisurin shel ahavah*, sufferings of love, the kind of pain a lover may occasionally cause to his beloved, and we were to accept these sufferings *"b'ahavah,"* with love. I have been taught that God is the lover of our people and that difficulties, like lovers' quarrels, are usually followed by greater love. I was familiar with the teachings of the Hebrew prophets and sages. "You alone have I singled out of all the families of the earth, that is why I will call you to account for all your iniquities," says the prophet Amos.[1] We were chosen not because we are better and thus to be treated favorably. We were chosen *to be* better, and therefore God demands and expects more from the Jewish people and therefore severely punishes us for our iniquities. I believed that God is in distress when his children are distressed, that "God is righteous in all His ways and kind in all His deeds."[2] I had lived all my young life with the pious belief that whatever happens, good or bad, is the will of God and is to be accepted without question and without complaint. I held on to my faith and belief in God's mercy even during the most difficult days of Nazi brutality.

After liberation and after I regained consciousness, however, I found myself confused and terribly lonely. I was grieving the loss of my family. I was depressed and overtaken by fear and uncertainty of my existence. I was then unable and unwilling to continue with the faith I had known and lived by since my childhood. I could not accept the idea that my faith and my prayers were better, or more sincere, than the faith and prayers of my father and mother. I was still alive, whereas they had been brutally murdered. I felt guilty having survived. I could not and would not believe that the prayers and faith of the millions of our martyrs were any less sincere than mine. And I became indifferent to faith and indifferent to the practices of Judaism. Religious observances became irrelevant and had lost meaning for me.

I began to question God's existence, for if he existed, he was to be a *Shome'ah tefillah* and kind and merciful. Why did he not listen to the prayers and pleas of the millions of the righteous and faithful? I have personally known thousands of Jews who have lived their lives with unshakable faith and with total devotion to God. Their acts of righteous deeds have been as numerous "as the seeds in a pomegranate."[3] Their faith has been without blemish, as have their prayers and their pleas; their tears surely have come from the depth of their hearts and souls. This was true of most of the people who perished. Why, I kept asking, had God not accepted their pleas and instead permitted the massacre of one-third of our people? If God is omniscient, omnipotent, merciful, and caring for his creation, as I was taught to believe, how could he tolerate so much pain, so much evil, so much destruction? These questions occupied my thoughts, boggled my mind, and disturbed my sleep.

My difficulty with belief and my internal religious struggle lasted a long time, but I did not wait too long to begin my return to religious observances. The first seeds for this return were planted in me three years after liberation. My experiences during those eight days of my first Passover festival in America with Riva and her parents were a turning point in my life and my way of life, and my spiritual pursuit began to turn its direction. I welcomed these changes, including my decision to observe the laws first and then perhaps understand them at a later time, knowing I might never have all the answers to my questions.

My acceptance of keeping and observing Torah and mitzvoth led to a more intensive search for knowledge and understanding. I began to attune my ears to and participate in discussions, debates, and lectures on the subject of faith. I studied religious texts and any book that touched on the subject of theology. My mind and heart were open to consider ideas and explanations that would help me recapture my faith and guide me on the path of understanding. I knew and accepted that every Jew is obligated to study, to know, to keep, and to do, and I followed that precept.

When I assumed the position of rabbi at Temple Emmanuel in Wakefield in 1964, my search intensified. As the spiritual leader of a community, I was bound to face my personal questions along with the questions of the young, bright intellectuals in that congregation. How could a compassionate God have permitted so much suffering and so many massacres during the long years of the Nazi reign? In my position of leadership, I frequently began to attend rabbinical conferences, conventions, and lectures where these questions were discussed. I read extensively on the topic of theodicy, and I began to develop my understanding of *emunah*, faith and belief. Indeed, every Jew is obligated to study, to know, to keep, and to do what is just and right.

In my intensive search for answers to the difficult theological questions, I found the story of Yosl Rakover in an anthology edited by Sidney Greenberg that moved me deeply.[4] At that time I believed this story to be a historical fact. Only some years later did I discover that the story of Yosl Rakover was a fiction created by Zvi Kolitz.[5] Fact or fiction, I have read the story several times and have always been moved emotionally when reading it, perhaps because my father and mother lived and died with unshakable faith, just like Yosl Rakover did. The same is true with most of the six million martyrs. When my father, like a great many of the other martyrs, I am sure, recited twice daily in his prayers, "In His Hand I trust my Spirit, my soul," he meant it fully, completely, and without reservation. And I became convinced that even if there was no one named Yosl Rakover, there were millions of Jews among the martyrs whose strength of faith and love of God was unshakable to their last breath of life.

Zvi Kolitz tells us that in the ruins of the Warsaw ghetto, concealed among heaps of charred stones and human bones, a sealed bottle was found. Inside it was the last testament written by a Jew in the last hours of his life. Yosl Rakover was a very pious Jew, a Hassid of the rebbe of Ger and was now in a cellar fighting the Germans during the end of the Warsaw ghetto uprising. By that time, he had lost his wife and four children. He knows that he will die soon. He is the only one still alive of the twelve who entered the bunker at the beginning of the uprising. In his last moments before he dies, he turns to God, in whom he believes with his whole heart, and says that he is proud of having the terrible honor of being a Jew, for he would be ashamed to belong to the people who have borne and raised the criminals responsible for the deeds that have been perpetrated against us. "I am proud of my Jewishness," says Yosl, "because being a Jew is an art. Being a Jew is hard. There is no art in being an Englishman, an American, or a Frenchman. It is perhaps easier, more comfortable to be one of them, but it is not more honorable. Yes, it is an honor to be a Jew." He continues by saying, "I believe in the God of Israel, even when He has done everything to make me cease to believe in Him. I believe in His laws even when I cannot justify His deeds." And Yosl Rakover concludes, "Here then are my last words to You, my angry God: 'None of this will avail You in the least! You have done everything to make me lose my faith in You, to make me cease to believe in You. But I die exactly as I lived, an unshakable believer in You. Praised be forever the God of the dead, the God of vengeance, of truth and judgment, Who will soon unveil his Face to the world again and shake its foundations with His almighty voice. Shema Yisroel! Hear Israel! The Lord is our God, the Lord is one, Into your hands, O Lord, I commend my soul.'"[6]

I do not know how many of the six million martyrs had the ability to articulate their thoughts before they died like Yosl Rakover did, but I am absolutely certain that a high percentage of them would certainly identify with every part of his thoughts and give consent to his testament of faith.

Yosl Rakover did not survive. Had he survived, he would have remained steadfast in his faith, believing exactly as he had before and during his suffering. I am convinced of that because I have seen many Holocaust survivors who remained believing and committed Jews exactly as they were before the Holocaust.

Yes, it is also historically true that Jewish suffering has often presented challenges to faith. The Holocaust may very well be the ultimate of all challenges faced by Judaism and the Jewish people. What was imposed on the victims of the Shoah was more than what they could endure, and the faith of many was shattered. Life in the ghettos, concentration camps, and death camps led to a serious crisis of religious beliefs for many Jews. Perhaps Auschwitz represents the source of the ultimate crisis of faith.

But it is also true that the Holocaust did not create a religious crisis for all the victims. I have met a great many survivors who continued in their faith after the Holocaust with the same fervor and devotion as before. They have been filled with gratitude to God for their miraculous survival and have not questioned God about their losses or their pain and anguish. Other survivors who had been nonbelievers became believers, with gratitude to God for their miraculous survival. I, too, am now grateful to God for helping me survive and giving me years to live. But my experiences and my losses had created a crisis in my faith and doubts in my belief in a beneficent Providence who hid his face from my loved ones and from so many other innocent victims, all of them created in his image. The problem of faith after the Holocaust has been a painful and complex legacy for many survivors, including me. The Holocaust raised mind-boggling questions that are not easily answered, if they can be answered at all.

At first, I felt guilty questioning God. I was raised in a home where I was taught that God's ways were not to be questioned. As a child, I heard my father and mother say on many occasions, in Yiddish, "*Got is gerekht un zain mishpet is gerehl*"—"God and his judgments are always right." They would also say, "*Me'tor nit fregen*"—"We must not question God's judgment."

Yet I ultimately realized that such inquiry was acceptable, even appropriate. I came to understand that faith did not mean simply to believe in God's existence but also to trust in him and to expect him to perform justice. I came to realize that the tradition of questioning God goes back to early days of Jewish history. In the book of Genesis we are told how Abraham, the first Hebrew, argued with God over the fate of the wicked people of Sodom and Gomorrah. He challenged God: "Will the Judge of the earth not do justice? Perhaps there are fifty righteous people in the city. Will You destroy the righteous and the wicked? Far be it for you to do such an injustice!"[7] It was Abraham's very belief in a righteous God that made him unable to tolerate such seeming injustice.

Judge Gideon, one of the great leaders of the Jewish people in the period of the Judges, some thirty-two hundred years ago, was also plagued by a similar question. After the Midianites and Amalekites oppressed the Israelites for seven years, an angel appeared to him and greeted him by saying,

"The Lord is with you!" Gideon then asked the angel, "If the Lord is with us, why has all this befallen us? Where are His wondrous deeds about which our fathers told us?"[8] Job, "the blameless and upright man, who feared God and shunned evil,"[9] when plagued with physical sufferings and with the loss of all his children and all his wealth, cursed the day of his birth. In great anger he cried out, "Perish the day on which I was born. . . . Why did I not die at birth, expire as I came out of the womb?"[10] The sages in the Talmud also asked the question, *"Rasha v'tov lo, tzadik v'ra lo?"*—"Why do the wicked prosper and the righteous suffer?"[11]

The questioning of God's absence in the concentration camps and in the death camps, I believe, is in the classical tradition of Judaism, and it is legitimate. The painful heart cries out, why did God hide his face and remain silent to the very end of the tragedy? Why were millions of good people left alone in concentration camps, ghettos, and forests in the midst of infinite despair?

My search for understanding continued. When I moved back to Worcester and began speaking about the Holocaust and my personal experiences of that period, I was bound to sort out further my own understanding of my personal *emunah*. My involvement with students, parents, and the community at large strengthened my resolve to find inner peace and to find answers to the many questions I struggled with.

I focused much of my attention on the general question of what we often see and observe around us: why do evil men prosper and righteous men suffer? As stated previously and recorded in the Talmud, the rabbis had raised this question some eighteen hundred years ago. Translating this question into contemporary concerns, people would continually ask, why did God allow the Shoah to happen? Why did he allow the massacre of six million Jews and unknown millions of non-Jews, all of them created in his image, all of them innocent men, women, and children? Why did the Nazi evildoers prosper for twelve long years? The answers recorded in the Talmud were not applicable and not satisfactory.

In the discussions on the subject we had, I would hear quoted from our liturgy as an answer to our dilemma, *"Mipnei chata'einu galinu me'artzeinu"*—"Because of our sins we were driven out of our land." Jews recite this prayer on all the Jewish festivals. Instead of blaming the Romans who were guilty of expelling us from our land, the author of this liturgy suggests that our misfortunes were due to our ancestors' and our own failings. In looking at the course of Jewish history, however, I find it hard to believe that the sufferings of our people in the twentieth century were due to the sins of our ancestors of twenty centuries ago. I cannot believe that their sins, nor our own sins, have been so terrible that we have deserved to suffer those terrible persecutions for two thousand years and climaxed those sufferings with a Holocaust. And I certainly reject the statement I have heard too often that the Holocaust was a punishment for our sins.

I firmly believe that the vast majority of the six million Jews murdered were good, decent people. Of the approximately three million Jews of Poland who were murdered, the vast majority of them were Torah scholars and observant Jews. And there were among them physicians, scientists, lawyers, writers, poets, businesspeople, intellectuals, musicians, and simple hard-working, good, and decent people. They did not deserve the punishment to die. All of them were committed to doing good for God's creation. I know, because I lived among them, in small cities, in large cities, and in villages. The Jewish communities in Poland were among the best of all Jewish communities in the world. They were the nucleus of world Jewry for more than four centuries. And among those who perished were about 1.5 million innocent children, who certainly committed no sins and did nothing wrong to deserve this kind of punishment. How could God hide his face when these children were savagely torn from their mothers and hurled like coal into the fiery furnace? This certainly cannot be answered with "*mipnei chataeinu*—"because of our sins."

I believe that all Jews who perished in the Holocaust were *kedoshim*, holy martyrs. This group includes the religious and the nonreligious, the Bundists and the Agudahniks, the Hasidim and the Mitnagdim, the Zionists and the anti-Zionists, and the secular and the assimilated Jews. They all were murdered only because they were *b'nei Avraham, Yitzhak v'Ya'acov*—children of Abraham, Isaac, and Jacob, that is, because they were Jews.

After years of serious searching, I have concluded and accepted that I may never find a satisfactory answer to these difficult and disturbing questions. Perhaps no answer is to be found until God himself reveals it: "For my plans are not your plans, nor are my ways your ways, declares the Lord. But as the heavens are high above the earth so are my ways and my plans above your plans."[12] But God expects us to have faith and to believe in him anyway. The book of Job also concludes that God did not grant humans the ability to comprehend all that is, neither in creation nor in what takes place in the world after creation.[13]

Ultimately, I have come to accept that not understanding God's ways is not a good enough reason for me to reject my belief in God's existence or to doubt my faith in him. We really cannot totally depend on our reasoning alone. While living a religious life of belief in God and faith in God's goodness, I have become convinced that life without faith is meaningless, lacking in direction and purpose, and potentially empty spiritually. I have become convinced that the Jewish people have no future without faith and tradition, that the Jewish people have no future without Judaism.

In my search to define my faith, I gleaned from the teachings of the prophets and sages, from rabbis and teachers of the classics of the Jewish faith, and from the Talmud and Midrash. I studied philosophical and theological ideas and concepts that would guide me in my religious belief and strengthen my faith. In time, I accepted three principles of belief that are essential and fundamental to my understanding and acceptance of my faith and my religious life: *hester panim*—God hiding his face; *behirah hofshit*—freedom of choice; and *Shome'ah tefillah*—God listens to human prayer.

With regard to *hester panim*—God hiding his face—I understand this to mean that sometimes God chooses to make his presence difficult to perceive; he is not responsive. This idea can be found numerous times in the Bible in the books of Isaiah, Job, and Psalms. But it is most clearly pronounced in the book of Deuteronomy as a form of punishment. As Moses addressed the people of Israel during the last year of his life, he warned them, in the name of God, that should they become unfaithful and forsake God's covenant, which he had established with them, "Then My anger will flare up against them, and I will abandon them and hide my countenance from them. They shall be ready prey; and many evils and troubles shall befall them."[14]

The biblical text is a harsh one, indeed. It speaks of abandonment, of God turning his face away from the people's suffering. We traditionally understand this to mean that betrayal of God's commandments, *hiding oneself* from one's responsibilities, unleashes the potential for chaos, which may affect both the good and the wicked, the guilty and the innocent alike. This passage poses perplexing questions: Why do the good and the innocent suffer? Is this just? Have we not been taught that God is just and kind? "God watches over those who love Him (the righteous) but destroys the wicked."[15]

Hester panim is also implicit in the story of the first murder recorded in the Bible, when Cain, in a moment of jealousy and rage, killed his brother, Abel.[16] Clearly, Cain was a murderer who let his jealousy and anger control him, but Abel was certainly innocent. The text does not mention a single wrong Abel had committed to deserve the punishment of death. Why, then, did God permit the killing of an innocent man?

I suggest that the Torah teaches us a very important lesson in this story. If a murderer is in our midst, there will surely be a victim and perhaps even an innocent victim. As a rule, God does not control our actions. He withdraws, leaving people to control their deeds, their rage, their jealousies, and their temptations. God expects humans to make their own decisions and settle their disputes amicably. He expects humans to act humanely of their own free will and not by his force.

The principle of *behirah hofshit*—freedom of choice—is also one of the basic principles of Judaism. As it says in the book of Deuteronomy, "See, this day, I set before you blessing and curse: blessing, if you obey the commandments . . . and curse, if you do not obey the commandments of the Lord, your God."[17] We also learn in Deuteronomy, "I put before you life and death, blessing and curse. Choose life."[18]

The twelfth-century Jewish philosopher Maimonides taught us that "free will is granted to every human being; if a person wishes to follow the good path and be good, he has the power to do so; if he wants to follow the evil way and be wicked, he is free to do so. . . . That is to say, the human species is unique in the world, there being no other species like it in this respect, namely that man by himself, using his own intelligence and reason, knows what is good and what is evil, without anyone preventing him from doing good or evil as he pleases."[19]

Humans are given the ability and freedom to choose their actions in accordance with their inner motives and ideals. In this sense, I believe, *hester panim* allows for freedom of choice. God does not usually interfere in the choices human beings make, thereby making them responsible for the consequences of their choices. He is a much greater God, allowing people to act in such a way as to realize their potential by making their own decisions. God has given full significance to his creation by allowing people to act freely. In a world with freedom of will, personal joy of discovery and achievement are possible. Freedom of choice gives people the opportunity to formulate values and develop scientific research and discovery. In such a world, God works not through coercion or manipulation but rather through the persuasive power of revelation, through his prophets, sages, and spiritual leaders, and through people of science and accumulated knowledge in every field of human endeavor and in every generation.

By hiding his face, God gives humans the opportunity to realize the divine purpose within each human being. I believe that the future is not a given and that not everything is predetermined. This is an open world in which humans can frustrate God's will or realize it. This is a world in which humans can achieve the ultimate good through inner growth and moral action. Conversely, they can perpetrate great evil. It is the task of humans to live and act in ways that influence the world for the good. The two concepts are thus interrelated. God hides his face so that we may have freedom of choice.

With regard to the third concept of my understanding of faith, *Shome'ah tefillah* (God listens to prayers), I have a problem believing that God cares only to hear our praises and thanksgiving. I grew up believing in God who answers prayers, and I have chosen to believe so now. "*Min hametzar karati yah anani vamerhav yah*"—"In distress I call on the Lord; He answers me and brings me relief."[20] But if people set out to destroy, I believe that God has a choice to either let them because of freedom of choice or to stop them because he wishes to protect them. He, too, has freedom of choice. He can choose to prevent tragedy from happening, or he can decide not to interfere. God also has the freedom of choice to accept our pleas or to ignore them. And we were not given the wisdom to understand everything or to comprehend why and how and when God makes his choices to act or not to act. I think this will remain a mystery until God himself reveals it to us.

These three concepts, *hester panim, behirah hofshit,* and *Shome'ah tefillah,* remain basic to my faith without conflict. God, as a self-limiting creator, willed an imperfect world so that humans could be free to perfect it or to destroy it. "*Asher bara elo-him la'asot*"—"God created the world to do."[21] But "to do" what? God created the world incomplete so that humans would complete it, care for it, fix it if broken, and make it continuously better and safer. He has charged humans with the responsibility of developing and guarding this beautiful but fragile and complicated universe. This way humans can become junior partners with God both for our good and for the good of future generations. He blessed us with the abilities to do this well, but he also gave us freedom of choice, which allows us to neglect this responsibility.

I have been born a Jew and have chosen to live with faith and to make the Jewish way of life of Torah and mitzvoth my life's journey. I believe that faith is a matter of personal choice, and I have chosen to believe, for this belief urges me and guides me on the path to fix the world and not to destroy it. Every individual, I am convinced, has it within his or her power to choose faith or reject it. Because I am a Jew who has chosen to affirm my Jewish identity, I have recognized that, as such, I am required to know, to study, to keep, and to observe the teachings of my tradition. As a Jew, there are actions I *must* or *should* do, as well as deeds that I *must not* or *should not* do. My duties and obligations as a Jew give identity and meaning to my existence.

As I see it, the harmony and order of the universe point to a creator who created a law-abiding nature in the universe, which does not change. The psalmist calls on the heavens, the sun, the moon, the stars, and the waters to praise God, "for He [God] commanded that they be created. He made them endure forever, establishing an order that shall never change *(hok natan v'lo ya'avor)*."[22] These observations are true and convince me of God's presence in nature, in history, and in humankind. Freedom of choice was given to Adam, the first man. He had the choice to eat or abstain from eating the forbidden fruit. He chose not to obey. Freedom of choice was given to Cain, who chose to kill his brother. This freedom of choice has existed throughout human history. It exists today and will exist forever, for it is unalterable. *It shall never change.*

The universe is an orderly and harmonious creation and not a whirlwind of chaos. The process of history reveals a God who cares. And humans, with all their imperfections, carry the proof of the divine creator. If they wish, people may find in their own lives signs of God's great power. "*Asher yatzar et ha'adam behokhma*"—"God created humans with wisdom."[23] The human body has so many wondrous and intricate parts, as does the wondrous creation of the universe, with its many galaxies and intricate yet orderly functions. Human intelligence is incapable of creating all this. God will not rebuild a ruined city or fix a broken bridge, but he gave human beings the ability to use their intellect and strength to build a city and to rebuild it should it be ruined. Yet God will mend a broken heart and comfort a troubled soul. "*Harofeh l'shvurei lev um'habesh l'atzvotam*"—"God heals broken hearts and binds up their wounds."[24] Only a supreme intelligent power could have created and caused the world and humans to function as they do. This is unalterable. God is bound by the nature of his creation—for he established them for all time, and it *shall never change.* Yes, indeed, I feel a trace of God in the Torah, in the Talmud, and in the classic commentaries; I feel a trace of God in history; and I feel a trace of God in everyday living. And, yes, I believe in a *Shome'ah tefillah,* in God who listens to and answers prayers. Because he, too, has freedom of choice, he may choose to listen and to grant our requests, or he may choose to reject them. He may choose to hide his face and not listen at all, for any reason he chooses.

It has been my choice to live with faith, to believe in God based on my conviction that this belief is strongly attached to authentic Judaism. From the opening words of Genesis, Jewish tradition asserts that God is the creator, that he is one, unique, and that his providence extends through human history. An awareness of God's presence pervades human creativity and achievements.

I believe that the survival of the Jewish people testifies to the idea that there is divine protection that will not allow us to disappear in spite of the attempts made by our enemies in every generation: "And yet, for all that, even by their being in the land of their enemies, I have not despised them and not rejected them in order to destroy them, to break my covenant with them, for I, God, am still their God."[25] Our survival as a people for four thousand years has been made possible by a mystical design for us to live with a sense of purpose. It is a design formed at the very beginning, at the very birth of our people, a design that we collectively agreed to live by, and we collectively do live by this covenant till this day. Jewish history in its totality is the epic of a people transcending its troubles and capable of pitying its persecutors, preserving its power of love in the midst of evil, and seeking to serve God and humanity from any location. It is the story of a people that not only has survived but also has remained civilized and sane; it is the story of a people with a special history and a special message. It is a history that is worthy not only of study but also of continuing.

Jewish history is unique. Its four-thousand-year existence beginning with nomad Abraham to the modern state of Israel is a mystery. Jews almost always lived within the context of other civilizations. Somehow the Jews managed to survive the death of one civilization and continue their cultural growth in another civilization that emerged at the time.[26]

The rebirth of the modern Jewish state of Israel is indeed a continuation of the mystery of Jewish history. I do not know of any other people in the history of the world that was driven out of its homeland, survived in exile for almost two thousand years, and then returned to rebuild its land with such success. Jews had no army since the Bar Kochba revolt against the Romans in the second century. As late as 1900 Palestine had been a barren, stony, cactus-infested patch of desert. Almost overnight Palestine has become a modern agricultural and industrial state, its desert replaced by fertile fields and planted with beautiful cities.

Nazi Germany was unable to end Jewish history, trying as hard as it did. And I firmly believe that the enemies surrounding Israel today will not succeed in their attempts to destroy the Jewish state. Our tradition has taught our people, and our people have learned the lesson well—a lesson of faith—as we patiently and faithfully waited for the day when we would return to our land and remain a free and independent nation forever.

I believe that faith and a love for Judaism can be acquired slowly, patiently, in regular daily doses: "When you sit in your house, when you walk by the way, when you lie down, and when you rise up."[27] Judaism is an ever-present dimension of daily living for every Jew; it is not a spectacular demonstration. Its symbol is the soft eternal light and the *kol d'mamah dakah*—the still small voice.[28] Faith requires steadiness, faithfulness, and patience.

I do not believe that theological speculations on the Holocaust will lead us to any understanding of it. I do not think it is of consequence to deal with esoteric speculation on the murder of six million innocent Jews and many millions of innocent non-Jews. We, who cannot explain the death of one single child from leukemia, may never succeed in interpreting the Holocaust through theology.

I do believe that the arena in which to confront the Holocaust is not the field of theology but the field of history and human behavior, the field of faith and hope. And confront the Holocaust we must. We must study the Holocaust and all the other evils and genocides committed by humans against humans during the twentieth century and take a pledge of remembrance, lest we forget!

We must study the cause of the vanished millions with even greater focus on how to prevent this evil from happening again. It might be helpful for us to reexamine the religious and humanistic values and structures that we live by. We must learn to live by theological modesty and be less dogmatic, less sure of ourselves, less arrogant, less hateful, and less prejudiced. And we must learn to be more accepting of differences and more tolerant of those who differ from us theologically, politically, culturally, racially, or in any other way.

Epilogue
Gratitude and Hope

As I look back to the years after my liberation from the Nazi terror, I realize that I have lived my life with bitter memories of persecution and irreparable losses. But I have also learned to live with a sense of gratitude for the joy of life.

I am grateful for having had the blessing of fifty-four wonderful years of sharing true love and a good and full life with Riva, of Blessed Memory.

I am grateful to have been blessed with my children, Meyer and Sue-Rita, and with my grandchildren, Jonah and his wife, Jessica; Liza; Sarah; and Daniel. I am very grateful to have the blessings of their love and affection. I am very grateful for having lived to see my first great-grandson, Ronan Michael (Mordekhai), son of Jonah and Jessica.

I am grateful for having had the opportunity to serve three congregations as teacher and rabbi for thirty-seven years and having acquired wonderful friends who have been my extended family and helped me to find satisfaction and fulfillment in my life despite the unforgettable losses and horror I sustained from the Nazi brutality.

I am grateful for the United States of America, the country that gave me the opportunity to start a new life and the freedom to practice my faith and to pursue happiness.

Above all, I am most grateful to God for having helped me to survive and for the opportunities I was given to live beyond the biblical years of G'vurot (Psalm 90:10). Every day I am inspired by the words of the psalmist who said:

Hashem elohai, shivati eleikha vatirpa'eni.
He'elita min Sh'ol nafshi hiyitani miyordi vor.
(Lord, my God, I cried out to You and You healed me.
You brought me up from Sh'ol [the netherworld]
Preserved me from going down to the pit.)
(Psalm 30:3–4)

I am grateful to God for having given me the opportunity to study and to teach, to be inspired and to inspire. I am grateful for having had the strength and the will to speak of the unspeakable and to share not only the horrors of the past but also a message for the future. I have urged my listeners to remember and to study the Holocaust and face up to it, learn from it, and draw valuable conclusions. The wounds of the past may be healed only if we stop transmitting hatred from generation to generation. I have tried to convince my listeners that the Holocaust is not only a Jewish problem but also a human problem. I have urged them to study the history of the twentieth century, during which time humans reached a new level in their scientific achievement. In fact, humans have reached incredible powers over self, over society, and over the physical environment. Humans have used their talents to develop an unbelievable amount of technology. Indeed, humans have made progress in practically every field of human endeavor in the twentieth century. As a result of their scientific and technological achievements, humans have reached new levels of human creativity, putting people on the moon, sending probes into space, and creating many extraordinary gadgets for our comfort and tools for our well-being.

Nevertheless, we have also reached an even higher level in our potential for evil and destruction. In addition to the Holocaust, there have been multiple destructive wars, genocides, and ethnic cleansings, and many millions of innocent men, women, and children have been put to death because of hate. Our scientific and technological achievements have allowed us to harness the power to destroy or to alter the human race and its physical and orderly habitat. This is the first time in human history that humankind seems capable of actions that can inflict terminal damage in our world. We now appear to have the ability to engage in actions previously considered impossible or unlikely.

My hope has been that in the twenty-first century we will have learned from the history of the twentieth century and that we will be wiser for it. I find myself deeply distressed frequently. Almost sixty years have passed since the defeat of Nazism, and we are now almost a decade into the twenty-first century, and yet there is no sign that we have learned anything from our recent horrors. Anti-Semitism is still around and getting stronger. Bigotry and hatred are still around and growing. There is good reason for concern for the future of our children and the future of our society. For that we cannot blame God. This has always been and will continue to be our responsibility and our challenge.

I hope for the time when the words of the Hebrew prophets will come true, when everyone will know "what is good and what it is that God requires of you, but to do justice, to love kindness, and to walk humbly with your God" (Micah 6:8); when all will "execute justice, deal loyally and compassionately with one another; do not defraud the widow, the orphan, the stranger and the poor, and do not plot evil against one another" (Zechariah 7:9–10); when "justice will well up like water, righteousness like an unfailing stream" (Amos 5:24); when "the wolf shall dwell with the lamb, the leopard lie down with the kid . . . nothing evil or destruction shall be done; for the world shall be filled with devotion to God as water covers the sea" (Isaiah 11:6, 9); for "have we not all one Father? Did not one God create us; why do we deal treacherously with one another?" (Malakhi 2:10).

And I hope with humility that my testimony will be an additional voice that cries out for individuals and nations to respect human lives and human rights and to eradicate hate and evil. For I firmly believe that human beings are just as capable of loving as they are capable of hating and that all of us are capable of tolerating differences and of eliminating racism, anti-Semitism, prejudice, and bigotry from our midst. May it be so speedily in our days.

Notes

Chapter 1

1. Yehuda Rosenthal, "Geshichte fun di yiden in Mlawa" [History of the Jews in Mlawa], in *Pinkes Mlawa* [Book (Notebook) of Mlawa], ed. Ya'akov Shatzki et al. (New York: Velt-Farband-Mlayer, 1950), 15.

2. Ibid., 24, quoting M. Balaban, *Historja Zydow w Krakowie* [History of Jews in Krakow] (n.p., 1931), 522.

3. Nahum Goldmann Museum of the Jewish Diaspora, "Mlawa" (Tel Aviv: Diaspora Museum, n.d.).

4. Rosenthal, "Geshichte," 25, quoting from A. G. von Hoelsche, "Mlawa, eine koenigliche Stadt in dem hier kein Jude wohnen darf" [Mlawa, a Royal City Where No Jew May Dwell There], in *Geographie und Statistik von West-Sud und Neu Ostpreussen* [Geography and Statistics of the South-West and New East Prussia](Berlin: F. Maurer, 1800), 497.

5. Rosenthal, "Geshichte," 13.

6. Goldmann Museum, "Mlawa."

7. David Kristal, "Zichronos" [Memories], in *Pinkes Mlawa*, 155.

8. Goldmann Museum, "Mlawa."

9. Ze'ev Jabotinsky, Zionist leader, writer, and orator, resigned from the World Zionist Organization and founded the more aggressive Revisionist Zionist movement in 1925.

10. The custom requires a married couple to light two candles on Friday night; in another tradition a candle is added after the birth of each child.

11. The *Siddur Sim Shalom* [Prayer Book "Grant Peace"] of the Rabbinical Assembly of New York has an interesting version of this prayer on page 720.

12. Shatzki et al., *Pinkes Mlawa*, 9.

13. *Mlawa Hayehudith* [Jewish Mlawa: Its History and Destruction], 2 vols., ed. David Shtokfish (Tel Aviv: Sh. Segal, 1984).

Chapter 2

1. Lucy Dawidowicz, *The War against the Jews, 1933–1945* (New York: Holt, Rinehart, and Winston, 1975), 56–69; Raul Hilberg, *The Destruction of the European Jews* (Chicago: Quadrangle Books, 1961), 45–53.

2. Yitzhak Alfasi, *Hasiduth Medor Ledor, Vol. 2* (Jerusalem: Machon Daat Yosef, 1998), 387–99.

3. William L. Shirer, *The Rise and Fall of the Third Reich* (New York: Simon and Schuster, 1960), 441, 407.

4. Martin Gilbert, *The Holocaust: A History of the Jews of Europe during the Second World War* (New York: Holt, Rinehart, and Winston, 1985), 58–59.

5. Shirer, *Rise and Fall*, 577.

6. Leni Yahil, *The Holocaust: The Fate of European Jewry, 1932–1945* (New York: Oxford University Press, 1990), 110–11.

7. Shirer, *Rise and Fall*, 447.

8. Gilbert, *Holocaust*, 64–65.

9. Ibid., 80–81.

10. Shirer, *Rise and Fall*, 872–78.

11. Dawidowicz, *War against the Jews*, 394.

12. American Jewish Committee, *American Jewish Yearbook, 1940–41* (Philadelphia: American Jewish Committee, 1941), 371.

Chapter 3

1. Nora Levin, *The Holocaust: The Destruction of European Jewry, 1933–1945* (New York: T. Y. Crowell, 1968), 171. The Einsatzgruppen were special killing squads. From the beginning of the Nazi invasion of Poland, their task was to follow the columns of the Wehrmacht, the German army, and round up the Jews and Polish intelligentsia for mistreatment and murder. Before the Germans attacked the Soviet Union in June 1941, the Einsatzgruppen's task was extended to "resolve the Jewish problem" and eliminate Communist leaders. Three thousand men drawn from special SS training camps served in the Einsatzgruppen. The officers of the units that rounded up and murdered Jews "were not hoodlums, perverts, or psychopaths. The great majority of them were university-educated, professional men. They became efficient killers" (Hilberg, *Destruction of the European Jews*, 177–256).

2. Levin, *Holocaust*, 171.

3. Aryeh Zimnowicz, "Azoy hot zich es ongehoibn" [This Is How It Started], in *Pinkes Mlawa*, 389–90.

4. David Kristal, "Ud Mutzal Me'eish" [A Brand Plucked from the Fire (Zecharaiah, 3:2)], in *Mlawa Hayehudith* 2:29–30.

5. *Mlawa Hayehudit*, 2:227.

6. Levin, *Holocaust*, 171.

7. *Mlawa Hayehudit*, 2:228.

8. Talmud Bavli, Gittin, 56a–56b.

Chapter 4

1. Levin, *The Holocaust*, 171; Hilberg, *The Destruction of the European Jews*, 177–256.

2. Kristal, "Ud Mutzal Me'eish," 29–30.

3. M. Tzanin, "Mlawa nochn churben" [Mlawa after the Holocaust], in *Mlawa Hayehudith,* 2:363, excerpted from his book *Iber Shtein un Shtok: A raize iber hundert choruv gevorene kehiles in Polin* [From Rock to Bottom: A View of a Hundred Destroyed Jewish Communities in Poland](Tel Aviv: n.p., 1952).

4. Zvi Perlo, "Mepi Nitzulim Shehigiu Artza" [From Testimonies of Survivors Who Immigrated to Israel], in *Mlawa Hayehudith,* 2:231. Perlo was president of the Irgun Yotzei Mlawa (Association of People from Mlawa) in Tel Aviv. He came to Israel many years before the Shoah. He collected testimonies from survivors who arrived in Israel.

Chapter 6

1. Kristal, "Ud Mutzal Me'eish," 30–31.
2. Tzanin, "Mlawa nochn churben," 364.
3. Ibid.
4. Genesis 32:25–30.

Chapter 7

1. The *Haggadah* is a decorated booklet with readings on the exodus from Egypt and related topics. The readings are recited at the seder on the first and second nights of the Passover celebration.

2. The *afikoman* is half a matzoh set aside at the beginning of the seder and eaten at the end of the meal, after which no other food may be eaten for the rest of the night. The Hallel, selections from the Book of Psalms, is recited on Jewish holidays, on the first day of the Hebrew month, and at the seder on Passover nights. The Four Questions, usually recited by the youngest child at the table, ask why this night (the Passover seder) is different from all other nights. The questions are as follows: Why is it that on all other nights during the year we may eat either bread or matzoh, but on this night we eat only matzoh? Why is it that on all other nights we may eat all kinds of herbs, but on this night we eat bitter herbs? Why is it that on all other nights we do not dip our herbs even once, but on this night we dip them twice? Why is it that on all other nights we eat either sitting or reclining, but on this night we eat in a reclining position?

Chapter 8

1. Perlo, "Mepi Nitzulim," 229.
2. Ibid., 230.
3. Ibid. Fela Ceitag was also helpful to the people of Mlawa when she worked for a dentist in Auschwitz-Birkenau. She is credited with saving the lives of many young women. She survived the war and lived in Jerusalem until her death in 2004.
4. Levin, *Holocaust,* 292–96.

Chapter 9

1. Dawidowicz, *War Against the Jews*, 135–39; Levin, *Holocaust*, 295; Hilberg, *Destruction of the European Jews*, 572–78.

2. Treblinka was a village northeast of Warsaw. After the Wannsee Conference, the Nazis chose this site, one of six, to be strictly a death camp. No other work was done but the labor of death. During one year 800,000 Jewish men, women, and children were exterminated there. The camp is also notable for having staged a heroic, albeit doomed, revolt. Gilbert, *Holocaust*, 286, 596–97.

3. Michael Berenbaum, *The World Must Know: The History of the Holocaust as Told in the United States Holocaust Memorial Museum* (Boston: Little, Brown, 1993), 137–50.

Chapter 10

1. Levin, *Holocaust*, 46, 50–51.

2. Berenbaum, *World Must Know*, 65, 104, 127.

3. Bezalel Mordowicz, "Antlofen fun Auschwitz" [Escaped from Auschwitz] and "Du'ach Rishon L'olam al z'va'ot Auschwitz" [First Report to the World about the Atrocities in Auschwitz], both in *Mlawa Hayehudith*, 2:116–45 (in Yiddish) and 146–64 (in Hebrew), respectively.

4. Shirer, *Rise and Fall*, 1356–70.

5. Levin, *Holocaust*, 701.

6. Gilbert, *Holocaust*, 774–75.

Chapter 11

1. Gilbert, *Holocaust*, 771–72.

2. Ibid., 790; Berenbaum, *World Must Know*, 8. When American troops liberated the Ohrdruf labor camp on April 4, 1945, four thousand inmates had died or been murdered there in the previous three months. Among them were Polish and Russian prisoners of war and Jews. When General Eisenhower visited the camp, he was so shocked that he immediately telephoned Prime Minister Churchill to describe what he had seen. He ordered American units in the area to visit the site so that they would understand what they were fighting against.

3. Lamentations 4:9.

4. Ezekiel 37:1–14.

5. Levin, *Holocaust*, 174. Theresienstadt (Terezin) is a city about forty miles from Prague, Czechoslovakia. The ghetto and concentration camp were initially described as a training and educational center for Jews, who would then go to Palestine. It was proclaimed as the "city which the Fuhrer has given the Jews" and promoted by a propaganda film with the name *Die Fuhrer schenkt den Juden eine Stadt* [The Fuhrer (Hitler) Grants the Jews the Gift of a Jewish State in Theresienstadt]. The first Jews sent there were Zionists. The Nazis initially intended it to be a "model camp" that could be shown to outsiders, but in reality it was a transit camp. From there Jews were

deported to the gas chambers and ovens of Auschwitz and Buchenwald. After liberation this location became for some time a displaced persons camp supported by the United Nations Relief and Rehabilitation Agency. See Levin, *Holocaust*, 174.

Chapter 14

1. Text from the *Haggadah*, read and chanted at the seder in home rituals on the first and second nights of Passover.
2. Text from the *Haggadah*, with my own thoughts.
3. *Haggadah*.
4. Ibid.
5. Ibid.; Psalm 118:18.
6. Exodus 24:7.
7. "God, who is full of compassion" is a memorial prayer for the deceased.

Chapter 15

1. "Prozdor" is a Hebrew word for a foyer or antechamber. The Hebrew College in Boston is a four-year afternoon program to earn a Hebrew College degree. To be accepted by the college, an applicant must first get a Hebrew high school degree from the Prozdor. Worcester offered this Prozdor four-year program so that a graduate of the Worcester Prozdor would be able to graduate at a relatively young age.

Chapter 17

1. Avraham Shaft, "Mah shekarah l'yehudei Mlawa" [What Happened to the Jews of Mlawa], *Mlawa Hayehudith*, 2:236–43.
2. Rosenberg, "In ghetto," 86–115.
3. Berenbaum, *World Must Know*, 180.
4. Mordecha Hilleli (Motek Beilowitz), "Hamachteret Hatzionit B'Auschwitz" [The Jewish-Zionist Underground in Auschwitz], *Mlawa Hayehudith* 2:191–97. Hilleli describes the Zionist youth underground in Auschwitz, which included young Jews from Mlawa.

Chapter 19

1. Amos 3:2.
2. Psalm 145:17.
3. Babylonian Talmud, B'rachot 57a.
4. Sidney Greenberg, ed., *Light from Jewish Lamps: A Modern Treasury of Jewish Thoughts* (Northvale, N.J.: J. Aronson, 1986), 91.
5. Zvi Kolitz, *Yosl Rakover Talks to God* (New York: Pantheon, 1999).
6. Ibid., 16, 17–18, 24–25.
7. Genesis 18:24–25.
8. Judges 6:13.

9. Job 1:1.

10. Job 3:11.

11. Talmud Bavli, Berachot 7a.

12. Isaiah 55:8–9.

13. Job, chap. 40–42.

14. Deuteronomy 31:16–17.

15. Psalm 145:17–20.

16. Genesis 4:8.

17. Deuteronomy 11:26–28.

18. Deuteronomy 30:19.

19. *Mishneh Torah* [The Book of Knowledge], 5:11.

20. Psalm 118:5.

21. Genesis 2:3.

22. Psalm 148:5–6.

23. Siddur [early morning private prayer].

24. Psalm 147:3.

25. Leviticus 26:44.

26. Max I. Dimont, *Jews, God and History* (New York: Simon and Schuster, 1962), ix.

27. Deuteronomy 6:7.

28. 1 Kings 19:12.

Glossary

afikoman	half a matzo set aside (or hidden for a child to find it) at the beginning of the seder and eaten at the end of the meal, after which no other food may be eaten for the rest of the night
Agudat Yisrael	Orthodox Jewish political group opposed to Zionism but supportive of the Jewish State in Israel
ahavah	love
Al Het	prayer of confession recited on the Day of Atonement
Arbeiter Ring	"Workmen's Circle"; social and cultural workers' organization
arbeit macht frei	German phrase meaning "Work Shall Make You Free"; engraved on sign over the gates at Auschwitz
Aron Hakodesh	Holy Ark where Torah scroll is placed in the synagogue
b'ahavah	with love
behirah hofshit	freedom of choice
Berihah	"escape"; underground movement to bring Jews to Palestine when it was under the mandate of the British, who did not permit the immigration of Jews to Palestine
bet (beis) midrash	religious house of study and prayer
Blockaltester	inmate in concentration camp who was head of a block
daven	to pray
death march	forced evacuation of inmates from concentration camps on foot; whoever was unable to continue in the march was shot to death

DP(s)	displaced person(s) who had no home to return to after the war
drosho (drasha)	religious discourse
Einsatzgruppen	SS death squads
Elijah's cup	cup of wine in honor of the prophet Elijah placed on seder table on Passover night
El Maleh Rahamim	"God full of Mercy"; prayer recited at funerals and on certain other occasions in honor of the deceased
emunah	faith, belief in God
Eretz Yisrael	Land of Israel; biblical name
erev	evening or day before Sabbath or holiday
gemainde	elected council of Jewish community leaders; see also *kehillah*
Gestapo	Acronym of *Geheim Staatpolizei*, secret state police of the Third Reich
Haggadah	special book for use of prayers, songs, poetry, and biblical verses used at the seder on the first two nights of Passover
Hakhsharah	"preparation"; movement of young Jews who wished to immigrate to Palestine and prepared themselves by hard work in factories, farms, and shops to gain experience and working skills to earn money for travel to Palestine
hallah	special egg bread made for the Sabbath
Hallel	praises to God; selections from book of Psalms recited on Jewish holidays, on the first day of the Hebrew month, and at the seder on Passover nights
Hamishlahat Ha-eretz Yisraelit	Jews from Israel who volunteered to work with survivors of the Holocaust in various displaced persons camps in Europe
Hasid (sing.), Hasidim (pl.)	very religious Jews who lived by unique philosophy of piety and joy in study and prayer; each Hasidic group has its own rebbe (rabbi, *tzaddik*) for guidance
Hasidism	teaching of Hasidic rabbis; founded by Yisrael Ba'al Shem Tov ("The Master of a Good Name" [1700–

1769]), who taught followers that one can reach spiritual connection with God through true love of God, joyous prayer, and compassion for fellow men

haskallah	enlightenment
havdalah	"separation"; prayer ritual recited in Jewish homes to separate holy Sabbath from ordinary days of the week
havurot	"circles"; circles of friends who meet for study, discussions, and socializing
hester panim	God hiding his face, not caring
hol hamo'ed Pesach	the four days between the first two days and the last two days of the eight days of the Passover festival; semiholidays
hol hamo'ed Sukkot	the five days between the first two days of the festival of Sukkot and the last two days of Shemini Atzcrat and Simhat Torah; semiholidays
Hovevei Tzion	lovers of Land of Israel, Zionists
Humash	Torah, Pentateuch, Five Books of Moses; first five books of the Bible (Genesis, Exodus, Leviticus, Numbers, and Deuteronomy)
huppah	canopy used at ceremony of Jewish wedding
Jewish state	State of Israel
Judenfrei, Judenrein	"Free of Jews"; declaration made after all Jews were expelled from a locale
Judenrat	Jewish council in the ghetto
Kabbalah	Jewish mysticism
Kabbalat Shabbat	evening services on Friday night welcoming Jewish Sabbath
kabbalist	Jewish mystic
Kaddish	memorial prayer recited by mourners during the first year after the loss of a family member and on the anniversary of the loss
Kapo (Capo)	Prisoner-trusty in charge of other prisoners in a concentration camp
kashrut	observance of dietary kosher laws

kedoshim	holy martyrs
kehillah	elected council of Jewish community; see also *gemainde*
kiddush	sanctification of the Sabbath over a cup of wine on Friday night at beginning of evening meal
kittel	white robe worn on High Holy Days by religious Jews
kosher	food prepared with permissible ingredients as prescribed by Jewish religious law
Kristallnacht	"Night of the Broken Glass," November 9–10, 1938, when mobs of Nazis attacked and destroyed Jewish businesses, homes, and synagogues
Lageraltester	inmate who serves as head of a concentration camp
Landrat	German chief officer of city or district
Luftwaffe	German air force
ma'ariv	evening prayers
maskilim	enlightened (modern) individuals
Messiah	"anointed one" who will come to redeem the world and bring peace to all nations
Midrash	explanations/commentaries on the Bible, including legends/stories teaching religious values
mikveh	bath house used for ritually purifying oneself
minhah	afternoon service, one of three daily services
minyan (sing.), *minyamin* (pl.)	quorum of at least ten men required for conducting congregational service; some congregations now including women in the counting
Mishnah	Jewish law accumulated over four centuries; basis for discussions in the Gemara; Mishnah and Gemara constitute the Talmud
Mitnaged (sing.), Mitnagdim (pl.)	opponents of Hasidim led by Rabbi Eliyahu of Vilna (1720–1797)
mitzvah (sing.), mitzvot (pl.)	religious commandment, act of kindness
Mizrahi	religious Zionist movement; easterner
Nuremberg Laws	severe anti-Jewish laws established in Nuremberg, Germany, in 1935

Parnes	leader or head of a Jewish community
Pesach	eight-day festival of Passover commemorating the exodus from Egypt some thirty-three hundred years ago (Exodus, chaps. 1–15)
Po'aei Tzion	workers-socialist Zionist movement
Purim	Jewish holiday based on story of Esther in the Bible
rebbe	Hasidic rabbi who leads a group of Hasidim
redemption	(usu.) to redeem, to eliminate human suffering
Revisionist Zionists	more aggressive Zionist movement organized by Ze'ev Jabotinsky
seder	"order"; Passover home celebration on first two nights of Passover; conducted in special order
selekzia	selection in concentration camps of those who were no longer able to produce
Shabbat	Sabbath, Saturday, seventh day of the week; Jewish day of rest
Shavuot	Feast of Weeks; occurs seven weeks after first day of Passover; celebrates anniversary of Ten Commandments given at Mt. Sinai (also agricultural festival)
shtibl (sing.), *shtiblach* (pl.)	place(s) of worship for Hasidim; consists of one or two rooms
shul	synagogue
Shulchan Arukh	code of Jewish laws
Shul Gass	Synagogue Street (street in Mlawa)
simha	joy; joyous occasion
Simhat Torah	rejoicing with Torah on ninth day of Sukkot festival
SS	black-shirted Nazi elite guard (German, Schutzstaffel)
Stubendienst	inmate in charge of room or hall where inmates live
Sukkot	festival of gathering in crops for the winter; during this festival Jews eat their meals in booths
ta'anit	fast day
Ta'anit Esther	fast of Esther; honors Queen Esther, who ordered all Jews to fast and pray to save them from annihilation by Haman

tefillah, t'fillah	prayer
tikun olam	fixing, repairing, improving the world
tish	table; table where rebbe shares meal with his Hasidim
Torah	Humash; first five books of the Bible (Genesis, Exodus, Leviticus, Numbers, and Deuteronomy); religious Jewish studies considered studying Torah
tzaddik	righteous and learned man who is pleasing to God and man; Hasidic rabbi
tzedakah (zedakah)	charity; righteous, kind act
vidui	confession of one's sins
Volkdeutsche	Polish citizens who were ethnically German
Wehrmacht	German army
yeshiva(s), yeshivot (pl.)	seminary of religious studies where one may earn rabbinic ordination
yetziat Mitzrayim	exodus from Egypt (Exodus, chaps. 1–15)
Yom Kippur	Day of Atonement; day of fasting and prayer
zekhut	privilege
zemirot	songs in praise of God and Torah and for the spirit of the Sabbath and the holy days